Challenge 21

Englisch für berufliche Gymnasien
Band 2 – Neue Ausgabe

Herausgegeben von
Hermann Fischer
Irene Hildenbrand
Karin Machan
Harald Peter
Dr. Hannelore Zimmermann

Ernst Klett Verlag
Stuttgart · Leipzig

Challenge 21
Band 2 – Neue Ausgabe

Herausgegeben von
Hermann Fischer, Münster; Irene Hildenbrand, Offenburg; Karin Machan, Münster;
Harald Peter, Freiburg; Dr. Hannelore Zimmermann, Donaueschingen

Beratende Mitarbeit
Kurt Walz, Giengen; Elke Uthoff, Osnabrück

Werkübersicht
Schülerbuch 978-3-12-801005-2
Teacher's resource book mit Lehrer-Service-CD-ROM und 2 Audio-CDs 978-3-12-801006-9
Vocabulary Notebook 978-3-12-801009-0
Unter www.klett.de (Challenge 21-Online) finden Sie alle wichtigen Informationen um Ihre Englisch-Abiturprüfung. Mit dem **EXAM TRAINING**, 978-3-12-801007-6 erhalten Sie die optimale Prüfungsvorbereitung.
Schülerpaket, bestehend aus 801007 und 801009 978-3-12-801013-7

1. Auflage   1 5 4 3 2 1 | 2012 2011 2010 2009 2008

Alle Drucke dieser Auflage können im Unterricht nebeneinander benutzt werden, sie sind untereinander unverändert. Die letzte Zahl bezeichnet das Jahr des Druckes.

www.klett.de

Redaktion: Helen Smyth.

Gestaltung: B2 Büro für Gestaltung, Andreas Staiger.
Reproduktion: Meyle + Müller Medien-Management, Pforzheim.
Druck: Offizin Andersen Nexö, Leipzig.
Printed in Germany.

ISBN 13: 978-3-12-801005-2

9 783128 010052

Contents

		Classroom phrases		II
		Vorwort		7

1 Changing lifestyles

		Getting started	photo collage, key words	8
Family statistics	9	Is there an even greater threat to children than lone parents?	*The Guardian*	9
		Listening comprehension The teenage dad	personal statement	10
Finding your own lifestyle	11	Grow Up? Not So Fast	*Time*	12
Staying young	13	Warning	poem	13
Health trends	14	Today's teenagers are less healthy than their parents	*The Independent*	14
The cost of smoking	15	Smoking in figures	statistics	15
Tattoos	16	Tattooists' new union to leave its mark on unregulated trade	*The Independent*	16
Modern communication	18	On the mobile	cartoons	18
		Hotspot	survey	19
Food trends	20	The Food Chains That Link Us All	*Time*	20

2 The world of work

		Getting started	cartoons	22
Young people and the job market	23	The shameful growth of a generation of 'neets'	*The Guardian*	23
Working women	25	Mothers held back under burden of their chores, says Cherie Blair	*The Independent*	26
Teleworking	27	Working at home grows in popularity	*The Independent*	27
		Listening comprehension Job satisfaction	interview	28
Entrepreneurial skills	29	Social Entrepreneur Of The Year: Calling all social visionaries	*The Independent*	29
		Hotspot	analyse and set up a *Juniorenfirma*, check the web	30
Intercultural competence Cross-cultural competence in business	31	Cross-cultural negotiations	online text	32
		Hotspot	intercultural competence poster	33

3 Consumerism

		Getting started	forms of advertising	34
Advertising	35	Opinions on advertising	statements	35
The rise of the new media	36	Media usage in the US	*The Guardian*	36
		Hotspot Advertising regulations, advertising campaigns	web search, presentations	38
Advertising standards	39	VW reviews complaints, pulls ad after all	*USA Today*	39
Targeting the consumer	40	Teachers' call for 'sexploitation' of children to end	*The Independent*	41
		Listening comprehension Consumer's paradise	novel extract	42
Shopping addiction	42	Is shopping your drug of choice?	*The Guardian*	43
Consumerism and values	44	Shopping is the true spirit of Christmas	*The Independent*	44
Too much choice	46	Text by Bill Bryson	non-fiction	47

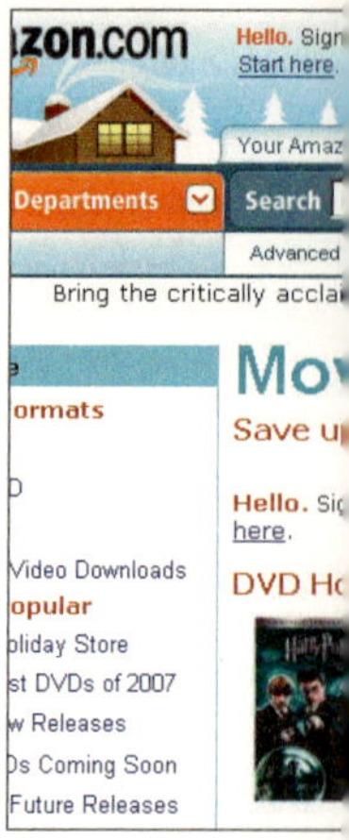

4 Multiculturalism

		Getting started	photos	48
Multicultural USA (1)	49	Xtra-File Hispanics in the USA		49
Multicultural USA (2)	50	America's Minutemen build their own fence against Mexican migrants	*The Guardian*	50
		Listening comprehension Believe in who you are	personal statement	51
Multicultural USA (3)	52	Legal Alien	poem	52
Multicultural Britain (1)	53	Xtra-File Britain's ethnic minorities		53
		Analysts name Britain's most racially diverse areas	*The Guardian*	54
Multicultural Britain (2)	55	Would-be settlers will have to pass the Britishness test	*The Guardian*	56
Multicultural Germany (1)	57	Xtra-File Ethnic minorities in Germany		57
Multicultural Germany (2)	58	Can Germany learn to live with Islam?	*BBC*	58

5 Energy and the environment

		Getting started	comic strip	60
An inconvenient truth	61	I need to wake up	song	61
		Listening comprehension The United Nations Climate Change Conference	speech	61
Climate change	62	Certainties and uncertainties of climate change	brochure	62
Alternative energy sources	64	How mirrors can light up the world	*The Guardian*	64
Disposing of nuclear energy	66	Radioactive waste: disposing of the myths	BNFL brochure	66
Energy & conservation	68	"Let our kids find their own oil."	fiction	68
Energy user no. 1: the car	70	Quotes	public statements	70
Alternative fuels for cars	71	Comparing Alternative Fuels For Cars	science journal	71
Car-sharing	72	Join the car club	*The Argus*	72
		Hotspot	research and report	74
Using energy – saving energy	75	Quiz		75

6 Technology and futurology

		Getting started	illustrations	76
Futurology (1)	77	Oops! They got it horribly wrong	quotes	77
		Listening comprehension The next fifty years	statements	78
Futurology (2)	79	Instant futures	*The Sunday Telegraph*	79
Teleportation	80	Beam me up, Scotty – one laser-beam encoded stream of information at a time	*The Independent*	81
Robotics	82	Robots could be babysitters of the future	*The Daily Telegraph*	82
Stem cell therapy	84	2 Friends, 242 Eggs and a Breakthrough	*The New York Times*	84
Human "spare parts"	86	Anna	novel extract	86
		Hotspot	research, discussion	87

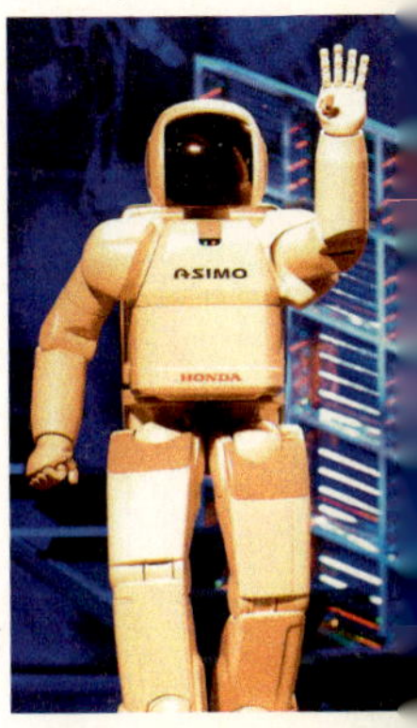

7 Space – the final frontier?

		Getting started	illustrations	88
Space travel (1)	89	Space oddity	song	89
		Listening comprehension The moon landing	live recordings	90
Space travel (2)	90	We must travel to the stars to save the human race, says Hawking	*The Independent*	91
		Xtra-File The International Space Station		92
Space travel (3)	92	The Big Question: Do we need to send people into space, or could robots do it better?	*The Independent*	93
Space tourism	94	Who's paying $200,000 for a few minutes in space?	*USA TODAY*	94
Satellites	96	Xtra-File Star Wars: the military use of satellites and space technology		96
		Satellites weigh Africa's water	*BBC News*, online article	97
Utopian short fiction	98	Tomorrow and tomorrow and tomorrow…	short story extract	98
UFOs and aliens (1)	100	Independence Day	screenplay extracts	101
UFOs and aliens (2)	104	So much space, so little time: why aliens haven't found us yet	*The Guardian*	105

8 USA: People, politics, perspectives

		Getting started	photos	106
The American dream	107	Schwarzenegger welcomes new U.S. citizens	speech	107
Americans about America	110	My America	personal statements	110
The melting pot	112	Out of many, one	*The Washington Post*	113
Fighting for the homeland (1)	114	Born on the Fourth of July	novel extract	114
		Listening comprehension For America	song	116
Fighting for the homeland (2)	116	The triumph of love	*The Sunday Times*	117
The right to bear arms	118	Hotspot	discussion, design a poster	118
		Lax gun laws sure to get off scot-free	*The Guardian Weekly*	119
		Xtra-File U.S. history and foreign policy		120

9 British politics – past and present

		Getting started	photo, caption	124
The Monarchy	125	The next 50 years of monarchy	statistics	125
Britishness	126	Debating race, identity, citizenship and culture	statements	126
		Hotspot	questionnaire, check the web	128
Intercultural competence (1)	129	The hidden rules of English behaviour	non-fiction	130
Intercultural competence (2)	131	Behaviour around the world	quiz	131
The legacy of Empire	132	Consequences of a colonial past	public statements	132
The Commonwealth (1)	133	Xtra-File The Commonwealth of Nations		133
		Xtra-File The Commonwealth and Europe		134
The Commonwealth (2)	134	India	speech	134
		21st century challenges	speech	135
		Listening comprehension Respecting difference, promoting understanding	speech	136
		Hotspot	research, speech	136
Britain and Europe	137	Britain's future tied to Europe	*The Japan Times*	137
		Listening comprehension Britain's role in Europe	interview	139
		Hotspot	check the web, design a front page (newspaper), poster	139

10 Globalization

		Getting started	photo collage	140
Global business	141	Globalisation shakes the world	*BBC News*	141
Food from around the globe	143	Carrier of culture	cartoon and quote	143
		Hotspot	show and tell	143
Better chances for Third World farmers	144	Trading up, A better deal	flier	144
		Listening comprehension The situation of women in Chile	*The Times*	145
Global understanding	146	English as lingua franca	*The Independent*	146
The language of tomorrow	147	Schools import China's teachers for lessons in 'language of tomorrow'	*The Independent*	147
Language barriers	148	The English Language	non-fiction	148
Global politics	150	Xtra-File Profile of the G8		151
Intercultural competence	152		quiz	152
		Hotspot	mind map	153

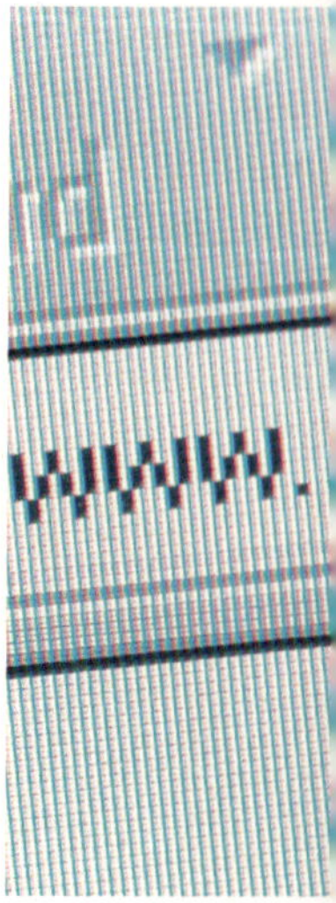

Skills files – overview 154

Vocabulary – English-German word list 189
Glossary of terms and literary terms 201
Acknowledgements and picture credits 204
Abbreviations and symbols 205
Irregular verbs 206
Map of Great Britain and Ireland 207
Map of the world: languages and countries with economic agreements 208
Back cover
- Map of the USA and Canada III
- Useful connectives IV
- Downloads IV
- Operatoren V

Vorwort

Neue Prüfungsformate

Die Anpassung des bewährten Lehrwerks an die neuen Anforderungen im Fach Englisch betrifft alle wichtigen Prüfungsformate: textbezogene Inhaltsfragen, Auswertung von visuellem und statistischem Material, Composition/Comment/ Essay, Übersetzung (englisch-deutsch) und Mediation. Die entsprechenden Prüfungsformen werden in den *Skills files* erklärt und im Aufgabenapparat vertiefend trainiert. Im Umschlag befindet sich eine Liste der gängigsten Operatoren, die in Prüfungen eingesetzt werden.

Ein intensive Prüfungsvorbereitung

Neben dem Lehrwerk empfiehlt sich der Einsatz des **Exam Training**, das gezielt die für die Abschlussprüfungen relevanten Kompetenzen trainiert. Die unterschiedlichen Prüfungsanforderungen in den einzelnen Bundesländern sind berücksichtigt und in Musterprüfungen eingearbeitet. Diese Prüfungen können unter **Challenge 21-Lehrwerk-Online** abgerufen werden.

Kompetenzen

Bundeslandübergreifend steht eine abwechslungsreiche Auswahl an fiktionalen und nicht-fiktionalen Texten zur Verfügung. Bei Wörtern und Eigennamen mit schwieriger Aussprache ist die Lautschrift in die Wortangaben integriert.
Der Erwerb und der Ausbau zentraler Kompetenzen in der Fremdsprache bilden einen besonderen Schwerpunkt: *Writing* und *speaking* werden ebenso berücksichtigt wie *business communication*, Präsentationen, handlungsorientierte Aufgaben, interkulturelle Kompetenzen und Internet-Projektarbeit. **Check the web** Aufgaben schaffen einen Anreiz im Internet aktiv zu werden, aber da manche Internet-Adressen schnelllebig sind, werden in der Regel keine spezifischen Adressen angegeben.

Struktur des Lehrwerks

Die klare Struktur des Lehrwerks sowie die Querverweise zu den detaillierten ***Skills files*** im Anhang sorgen für eine hohe Benutzerfreundlichkeit. Durch den modulhaften Aufbau der einzelnen Units kann jede Lehrkraft die Progression selbst bestimmen.

Referenzwerk

Die umfangreichen ***Skills files*** machen **Challenge 21** zu einem wertvollen Referenzwerk, in dem Antworten auf lektionsunabhängige Fragen zu finden sind: Was ist Mediation? Wo liegen die Besonderheiten im *business English*? In den **Xtra-Files** wird Zusatzmaterial angeboten, das unabhängig von der Unit eingesetzt werden kann. Eine alphabetische Wortliste, ein Glossar literarischer Begriffe sowie einige Landkarten runden das Angebot ab.

Wortschatz und Hörverständnisarbeit

Die Wortschatzarbeit findet besondere Berücksichtigung im **Vocabulary Notebook**. Vertonte Lesetexte sowie *Listening comprehension* Aufgaben auf den CDs im **Teacher's resource book** sind die Grundlage für gezieltes Hörverständnistraining.

Service im Internet

801005-0001

Unter **Challenge 21-Lehrwerk-Online** (unter www.klett.de) finden Sie eine Auswahl der im Schülerbuch abgedruckten Vokabeln als MP3s. Einfach unter www.klett.de auf „Lehrwerk-Online" gehen und in das Suchfeld den Online-Link eingeben. Der passende Link befindet sich immer auf der ersten Seite der Unit.
Unter Lehrwerk-Online können **Grammatikthemen** selbstständig nachgelesen werden. Sie geben den Link ein und kommen zu einer Übersicht, von wo aus Sie zum gewünschten Grammatikthema weiterklicken können.

Erfolgreich Englischkenntnisse vertiefen und erweitern – hierzu leistet **Challenge 21 Band 2 – Neue Ausgabe** einen wesentlichen Beitrag.
Allen Nutzern dieses Lehrwerks viel Erfolg wünscht

das Challenge-Team

Unit 1 Changing lifestyles

801005-0001

patchwork family

advertising family

lesbian couple

divorced couple

nuclear family

stepfamily

one-parent family

extended family

childless couple

gay couple

Getting started

1 Look at the photos, and the family types and household arrangements in the boxes. Which term(s) would you match with each photo? Give reasons.
2 Think of suitable definitions for the terms in the boxes.
3 In your opinion, which family types/household arrangements are becoming more common? Which ones are becoming less common? Try to explain these trends.

→ **Illustrations and photos**
See *skills file* on page 158.

Family statistics

2|1

Is there an even greater threat to children than lone parents?

Panics grip the nation with such ease. When the Office of National Statistics published a bundle of figures last week, it set all the usual Cassandras wailing. Here's the figure that frightened them: "Children in Britain are three times more likely to live in one-parent households than they were in 1972." This is absolutely true. Nearly a quarter of children (24%) now live with one parent – though that still means 76% live with two parents. Most people's ideal is to bring up children with two happy parents, but many fail.

"So who are the single parents?"

So who are the single parents? Most have been married: 55% are divorced, separated or widowed. Most of the other 45% were cohabiting when their children were born. Seventy-four per cent are over the age of 30 and only 12% are under 25, so we are not talking about teen pregnancy (which has fallen). Nor is it a permanent state: on average people stay single parents for only five and a half years.

What causes panic is the idea that bad things are "on the rise", to use the BBC's words, raising spectres of ineluctable moral decline. "On the rise" suggests an ever-upward graph where soon no child will live with two parents. Where will it all end?

Yet the rise the Office of National Statistics reported was minute. In 10 years, the number of children living in single-parent families has gone up by just 3%. The poorest are most likely to part due to financial pressure. It leads to rows about men spending children's money on a drink or a bet. Research shows that when mothers control the cash, more is spent on children and housekeeping. Hard-pressed mothers may turn out men who not only can't provide but also drain the household budget.

It is not that, as the right claims, the state gives more to single mothers: it doesn't. Now tax credits are paid to the main childcarer, usually the mother, but the money is often paid into a joint account.

"There are happy and unhappy homes, married or not."

Why is there this perennial hand-wringing over one-parent families? Because the statistics show their children are in danger of doing worse. But the figures also suggest that once you control for poverty, the difference fades. There are happy and unhappy homes, married or not. Mothers often leave marriages if they fear fathers are doing their children damage: crime runs in families, as do drugs, drink, violence and bullying. Walking away can be the right thing to do.

Look carefully again at the devastating recent Unicef report that put Britain near the bottom for children's wellbeing. Commentators rushed to say that single parenthood is the cause. But the charity One Parent Families points to evidence suggesting that it is nothing of the kind. In those same Unicef tables, who comes top for children's wellbeing? Sweden, Norway, Finland and Denmark took the top four places. Yet they are all in the top ranks too for the highest number of children brought up by lone parents. They are not rearing generations of sociopaths. On the contrary, they rank high in adult happiness charts, too.

By Polly Toynbee, *The Guardian*, www.guardian.co.uk, April 17, 2007 – 526 words.

1 **to grip** to take hold of s.o.'s mind · 3 **a bundle of figures** some new data · 3 **to set the Cassandras wailing** to make pessimistic people cry out · 16 **to cohabit** to live together without being married · 19 **pregnancy** period when a mother expects her baby · 24 **spectre** ghost, *here:* threat · 24 **ineluctable** unavoidable · 24 **moral decline** loss of good standards of behaviour · 25 **ever-upward** steadily rising · 25 **graph** diagram · 29 **minute** [maɪ'nju:t] very small · 33 **row** [raʊ] fight · 38 **to drain the household budget** to spend the money that the family has to live · 39 **to claim** to argue · 43 **joint** shared · 44 **perennial hand-wringing** *ständiges Klagen* · 49 **to fade** to become less obvious · 52 **to run in the family** to stay the same over several generations · 55 **devastating** terrible · 59 **charity** organization that helps people in need · 59 **to point to evidence** to show facts · 66 **to rear** [rɪə] to bring up · 67 **sociopath** mentally disturbed person

Before you read: "Is there an even greater..." on page 9.

1 Look at the photos on page 8 again. Describe your own picture of the ideal family.

Understanding the text

2 Summarize the latest findings published by the National Office of Statistics.
3 According to the article, for what reasons do people find themselves bringing up a child without a partner?
4 Explain why poor couples seem to separate more often than wealthy ones.
5 "The children of one-parent families are especially likely to have problems later in life." Find arguments in the text which support or contradict this statement.

A step further: Cartoon

6 Describe the cartoon below. What main point does it make?
7 To what extent does the cartoon agree with or contradict the *Guardian* article?

→ **Cartoons**
See *skills file* on page 155.

"Why can't WE be a single parent family?"

Translation

8 Translate from L 4, "Here's the figure..." to L 21 "... five and a half years" into German.

→ **Translation**
See *skills file* on page 165.

1|1

Listening comprehension

The teenage dad

The text you are going to hear is about the issues faced by one young father. Listen to Aaron Nixon, 16, from East London, who was 15 when his son, Bobbey, was born.

Finding your own lifestyle

Before you read: "Grow up? . . ." on page 12.

1 What are your plans for the future? Consider career, family situation, housing, friends, hobbies, travel, etc.

Understanding the text

2 Describe the lifestyles enjoyed by Michele, Ellen, Nathan, Corinne, Marcus and Jennie.

3 Summarize how the lifestyles of young people have changed during the last three decades.

4 What have social scientists recently found out regarding people in their early twenties?

5 According to the writer, what are the positive points of being a "twixter"?

6 Why are some scientists worried about the twixters?

Language and style

7 Explain what is meant by the following phrases.

a) "twentysomething Peter Pans" ‹L 17–18›

b) "transitional never-never land between adolescence and adulthood" ‹L 34–35›

8 Translate these figurative expressions from the text into German.

a) "hopping from job to job and date to date" ‹L 21–22›

b) "the iron cage of adult responsibility" ‹L 36–37›

c) "they're reaping the fruit of decades of American affluence and social liberation" ‹L 44–46›

d) "young people ... search their souls and choose their life paths" ‹L 47–48›

e) "whatever cultural machinery used to turn kids into grownups has broken down" ‹L 52–53›

f) "moral backbone" ‹L 54›

→ **Figurative language**
See *glossary* on page 202.

9 The writer asks a lot of questions in his article, cf. L 16–18. What effect does this have on the reader?

10 Find synonyms for these words in the text.

a) middle	c) in-between	e) legitimate
b) not permanent	d) all the time, always	f) to concentrate on

Your opinion

11 a) What do you think of the lifestyles of the young people in the article?

b) In what way, if at all, would this lifestyle fit in with your plans for the future?

Essay/Composition

12 Would you personally like to live like the people in the text for a couple of years, or not? Write an essay giving your point of view. You can refer to the arguments you collected in task 11.

→ **Essays/Compositions**
See *skills file* on page 157.

Role play

13 Form groups of four to six people. Set up a radio programme with an interviewer and some young people who have different opinions about the right time to start a family and have a regular job. Think of arguments you could use to support each position. You can refer back to your essay in task 12 for ideas. Write a short role play and act it out in class.

Grow Up? Not So Fast

Michele, Ellen, Nathan, Corinne, Marcus and Jennie are friends. All of them live in Chicago. They go out three nights a week, sometimes more. Each of them has had several jobs since college; Ellen is on her 17th, counting internships, since 1996. They don't own homes. They change apartments frequently. None of them are married, none have children. All of them are from 24 to 28 years old.

Thirty years ago, people like Michele, Ellen, Nathan, Corinne, Marcus and Jennie didn't exist, statistically speaking. Back then, the median age for an American woman to get married was 21. She had her first child at 22. Now it all takes longer. It's 25 for the wedding and 25 for baby. It appears to take young people longer to graduate from college, settle into careers and buy their first homes. What are they waiting for? Who are these permanent adolescents, these twentysomething Peter Pans? And why can't they grow up?

Everybody knows a few of them – full-grown men and women who still live with their parents, who dress and talk and party as they did in their teens, hopping from job to job and date to date, having fun but seemingly going nowhere. Ten years ago, we might have called them Generation X, or slackers, but those labels don't quite fit anymore. This isn't just a trend, a temporary fad or a generational hiccup. This is a much larger phenomenon, of a different kind and a different order.

Social scientists are starting to realize that a permanent shift has taken place in the way we live our lives. In the past, people moved from childhood to adolescence and from adolescence to adulthood, but today there is a new, intermediate phase along the way. The years from 18 until 25 and even beyond have become a distinct and separate life stage, a strange, transitional never-never land between adolescence and adulthood in which people stall for a few extra years, putting off the iron cage of adult responsibility that constantly threatens to crash down on them. They're betwixt and between. You could call them twixters.

Where did the twixters come from? And what's taking them so long to get where they're going? Some of the sociologists, psychologists and demographers who study this new life stage see it as a good thing. The twixters aren't lazy, the argument goes, they're reaping the fruit of decades of American affluence and social liberation. This new period is a chance for young people to savor the pleasures of irresponsibility, search their souls and choose their life paths. But more historically and economically minded scholars see it differently. They are worried that twixters aren't growing up because they can't. Those researchers fear that whatever cultural machinery used to turn kids into grownups has broken down, that society no longer provides young people with the moral backbone and the financial wherewithal to take their rightful places in the adult world. Could growing up be harder than it used to be? […]

Jeffrey Arnett, a developmental psychologist at the University of Maryland, favors "emerging adulthood" to describe this new demographic group […]. It's too easy to write them off as overgrown children, he argues. Rather, he suggests, they're doing important work to get themselves ready for adulthood. "This is the one time of their lives when they're not responsible for anyone else or to anyone else," Arnett says. "So they have this wonderful freedom to really focus on their own lives and work on becoming the kind of person they want to be." […]

But is that all there is to it? Is it that they don't want to grow up, or is it that the rest of society won't let them?

By Lev Grossman, *Time*, www.time.com/time, January 16, 2005 – 623 words.

5 internship work experience in a company · **6 frequently** often · **11 median** middle value in a sequence · **24 Generation X** *(US)* generation born between 1964 and 1979 · **24 slacker** term used especially in the 1990s to describe s.o. who is unmotivated and aimless · **26 fad** short-lived fashion · **26 generational hiccup** [dʒenəˌreɪʃənl ˈhɪkʌp] temporary problem experienced by one generation · **29 shift** change · **34 a transitional never-neverland** *(figurative)* period in which s.o. does not seem to get older · **36 to stall** to stick · **36 iron cage** *(figurative)* pressure · **38 betwixt and between** between two states · **42 demographer** scientist who does research into population changes · **45 to reap** [ˌriːp] **the fruit of s.th** *(figurative)* to enjoy the result of one's hard work · **45 affluence** financial well-being · **47 to savor** to enjoy · **54 backbone** *(figurative)* strength of character · **55 financial wherewithal** [faɪˌnænʃl ˈweəwɪðɔːl] the money one needs to live

Staying young

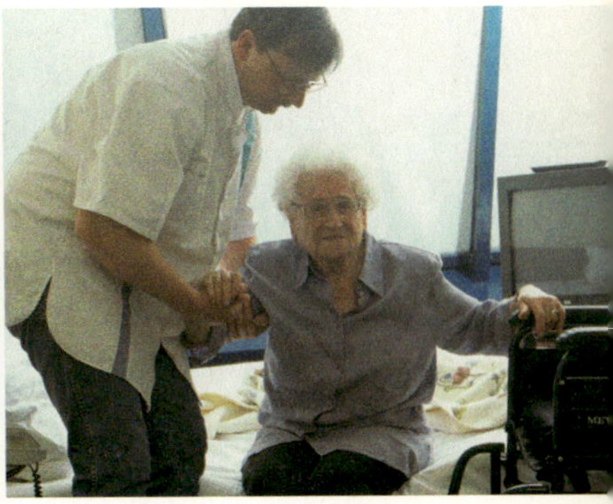

Before you read

1 How does society expect old people to behave? Make a list of expectations.
2 Look at the pictures on this page. In your opinion, which older people are "typical" and which aren't? Give reasons for your answers.

2|4

Warning

When I am an old woman I shall wear purple
With a red hat that doesn't go, and doesn't suit me,
And I shall spend my pension on brandy and summer
gloves
And satin sandals, and say we've no money for butter.
I shall sit down on the pavement when I'm tired
And gobble up samples in shops and press alarm bells
And run my stick along the public railings
and make up for the sobriety of my youth.
I shall go out in my slippers in the rain
And pick the flowers in other people's gardens
And learn to spit.
You can wear terrible shirts and grow more fat
And eat three pounds of sausages at a go
Or only bread and pickle for a week
And hoard pens and pencils and beermats and things
in boxes.
But now we must have clothes that keep us dry
And pay our rent and not swear in the street
And set a good example for the children.
We must have friends to dinner and read the papers.
But maybe I ought to practise a little now?
So people who know me are not too shocked and
surprised
When suddenly I am old, and start to wear purple.

From *Selected Poems* by Jenny Joseph, London: Bloodaxe Books Ltd. 1992 – 207 words.

2 to not suit s.o. to not look good on s.o. · **3 pension** ['penʃn] monthly sum of money one receives after retiring · **6 pavement** *Gehsteig* · **7 to gobble** ['gobl] to eat a lot quickly · **7 sample** *Kostprobe* · **8 railings** *Geländer* · **9 sobriety** [səʊ'braɪətɪ] *here:* being serious, sensible · **12 to spit** *spucken* · **14 at a go** at once · **15 pickle** *saure Gurke* · **16 to hoard** to collect in large numbers · **16 beermat** *Bierdeckel* · **19 to swear** to say bad words

Understanding the text

3 Paraphrase the poem in no more than two sentences.
4 Describe the woman who is speaking in the poem. How old would you say she is? Describe her personality.
5 Describe the tone of the poem.
6 The content of the poem can be divided into three parts. Give line examples to show where each part starts and ends, and explain your choices.

→ **Tone**
See *glossary* on page 203.

Health trends

Before you read

1 What do you personally do in order to keep fit and stay healthy?
2 What unhealthy habits, if any, do you have?

Today's teenagers are less healthy than their parents

Today's adolescents are the first generation to have grown up less healthy than their parents, doctors said yesterday.

Alcohol, tobacco, drugs, obesity and sexually transmitted diseases have replaced childhood infections of the past, such as tuberculosis and polio, and are exacting a greater toll. The difference is that the modern threats to teenagers' health are preventable.

Between 1970 and 2000, obesity in adolescents has increased fourfold; sexually transmitted diseases have increased threefold; teenage pregnancy rates in Britain are the highest in Europe (despite a recent fall); drinking has increased; smoking rates are unchanged since 1982; and suicide is slightly up in the 30-year period (despite a recent decrease), figures show. The trends are highlighted in a series of papers on adolescent health published by *The Lancet* today, which the journal says is an area of medicine that remains "neglected, marginalised or ignored".

Adolescence is the time when teenagers start smoking, drinking and having sex – behaviour which could have a huge impact on their long-term health, the journal said. But, it added, the opportunity to intervene was being missed.

Speaking at the launch of the series in London yesterday, Russell Viner, a specialist in adolescent health at University College Hospital, said the ages at which young people were permitted to vote, drink, drive or buy cigarettes were out of kilter with their biological and social maturity.

Many young people remained tied to their families until well into their twenties, despite having become biologically mature in their early teens. The modern mismatch between biological maturity and social maturity, marked by marriage or financial independence, had coincided with an increase in risky behaviour leading to injuries, mental disorders and suicides.

By Jeremy Laurance, *The Independent*, news.independent.co.uk, March 27, 2007 – 278 words.

5 transmitted passed on to s.o. else · **7 to exact a greater toll** [ɪɡˌzækt ə ˌɡreɪtə 'təʊl] *here:* to cost many lives · **11 fourfold** four times as much · **17 to highlight** to point out · **20 neglected** not given enough attention · **20 marginalised** treated as if it were unimportant · **25 to intervene** to step in in order to prevent s.th. · **26 launch** *here:* publication · **29 to permit** [pə'mɪt] to allow · **30 to be out of kilter** to not match · **31 maturity** [mə'tjʊərətɪ] *Reife* · **37 to coincide** [ˌkəʊɪn'saɪd] to occur simultaneously · **38 mental disorder** psychological problems

Understanding the text

3 Describe how teenagers' health problems have changed over the last thirty years.
4 Explain why adolescence is an important time for someone's later health.
5 Explain the difference between "social maturity" and "biological (maturity)" ‹L 31›?

Discussion

6 Discuss whether teenagers are really less healthy than their parents.
7 Suggest ways in which you can improve health by means of lifestyle changes. In your opinion, which health risks are beyond your control?

→ **Discussions**
See *skills file* on page 177.

Mediation

8 Find the most impressive facts in the article and create a short flier in German, warning teenagers about recent negative health trends in their age group. Outline the health risks they may face.

→ **Mediation**
See *skills file* on page 158.

The cost of smoking

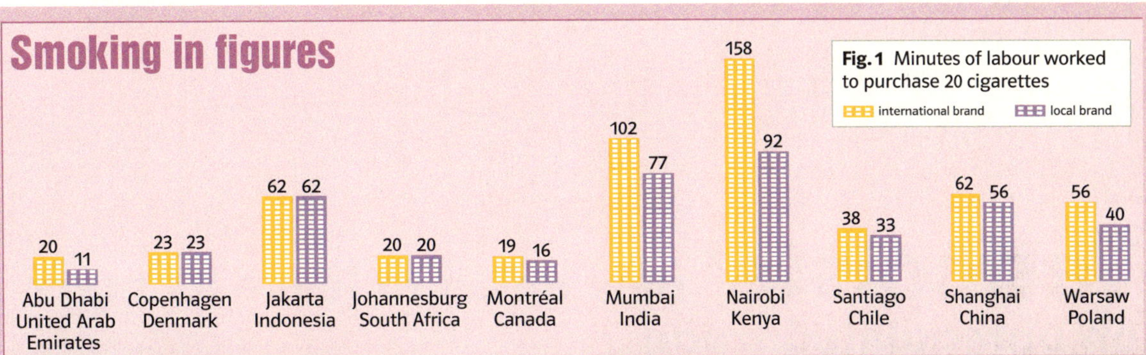

Fig. 2 A pack of an international brand of cigarettes will buy…

one and a half kilos of cucumbers in Georgia

a dozen eggs in Panama

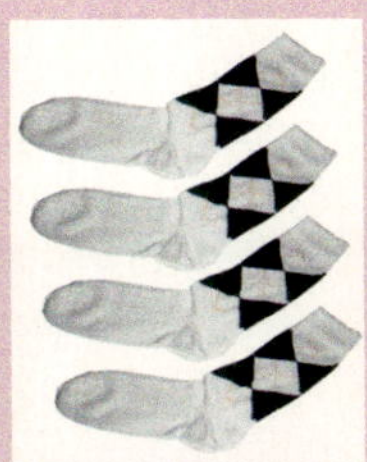
four pairs of cotton socks in China

a dozen coconuts in Papua New Guinea

one kilo of fish in France

six kilos of rice in Bangladesh.

Source: *The Tobacco Atlas*, Dr. Judith Mackay and Dr. Michael Eriksen, World Health Organisation publication, 2002.

Understanding statistics

1 Work in pairs. Make a list of the main facts you have learned from the statistics.
2 Where are cigarettes most expensive? Where are they least expensive?
3 Which of the equivalents of a pack of cigarettes do you find the most impressive? Give reasons for your answer.

→ **Statistics**
See *skills file* on page 161.

Discussion

4 Smoking has been restricted in some areas in Germany. How do you personally feel about these restrictions? Discuss arguments for and against restricting where people can smoke.

→ **Discussions**
See *skills file* on page 177.

Mini-project

5 a) Work in small groups. Think of arguments in favour of and against: smoking; the ban on smoking in public places.
b) Write the arguments in the form of key sentences on separate sheets of paper and use them to create a poster to display in your classroom.

Tattoos

Before you read

1 Look at the picture on page 17. Would you like to have tattoos similar to the man's, or not? Give reasons.

2 a) Find out how many of your classmates have tattoos or piercings, and why they decided to have these done.
b) Did they have any problems afterwards, e.g. health problems or trouble with their parents?

3 How might someone feel about their piercing or tattoo when they are older? What problems might they have?

→ **Illustrations and photos**
See *skills file* on page 158.

Tattooists' new union to leave its mark on unregulated trade

The first trade union for Britain's 1,500 tattooists and body-piercers was announced yesterday after the GMB said it was setting up a branch to represent their interests.

Body art, once the preserve of a minority of aficionados and drunken sailors or husbands-to-be on a stag night, has boomed in the past decade. An estimated two million Britons now have a tattoo or a piercing with celebrities such as David Beckham, Britney Spears and even Zara Phillips, daughter of the Princess Royal, proudly sporting their adorned bodies.

But as the industry has expanded from a few hundred studios nationwide to more than 500 in London alone, so too has the potential for untrained operators to set themselves up in a trade that remains largely unregulated.

Naresh, a tattoo artist for 16 years in north London, who will be the GMB's branch representative, said: "The art has changed beyond recognition. It used to be that people would come into a studio, point to a picture and that is what they would get."

"Now, we get people from barristers to surgeons coming knowing exactly what they want. It is possible to set up with little or no training."

"As a union we can give tattooists and body piercers the collective voice they have never had to set minimum standards and create the sort of qualifications that we think will work."

Body piercers and tattooists, whose arts derives from the Tahitian word "tataou", meaning tapping the skin, are regulated by two items of legislation – one which prevents anyone aged under the age of 18 from having a tattoo, and general health and hygiene rules which are enforced by local authorities.

The sudden increase in body piercings has given rise (to fears) among health

Headline: **to leave a mark on s.th.** to influence s.th. · **unregulated** not covered by rules · **trade** *here:* business

2 **to announce** to make public · 3 **GMB** Britain's General Union · 5 **preserve** [prɪ'zɜ:v] privilege held by a certain group · 6 **aficionado** [əˌfɪʃɪən'ɑ:dəʊ] fan · 7 **stag night** *(BE) Junggesellenabend* · 8 **estimated** calculated roughly · 12 **to sport** to show proudly · 12 **adorned** decorated · 20 **to change beyond recognition** to undergo great changes · 24 **barrister** *(BE)* lawyer who works in a court of law · 25 **surgeon** ['sɜ:dʒən] doctor who performs medical operations · 29 **the collective voice** *here:* shared power · 34 **to tap** to make a cut · 40 **to give rise to** to cause

Understanding the text

4 Describe how tattooists' customers have changed during the last few years.
5 Outline the benefits a tattooists' union would have both for tattooists and their customers.
6 Which laws regulate body piercers and tattooists at present?
7 In what way(s) are the people who get piercings or tattoos at risk?

Further activity: Role play

8 Imagine a scene where a teenager comes home with a piercing or tattoo, and tells one parent about it. Work with a partner. Write a short role play and act it out in class: one person takes the role of the parent, the other person is the teenager.

Your opinion

9 Apart from piercings and tattoos, what other fashions could create a health risk? Give examples.

professionals that poor hygiene and techniques are responsible for the growing prevalence of injuries and infection.

A survey by the Royal College of Nursing of GPs in Rochdale found that 95 per cent had dealt with medical complications resulting from a body piercing. More than three quarters of the problems involved infections.

Tattooists are also concerned that untrained operators are flouting hygiene rules which, in extreme cases, can lead to the transmission through dirty needles of diseases such as hepatitis B and C, and HIV.

John McKechnie, a tattooist for 30 years who runs the Naughty Needles studio in Bolton, said: "Tattooing machinery is too easily obtainable and all too often untrained people don't know about strict hygiene rules. It's about time we sorted out a union."

By Cahal Milmo, *The Independent*, news.independent.co.uk, January 19, 2005 – 424 words.

42 prevalence occurrence · **50 to flout rules** to break rules · **51 transmission** *here:* passing an infection on to s.o. else · **56 easily obtainable** easy to get

Modern communication

Before you look

1 Think of captions to go with each cartoon. Compare your version with what others in your class suggest and choose the most appropriate one.

On the mobile

A

C

B

D

2 Try to match the original captions below with the correct cartoon.
What's that? • I know you're on the bus, I'm just behind you. • Stop talking now class. • Typical men, always bragging about whose is smallest.

to brag to boast

Working with the cartoons

3 Outline the aspects of modern communication shown in each cartoon in one or two sentences, e.g. advantages, disadvantages, developments or effects of modern communication.

4 Draw a mind map relating to modern communication. Start with the aspects addressed in the cartoons and add any other key ideas you can think of.

→ **Cartoons**
See *skills file* on page 155.

→ **Mind maps**
See *skills file* on page 186.

Hotspot

Work in pairs or a small group. Prepare and carry out a survey in your class (or year group) to find out which types of communication people mainly use.

a) Use the ideas below to devise questions (Q.) and answers (A.).

b) Analyse the answers you get and draw conclusions.

c) Present your results in graphs and diagrams, and summarise your conclusions in the form of a text.

Using the internet

Q.: Own PC / notebook?
A.: Yes / No
Q.: internet access?
A.: Yes / No
Q.: Where: at home? school? ...?
A.: multiple choice
Q.: Use internet for?
A.: multiple choice: information / games / mailing / chatting / shopping / studying / music / homework / ...
Q.: Two most frequently used options?
A.: open-end
Q.: Time spent online per day / week / month?
A.: multiple choice
Q.: How much / spend?
A.: multiple choice
Q.: Who pays?
A.: multiple choice

Using mobile phones

Q.: What age / first mobile?
A.: multiple choice: under 6 years / 6 – 10 years / 10 – 14 years...
Q.: Used mostly?
A.: multiple choice: talking / sending and receiving text messages / taking photos / listening to music / playing games / ...
Q.: How often use per day?
A.: multiple choice
Q.: Average costs per month
A.: multiple choice
Q.: Who pays?
A.: multiple choice

Communicating

Q.: How often write / receive?
A.: Table with multiple choice: fax / mail / postcard / letter / text message – per hour / day / week / ...

→ **Questionnaires and surveys**
See *skills file* on page 168.

Food trends

Before you read

1 a) What is your favourite food? Where does it come from or how is it produced?
b) How healthy is this food?

Understanding the text

2 Explain why new food products have become more common over the past 50 years.

3 Outline other changes with regard to food supplies that have happened in that period.

4 Which eating patterns have not been changed by globalization?

5 What kinds of food are fashionable nowadays? Which foods are definitely "out"?

The Food Chains That Link Us All

[…] The famous dictum of the early 19th century French gastronome Jean Anthelme Brillat-Savarin, "Tell me what you eat and I will tell you who you are," should be expanded. Tell me what you eat and I will tell you who you are, where you live, where you stand on political issues, who your neighbors are, how your economy functions, your country's history and foreign relations, and the state of the environment. By looking at food, the age we live in is better understood. […]

All of the processes by which cooks were introduced to new products and new ideas (and, in fact, most of history) began to speed up in the 19th century as transportation became faster – an acceleration so relentless that over the past 50 years the changes have seemed bewildering. Today trade is swift and global, and therefore food no longer reflects its place or time. No longer do you know where you are or what month it is by the food that is available. Every day organic vegetables from California, freshly caught turbots packed in dry ice from France, fresh Portuguese sardines, New Zealand oysters and smelly durian from Asia land in the airports of the world. More than ever in our history, we are now offered endless choices in food. But we may be embracing this excitement at the cost of the erosion of our own cultures.

Globalization has not led to equality […]. Food remains classist. The poor still eat mostly carbohydrates and fats, while the rich get the

1 dictum saying · **2 Jean Anthelme Brillat-Savarin** [ˈʒɑːnɑːnˌtelm briːˌjæsævəˈraːn] · **13 to speed up** to become faster · **15 acceleration** quickening · **15 relentless** fierce · **16 bewildering** confusing · **17 swift** fast · **18 to reflect s.th.** *here:* to give information about · **21 turbot** [ˈtɜːbət] *Steinbutt* · **23 durian** [ˈdjʊərɪən] type of fruit native to South-east Asia · **26 to embrace** *(figurative)* to welcome

Further activities: Your opinion

6 In what ways is food production linked to environmental protection? How important is this issue for you when you go shopping?

7 Apart from environmental issues, what other ethical reasons can you think of why we should, or should not, buy and eat certain kinds of food?

Check the web and Essay/Composition

8 You are familiar with the term "fast food" but some time ago a "slow food" movement was created. Find out about this new movement, e.g. where it was begun and what its aims are.

9 List the pros and cons of slow and fast food. You can refer back to task 8. Write an essay in which you state your opinion on the best way to eat nowadays.

→ **Essays/Compositions**
See *skills file* on page 157.

Mind map

10 Work in groups of four. Make a list of all the positive and negative lifestyle trends you have learned about in this unit. Use these ideas to draw a mind map. You can also include new ideas. Compare your mind map to those of the other groups.

→ **Mind maps**
See *skills file* on page 186.

protein – something that can even be seen in the difference between airline meals in first class and economy. […] Most of the great cities of the world, once refuges for the poor, are increasingly enclaves for the wealthy where cooks and even farmers can experiment without considering cost. […]

Farmers traditionally like to grow crops as large as possible because the ratio of weight to effort is better. People like baby vegetables because they are cute – tiny carrots, peanut-like squash and bean-sized Brussels sprouts. If the customer pays enough, the farmer will pick the vegetable when it's tiny. Precious small radish-sized potatoes from white to purple, and very waxy to very floury, sell in New York City for a price per size comparable to Manhattan real estate. The wealthy, of course, reject industrial farming, which was always intended to mass produce for the poor (and yet has failed in its greatest goal: to end world hunger). […]

Industrial food is out of fashion. Today there is a global market for organic fruits and vegetables, free-range birds, oysters from microbeds. Technology is in. Genetically modified food offers many opportunities, not the least of which is crops that are so insect repellent they need no pesticides. But – to the fury of some farmers – some of the same people who reject pesticides and call for organic food are now calling for a ban on genetically modified food. The argument, though a bit murky, is powerful. While there is no solid proof of the evils of such food, why trust hi-tech food from the same corporations that brought us industrial food?

Climate change is also changing our food, particularly through its impact on that great supplier, the ocean. Water is becoming not only warmer but less salty. The oceans, however, have been assaulted with not only climate change, but with pollution and destructive industrial fishing. Many predictions about seafood stocks are dire. Will most of them be seriously depleted by the year 2048, as one marine biologist recently predicted? […]

To understand the food of today, the past must be remembered. For the same reason, if future historians want to look back at what life was like in the early 21st century – the technological and information revolutions, the blessings and dangers of globalization, the challenges to the survival of a healthy planet – they would do well to look at our food. Changes in food have always been a function of changes in society. We are – and will always be – what we eat.

From *Time* specials, www.time.com, July 9, 2007 – 673 words.

34 refuge ['refju:dʒ] safe place · **34 enclave** area reserved for a specific group · **38 ratio** ['reɪʃɪəʊ] proportion · **40 squash** a kind of pumpkin · **41 Brussel sprout** *Rosenkohl* · **43 precious** ['preʃəs] expensive · **44 waxy** shiny · **46 real estate** houses and land · **52 free-range birds** chickens, etc. which are allowed to move around freely · **55 insect repellent** unattractive for insects · **55 pesticide** chemical substance that kills insects · **60 murky** unclear · **68 to assault** to attack · **70 dire** [daɪə] terrible · **71 depleted** greatly reduced

Unit 2 The world of work

801005-0002

A Sorry, Mr Wilkins, no hard feelings – but from your CV I don't think you would be right for this company.

B Looks like your spell check was turned off when you prepared your resume.

Getting started

1 Work in pairs and describe one of the above cartoons. Work out what its message is.
2 Which aspect(s) of the "world of work" does the cartoon relate to?
3 Present your ideas in class.

→ **Cartoons**
See *skills file* on page 155.

Young people and the job market

Before you read

1 Unemployment can have serious implications for those who find themselves without work. Think of ways in which unemployment affects these people and collect your ideas in a mind map.

→ **Mind maps**
See *skills file* on page 186.

The shameful growth of a generation of 'neets'

A growing army of young people in Britain is being left behind. That's the conclusion of a recent report by the Prince's Trust, which exposed the crisis of "neets" – young people aged 16 to 24 not in education, employment or training.

Relatively low unemployment masks almost 1.3 million "neets", a lost generation that has grown by 15% since 1997. The failure to tap their potential undermines social cohesion, damages the economy, and puts a growing strain on the exchequer. The report estimates the cost at £3.65bn a year. [...]

Vocational qualifications often fail to harness and develop practical talents, partly because there is no clear progression route from one vocational qualification to the next, equivalent to the academic route of GCSEs, A-levels and degrees.

Most people's vision of an apprenticeship is of an eager young learner acquiring, at the elbow of an experienced craftsman, key competences in a valued, skilled job. But the reality is quite different. Many have become "virtual": it is possible to complete your training without ever having set foot in the workplace.

New, programme-led apprenticeships, introduced in 2003, enable apprentices to begin their training at a college or training provider even if they have yet to secure a work placement.

The authors of a London School of Economics study in 2003 concluded that we have created a complex academic system of vocational qualifications because of a lack of consensus about what vocational education is actually for. [...] Vocational education should be about providing a rigorous pathway for students who wish to acquire a craft. It should be rooted in the practical

An instructor demonstrates a manufacturing process to apprentices.

acquisition of the skills necessary to do particular jobs.

Lack of clarity about purpose, which has handicapped curriculum reform in the past, may undermine the new 14–19 diplomas. Fears persist that they will not contain sufficient practical learning to engage young people and provide a useful step to employment. The minister for higher education and lifelong learning said recently in parliament: "It is important that we do not pigeonhole them as exclusively vocational ... Those diplomas will provide a blend of practical and theoretical learning."

To succeed, diplomas must provide students with the opportunity to acquire genuine skills in the best environment. Barriers must be broken

3 to expose s.th. to publish s.th. that was unknown · **8 to tap** to use · **9 social cohesion** [ˌsəʊʃlkəʊ'hiːʒn] feeling that one is part of a community · **10 strain** pressure · **11 exchequer** [ɪks'tʃekə] *(GB)* Ministry of Finance · **13 vocational** *Berufs-* · **13 to harness** to use · **19 eager** ['iːgə] willing · **19 to acquire** to get · **20 craftsman** a skilled worker, especially who makes things by hand · **28 work placement** *Praktikum* · **32 lack of consensus** disagreement · **36 to be rooted in** to be firmly based on · **37 acquisition** *here:* learning · **39 clarity about purpose** knowing exactly what one wants · **40 curriculum** subjects one studies at college · **41 14-19 diplomas** *(GB)* qualifications that will allow 14-19-year-olds to study in a vocational area · **41 to persist** to continue · **42 sufficient** [sə'fɪʃənt] enough · **47 to pigeonhole** ['pɪdʒənhəʊl] to classify · **48 blend** mixture · **51 genuine** ['dʒenjʊɪn] real down between schools and FE colleges, because schools alone simply do not have the facilities or the resources to deliver all 14 diplomas. Genuine workplace experience should be a compulsory element of all diplomas, so students can be taught – and inspired – by experienced, skilled craftsmen.

To be part of a clear vocation path, diplomas must be fully integrated with apprenticeships and higher vocational qualifications, such as foundation degrees.

While we waste a generation's potential, we add to their number, as 45,000 16-year-olds leave school each year functionally illiterate and/or innumerate. This sad, forgotten generation can only look forward to a future of unemployment as demand for unskilled labour plummets.

To compensate for these failures, we import skills through mass immigration, masking the ill effects of the government's failure to build a vocational training regime sufficiently rigorous and appealing to satisfy economic needs and to inspire those with practical aptitudes. Until we build such an attractive vocational path, we will continue to cheat the lost generation of their chance to prosper.

By John Hayes, Shadow Minister for Vocational Education, *The Guardian*, April 24, 2007 – 548 words.

53 **FE college** *short for* Further Education college · 54 **facilities** *here:* equipment, classrooms, etc. · 56 **compulsory** obligatory · 63 **foundation degree** *(GB)* university degree combining study and work experience in a company · 66 **illiterate** unable to read and write · 67 **innumerate** unable to do mathematics · 69 **to plummet** to fall sharply · 70 **to compensate for** to correct · 71 **to mask** to hide · 74 **appealing** attractive · 75 **aptitude** ability · 78 **to prosper** to do well in life

Mediation: English-German

2 You are doing an internship in a German company. Your instructor asks you to sum up the information on "neets" in German in ten sentences. Explain who "neets" refers to; what demands for change in vocational training John Hayes makes; the reasons why these changes are necessary.

Mediation
See *skills file* on page 158.

Research

3 Search the internet for statistics on current unemployment rates in:
a) Germany
b) the European Union
c) the United Kingdom
d) the USA.

4 Which specific groups do the statisticians consider when collecting unemployment statistics?

Mediation and presentation

5 Imagine you work in a German company with business partners abroad. In the near future, your boss is going to be visited by some Chinese business partners. He asks you to prepare a short presentation on the *"duales Ausbildungssystem"* in Germany. You can use a search engine and these two German key words to find information. Sum up the most important ideas about the German dual vocational education system in English. Prepare a transparency with key words to use in your presentation. You will find useful vocabulary in the text.

Mediation
See *skills file* on page 158.
Presentations
See *skills file* on page 160.

Check the web
en.wikipedia.org

Working women

Before you read: "Mothers held back..." on page 26.

1 Analyse the statistics below.

→ **Statistics**
See *skills file* on page 161.

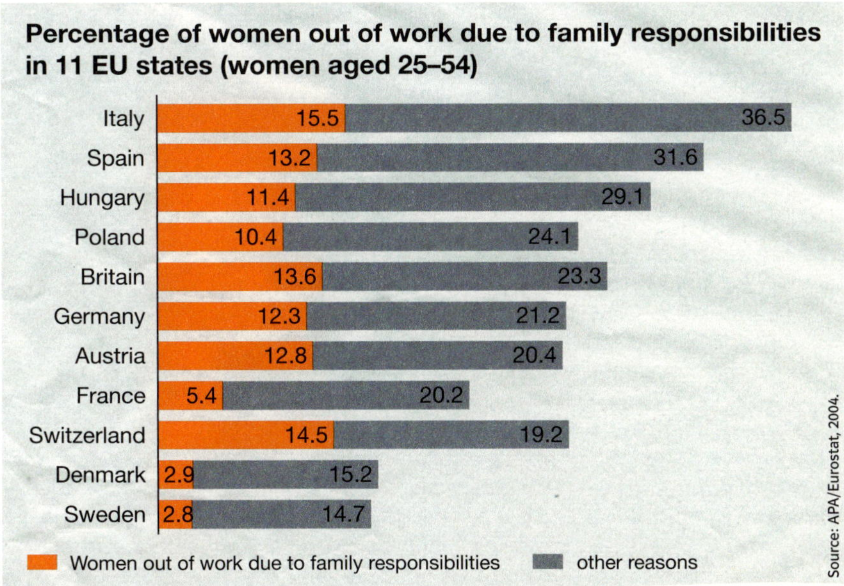

2 Why might Sweden have a much lower proportion of women out of work due to family responsibilities than Britain?

3 What consequences does the higher level of employment among women probably have for Swedish families?

Summary

4 a) Summarize the important points of the text on page 26 in table form. Draw a table with two columns on a sheet of paper. The left-hand column is for the following "prompts":

→ **Summaries**
See *skills file* on page 164.

Prompts	Related information
– mothers are the primary parent	
– the glass ceiling	
– care responsibilites in families	
– long-term solution(s).	

b) Scan the text and fill in the related information in key words in the right-hand column.

Role play: Dialogue

5 Work in pairs. A married couple with one child both work to support the family. However, the wife is also mainly responsible for the housework. She wants to convince her husband to share the housework more fairly. Think of arguments she may use. Also think of arguments her husband may use. Act out the dialogue.

Translation

→ **Translation**
See *skills file* on page 165.

6 Translate ‹L 31–47› into German: "Mrs Blair said yesterday ... she warns".

Mothers held back under burden of their chores, says Cherie Blair

Men must do more to help ease the domestic burden shouldered by women, Cherie Blair has told a conference on the family and the future role of carers.

Mrs Blair, who once said that she felt she might fall off the "tightrope" when balancing her career with her family life, called for more support for mothers who still hold down jobs.

She told the London conference, which was organised by the left-of-centre think tank, Demos, that mothers remained the "primary parent" responsible for "buying children's presents and clothes, making sure the fridge was stocked or writing Christmas cards".

"A baby is born. A child develops a high fever. The boiler breaks down. A parent suffers a stroke. These are the everyday events that throw a working woman's delicate balance between work and family into chaos," said Mrs Blair.

This is not the first time Mrs Blair, a judge, high-profile barrister and mother of four, has complained about men not doing their fair share of housework.

In 2003 she told a conference on women's and human rights in Australia that more women worked than ever before but they still shouldered the burden of housework and child care.

In an aside to the audience she said: "I am always quite astonished when I read surveys about how many hours [of housework] men are supposed to do, because in my experience they don't do any at all."

Mrs Blair said yesterday it was time to lift the "glass ceiling" in the home, where women are held back under the burden of their chores and responsibility for children and elderly parents.

"That's life, we tell each other," she said. But care, she argued, can no longer be considered a private matter. "We need to find ways to make the invisible visible, to uncover and celebrate the value of unpaid work."

She pointed to the cost to society when things went wrong at home. "Think of the growing number of children in care, the millions of pounds spent on the youth justice system. This is because the care work that takes place in families has a wider social value."

Women "sandwiched" between caring for elderly relatives and dependent children risk losing out on earnings that they will need to support their own retirement, she warns. [...]

But she adds: "The current reliance on this kind of informal care is unlikely to be sustainable. One way, of course, of finding a long-term solution to these challenges is by involving fathers more in care."

She points to a "quiet revolution" among men who increasingly want to play an active role in their children's care.

"The Government has begun to talk about the importance of men's role as active fathers, not just as breadwinners. It has introduced supportive legislation such as two weeks' statutory paternity leave. But society will need to do more in the future to help them."

In the absence of policies specifically targeted at "helping and supporting fathers", the traditional gender divide will be reinforced, she says.

"Due to the stubborn pay gap, inflexible working patterns and an entrenched working culture, men will end up remaining in the workplace rather than sharing caring responsibilities at home."

By Robert Verkaik, *The Independent*, March 22, 2007 – 541 words.

Heading: **burden** a lot of work · **chore** [tʃɔː] *here:* housework; **Text: 1 to ease s.th.** to make s.th. easier · **4 carer** person who looks after a sick or old person at home · **6 tightrope** *(figurative) Hochseil* · **8 to hold down** to keep · **10 think tank** organization that does research · **18 delicate** *opposite of* stable · **27 aside** remark that is not directly connected with the subject being discussed · **31 glass ceiling** *(figurative)* barrier that stops certain groups from getting the best jobs in a company · **45 to lose out on s.th.** to miss a chance · **47 retirement** time when one no longer works after a certain age · **48 reliance** [rɪˈlaɪəns] depending on s.th. for help · **49 sustainable** which can be kept going for a long time · **58 statutory paternity leave** [ˌstætjətrɪ pəˈtɜːnətɪˌliːv] period of time allowed to fathers by law to look after children · **64 stubborn** *(negative)* unchanging · **65 entrenched** fixed

Teleworking

Before you read

1 What kinds of employment contracts are usually offered to employees in developed countries? Make a list.

Working at home grows in popularity

Billions of people have ditched the commute to the office in favour of working from home – and the number of home-based workers is set to rise dramatically.

According to research [...] by consumer think tank the Future Foundation, 8.6 per cent of the work force – 2.5 million people – work from home for one or more days a week.

It expects that number to rise by 200,000 a year for the next four years. By 2020, it reckons that 16 per cent of the working population will be at least partially based at home.

Employers increasingly allow well-paid, high-flying professionals, as well as traditional teleworkers, to work away from the office. The report, commissioned by Brother, the electronics and manufacturing company, also identifies a new type of worker, who is based at the office but e-mails clients from their BlackBerry on the train or makes work-related phone calls from home. Describing them as "freE workers", it says this group accounts for 46 per cent of the work force but will rise to 80 per cent by 2020.

"The question by then will be not who sometimes works at home but who doesn't," says report author William Nelson. "There are positive benefits to skipping the daily commute and increasing productivity by working at home. Highly-skilled workers who are in demand may find their company would rather allow them to work flexibly, rather than lose them."

In a separate report, published recently by the Management Consultancies Association, a third of the 1,200 respondents claimed that remote working is now common in their organisation. However, despite the potential gains for the employer, 93 per cent said it was the employees who were choosing to work away from the office, rather than their employer encouraging them to do so.

It also found that the majority of companies were unwilling to fund the arrangements. Only 40 per cent said that their employer covered the costs of remote working.

The Flexible Working Regulations, which came into force in 2003, provide parents with children under six – or 18 if the child has a disability – with the right to request flexible working arrangements, which may include working from home.

The employment solicitor James Upton, from Hill Dickinson Solicitors, says: "This means an employer has to follow certain procedures to consider their request for flexible working. It doesn't mean they are automatically able to work from home. Neither does it mean that employees without children can't ask their boss to let them work from home."

If you're a valued employee with bags of experience, you're more likely to convince your employer that you can work from home effectively, than if you're fairly junior, only started last month and need constant supervision. [...]

By Joanne O' Connell, *The Independent*, September 24, 2005 – 455 words.

1 to ditch to give up · **3 to be set** to be expected · **10 to reckon** to suppose · **11 partially** part of the time · **13 high-flying** very successful · **15 to commission s.th.** to officially ask s.o. to do s.th. · **21 to account for** to be a particular number · **25 to skip s.th.** to stop doing s.th. · **27 in demand** *here:* needed by companies · **32 remote working** teleworking · **34 gain** advantage · **39 to fund** to finance · **44 disability** a handicap · **47 solicitor** *(BE)* lawyer · **54 valued** respected · **55 you're more likely to** you have a better chance · **58 supervision** guidance in one's work

Understanding the text

2 Describe the trends which Future Foundation research has discovered with regard to working from home in Britain.
3 Explain what is meant by the term "freE workers" ‹L 20›.
4 According to the text, what are the benefits of working from home?
5 Who usually takes the initiative when it comes to working from home?

A step further: Cartoon and text

6 Describe the cartoon and relate it to the text.

→ **Cartoons**
See *skills file* on page 155.

"I suppose you realize that when I tell everyone back at the office about this you won't be able to tele-commute anymore."

Essay/Composition

7 Comment on the benefits and inconveniences of teleworking for both employers and employees.

→ **Comments**
See *skills file* on page 155.

1|2

Listening comprehension

Job satisfaction

Oxfam International is a confederation of 13 organizations which work together with more than 3,000 partners in over 100 countries to find long-term solutions to poverty and injustice.
Listen to an interview with the director of Oxfam in Britain, Barbara Stocking.

Entrepreneurial skills

entrepreneur /ˌɒn.trə.prəˈnɜː/
someone who starts their own business, especially when this involves risks

Cambridge Advanced Learner's Dictionary, 2003.

Before you read

1 Look at the definition of an entrepreneur. In your opinion, which characteristic traits and attributes does an entrepreneur need? Make a list of adjectives and be prepared to explain them. You may use a dictionary.

Social Entrepreneur of the Year: Calling all social visionaries

2|5

The social entrepreneur, rather than looking to maximise profits, seeks to maximise the good of society. If you think you fit the bill, enter the contest launched today by *The Independent*.

Dr Muhammad Yunus

Have you launched a business that does more than simply make as much money as possible? If so, *The Independent* wants to hear from you. [...] We (are) launch(ing) an important new contest to find the UK's most successful social entrepreneurs.

Why do we think this is important? Well, the traditional view of successful entrepreneurship is that the more money a business makes, the better. Yet there are a growing number of entrepreneurs, both in this country and around the world, whose desire for money is to use it to transform society.

But what exactly is social entrepreneurship?

The term has become something of a buzzphrase. In some ways, it's easier to start by talking about exactly what social entrepreneurship is not.

For example, this is not just another way of describing a charitable organisation or foundation. Nor is it about campaigning – social entrepreneurship always offers practical alternatives to inequitable states of affairs. Similarly, social entrepreneurship is more than corporate social responsibility and it doesn't require you to run a not-for-profit or non-governmental organisation. [...]

To define a social entrepreneur, think Sir Richard Branson crossed with Mother Teresa. That is, think about blending good business skills with charitable instincts.

Rather than seeking to maximise profits, as businesses must do, the social entrepreneur seeks to maximise the good of society. And while a mainstream business entrepreneur creates products and services that will generate profits, the social entrepreneur responds to market failures, coming up with goods and services, or approaches to accessing them, that business cannot because the financial rewards are not high enough and the risk is too great.

A social entrepreneur's chief contribution does not come from an ability to set up hospitals, schools or centres for the physically or mentally disabled. Rather, it comes from the capacity to envisage what does not exist and make it happen.

The Nobel Peace Prize laureate, Muhammad Yunus, is the perfect example. He was deemed borderline sane as he struggled to launch his "bank for the poor" in Chittagong, Bangladesh.

From *The Independent*, news.independent.co.uk, May 4, 2007 – 376 words.

2 to seek, sought, sought to try · **3 to fit the bill** to be suitable · **5 to launch** to start · **17 buzzphrase** a fashionable expression · **21 charitable** which helps people in need · **23 inequitable** unfair · **24 state of affairs** situation · **25 corporate** *here*: as shown by companies · **30 to blend** to mix · **35 mainstream** conventional · **38 approach** a way of dealing with s.th. · **39 to access** *here:* to reach · **40 reward** *here:* money one makes · **44 disabled** handicapped · **45 to envisage** [ɪnˈvɪzɪdʒ] to imagine · **47 laureate** winner of a prize · **48 to deem** to consider · **48 borderline sane** almost mentally ill

Understanding the text: "Social entrepreneur..." on page 29.

2 Compare a conventional entrepreneur with a social entrepreneur, who may enter the contest.
3 What does social entrepreneurship not mean?
4 Outline the social entrepreneur's main goal.
5 Explain why social entrepreneurs can also be called 'social visionaries'.

Mediation (alternative to understanding the text)

6 The owner of a German, medium-sized company has found *The Independent* article on the internet. He asks you to explain, in German, the difference between a conventional entrepreneur and a social entrepreneur. Make a table with two columns and list the main differences as mentioned in the text, in German.

→ **Mediation**
See *skills file* on page 158.

Internet research and presentation

7 "Social entrepreneurship is more than corporate social responsibility." ‹L 24› Use the internet to find out what the latter term means.
a) How is 'corporate social responsibility' defined?
b) How would you translate the term?
c) Suggest reasons why CSR is also criticized. You can check the wikipedia website to find ideas.
d) Prepare a transparency with the main ideas you have come up with about corporate responsibility and present them in class.

→ **Presentations**
See *skills file* on page 160.

Translation

8 Translate lines 32 to 46 into German. Start with "Rather than... " down to "... make it happen."

→ **Translation**
See *skills file* on page 165.

Hotspots

a) **1** Some schools in Germany have a so-called *"Juniorenfirma"*. Find out which class at your school is in charge of it. Then prepare a list of questions in English to ask the students involved. Collect information that you can use to create a leaflet about this 'company' in English. You can present your findings at the end of this short project.
2 If there is no such *"Juniorenfirma"* in your school, imagine you are asked to set one up. Which services and products could you offer in your school? How could you run the company along social entrepreneurial lines? List your services and products, invent a marketing slogan to go with each item and think up a name for your company. Also think of slogans to underline the social entrepreneurial aspects of your company.
b) Bill Gates is one of the richest people in the world and also one of the most successful entrepreneurs ever. Find out whether he may also be called a social entrepreneur. You can use the internet to find information.

Check the web
www.google.com
www.excite.com

Intercultural competence: Cross-cultural competence in business

Before you read: "Cross-cultural negotiations" on pages 32–33.

1 Study the following situations A–C and explain what you think went wrong.

Situations

A A German company is about to establish business contacts in South America. The German delegation is to meet the potential business partners from Brazil at 2 pm in the conference room of a first-class hotel where the Brazilians are staying. At 2.15 pm the Germans are still waiting alone in the conference room. At 2.30 pm the situation has not changed. At 2.35 pm the Brazilians show up, greet the Germans very politely and are ready to get down to business. The Germans are not amused.

B An American spends a year working in Britain for the European subsidiary of his American employer. He shares his office with Susan Smyth. When she shows up one morning, wearing a white suit, he says to her: "Wow, I like your pants!" Susan turns red and leaves the office.

C George W. Bush was received by Pope Benedict XVI. During the audience they sat opposite each other. George W. Bush had his legs crossed. When Pope Benedict XVI asked Mr Bush a question, the latter replied: "Yes, sir."

Understanding the text

2 Create a table to provide an overview of how particular behaviour is interpreted differently around the world.

Example:

Behaviour	Countries and rules
strong eye contact	US, UK, northern Europe = confidence, sincerity South America = trustworthiness Japan = rude and should be avoided

Language

3 Find opposites in the text for the following adjectives.

a) long | c) unimportant | e) different
b) polite | d) strong, firm

4 Think of adjectives that belong to the same word families as these nouns.

a) values ‹L10› | d) trustworthiness ‹L21› | g) information ‹L78›
b) confidence ‹L20› | e) distance ‹L27› | h) speech ‹L84›
c) sincerity ‹L21› | f) urgency ‹L40› | i) depth ‹L98›

Cross-cultural negotiations

Let us look at a brief example of how cross-cultural negotiation training can benefit the international business person:

There are two negotiators dealing with the same potential client in the Middle East. Both have identical proposals and packages. One ignores the importance of cross-cultural negotiation training believing the proposal will speak for itself. The other undertakes some cross-cultural training. He/she learns about the culture, values, beliefs, etiquette and approaches to business, meetings and negotiations. Nine times out of ten the latter will succeed over the rival. This is because 1) it is likely they would have endeared themselves more to the host negotiation team and 2) they would be able to tailor their approach to the negotiations [...]. By way of highlighting this, a few brief examples of topics covered in cross-cultural negotiation training shall be offered.

Eye Contact: In the US, UK and much of northern Europe, strong, direct eye contact conveys confidence and sincerity. In South America it is a sign of trustworthiness. However, in some cultures such as the Japanese, prolonged eye contact is considered rude and is generally avoided.

Personal Space & Touch: In Europe and North America, business people will usually leave a certain amount of distance between themselves when interacting. Touching only takes place between friends. In South America or the Middle East, business people are tactile and like to get up close. In Japan or China, it is not uncommon for people to leave a gap

of four feet when conversing. Touching only takes place between close friends and family members.

Time: Western societies are very 'clock conscious'. Time is money and punctuality is crucial. This is also the case in countries such as Japan or China where being late would be taken as an insult. However, in South America, southern Europe and the Middle East, being on time for a meeting does not carry the same sense of urgency.

Meeting & Greeting: Most international business people meet with a handshake. In some countries this is not appropriate between genders. Some may view a weak handshake as sign of weakness whereas others would perceive a firm handshake as aggressive. How should people be addressed? Is it by first name, surname or title? Is small talk part of the proceedings or not?

Gift-Giving: In Japan and China gift-giving is an integral part of business protocol, however in the

1 brief short · **2 to benefit** to be useful · **4 negotiator** s.o. who wants to come to an agreement with others · **12 the latter** the last in a list · **13 to endear oneself** to make others like one · **14 host** which receives a group of visitors · **15 to tailor** to adapt · **16 by way of** as a means of · **20 to convey** to express · **21 sincerity** meaning what you say · **30 tactile** physical · **32 to converse** to talk to s.o. · **34 clock conscious** finding punctuality important · **35 crucial** ['kru:ʃəl] decisive · **37 insult** rudeness · **40 urgency** importance · **45 to perceive** to see · **46 to address s.o.** to speak to s.o. · **48 proceedings** series of actions, e.g. at a meeting · **50 integral** ['ɪntɪgrəl] important

Hotspot

Create an intercultural competence poster for visitors to your town. List points that they may find unusual about German culture and advise them on what kind of behaviour is expected of them.
You may include the following aspects: sorting waste and being environmentally conscious, punctuality, smoking in public places, using public transport, mealtime etiquette, etc.

US or UK, it has negative connotations. Where gifts are exchanged should one give lavish gifts? Are they always reciprocated? Should they be wrapped? Are there numbers or colours that should be avoided?

All the above in one way or another will impact cross-cultural negotiation and can only be learnt through cross-cultural training. Doing or saying the wrong thing at the wrong time, poor communication and cross-cultural misunderstandings can all have harmful consequences.

Cross-cultural negotiation training builds its foundations upon understanding etiquettes and approaches to business abroad before focusing on cross-cultural differences in negotiation styles and techniques.

There are three interconnected aspects that need to be considered before entering into cross-cultural negotiation.

The Basis of the Relationship: in much of Europe and North America, business is contractual in nature. Personal relationships are seen as unhealthy as they can cloud objectivity and lead to complications. In South America and much of Asia, business is personal. Partnerships will only be made with those they know, trust and feel comfortable with. It is therefore necessary to invest in relationship building before conducting business.

Information at Negotiations: Western business culture places emphasis on clearly presented and rationally argued business proposals using statistics and facts. Other business cultures rely on similar information but with differences. For example, visual and oral communicators such as the South Americans may prefer information presented through speech or using maps, graphs and charts.

Negotiation Styles: the way in which we approach negotiation differs across cultures. For example, in the Middle East rather than approaching topics sequentially negotiators may discuss issues simultaneously. South Americans can become quite vocal and animated. The Japanese will negotiate in teams and decisions will be based upon consensual agreement. In Asia, decisions are usually made by the most senior figure or head of a family. In China, negotiators are highly trained in the art of gaining concessions. In Germany, decisions can take a long time due to the need to analyse information and statistics in great depth. In the UK, pressure tactics and imposing deadlines are ways of closing deals whilst in Greece this would backfire. [...]

From *Kwintessential Ltd website*, www.kwintessential.co.uk – 755 words.

51 **connotation** a certain idea that we link with a word · 52 **lavish** generous · 53 **to reciprocate** to give in return · 55 **to impact** to have an effect on · 70 **contractual** agreed in a contract (= *Vertrag*) · 72 **to cloud s.o.'s objectivity** to make s.o. less objective · 77 **to conduct** to do · 89 **sequentially** one after another · 92 **consensual agreement** decision with which everyone is happy · 96 **concession** compromise · 99 **to impose s.th.** to make everyone accept s.th. · 100 **to backfire** to go wrong

Unit 3 Consumerism

801005-0003

Getting started

1 Describe the different forms of advertising shown above and say what you think of them.
2 Which forms of advertising do you regularly encounter? How do you react to them?
3 Which other forms of advertising are part of our daily lives? Think of some examples.

Advertising

Opinions on advertising

2|7

A Advertising may be described as the science of arresting the human intelligence long enough to get money from it.

Steven Leacock, Canadian economist & humorist (1869–1944)

D What is the difference between unethical and ethical advertising? Unethical advertising uses falsehoods to deceive the public; ethical advertising uses truth to deceive the public.

Vilhjalmur Stefansson, Canadian explorer & ethnologist (1879–1962)

B Advertising is the greatest art form of the twentieth century.

Marshall McLuhan, Canadian social scientist (1911–1980)

E Many a small thing has been made large by the right kind of advertising.

Mark Twain, US humorist and novelist (1835–1910)

C Advertising is legalized lying.

H.G. Wells, British author (1866–1946)

G Advertising is the modern substitute for argument; its function is to make the worse appear the better.

George Santayana, US (Spanish-born) philosopher (1863–1952)

F You can tell the ideals of a nation by its advertisements.

Norman Douglas, Scottish author (1868–1952)

100 words

A: **to arrest s.th.** to make s.o. pay attention to s.th. · **D:** **falsehood** lie

Your opinion

1 Explain what you understand by each of the quotations above and then give your opinion on how true you think each statement is.

2 What is advertising in your opinion? Collect statements of your own in class which begin with "Advertising is …".

Essay/Composition

3 Choose one of the above quotations and write an essay discussing the point made. Use real examples from the world of advertising to support your viewpoint. Write about 250 words.

→ **Essays/Compositions**
See *skills file* on page 157.

The rise of the new media

Media usage in the US

If you are reading this as you surf the internet while the TV is on, the radio is playing and you are listening to music on your personal stereo you are already tapping into the American way of media multitasking.

Data released by the US census bureau today forecasts that Americans will spend a total of 65 days watching TV next year and 41 days listening to the radio. A week each will be given to reading newspapers and surfing the internet.

All that reading, surfing and listening will occupy 3,518 hours of the average American adult's year – the equivalent of almost five months. But such indolence doesn't come cheap. The average American, says the survey, will spend $936 (£475) on media in the coming year.

The information comes in the 126th statistical abstract, which collates data from census bureau studies as well as international organisations, non-profit-making groups and the private sector. The abstract, which has been published most years since 1878, makes comparisons with previous years as well as providing forecasts.

Internet boom

Thus the survey shows that 97 million adult internet users looked for news online in 2005, 92 million bought a product online and 91 million made an online travel reservation. About 16 million Americans used a social or professional networking site such as MySpace, and 13 million created a blog in 2005, with 39 million reading someone else's blog.

The information on internet usage is based on telephone surveys of 2,500 US adults carried out in September 2005 by the Pew Research Centre. The survey also showed that 25 million Americans downloaded videos to their computers, and 24 million remixed material found online to make their own creation.

Despite much speculation about the death of old media and the rise of the new, reading a newspaper and surfing the internet will each consume the same amount of the average American adult's time next year, the census bureau says.

Nevertheless, a week spent reading the news on the internet represents a significant change in habits. Ten years ago, according to a Pew report in the summer, one in 50 Americans regularly got their news from the internet. Today the figure is one in three. But the figures show that the rate of increase in online news readership has slowed since 2000, suggesting, says the report, that "online news has evolved as a supplemental source that is used along with traditional news media outlets. It is valued most for headlines and convenience."

"This new census bureau material highlights just how dramatically we have moved into the information age," said Lee Rainie, director of the Pew internet and American life project. "Pick any metric you like and you'll see that the volume of information and media in people's lives has grown, the velocity of that information as it circulates in their lives has increased, and the variety of information has exploded." […]

From "Snapshot of the US: 65 days in front of the TV and five months of media" by Dan Glaister, *The Guardian*, December 15, 2006 – 482 words.

3 to tap into s.th. *here:* to be familiar with s.th. · **10 to occupy** ['ɒkjʊpaɪ] to fill a period of time · **12 indolence** ['ɪndələns] laziness · **17 to collate** to gather and compare · **44 significant** large and important · **44 habit** usual behaviour · **51 supplemental** additional · **51 along with** together with · **52 to value** to consider important · **53 convenience** [kən,vi:nɪəns] *here:* being easy to use · **56 Rainie** ['reɪni:] · **57 metric** *here:* way of measuring s.th. · **59 velocity** speed

Understanding the text

1 What is meant by the term "media multitasking" ‹L 43›?

2 What are the main things that adult internet users do on the internet?

A step further: Cartoon and quotation

3 Describe the cartoon. What additional aspect of media usage does the cartoon refer to?

→ **Cartoons**
See *skills file* on page 155.

"They're books, dad needs them for reading."

4 "A week spent reading the news on the internet represents a significant change in habits." ‹L 43–44› What implications does this statement have for newspaper readers, advertisers and newspaper publishers?

Working with the text: Interview

5 A journalist is interviewing an expert from the US census bureau about media usage in the US. Invent the journalist's questions and formulate answers based on the information given in the text.

Example:

How many days will Americans probably spend listening to the radio next year?

They will spend a total of 41 days listening to the radio.

Working with words

6 Find words in the text which mean the following:

a) *Musik hören*
b) *im Internet surfen*
c) *Geld ausgeben für*
d) *Information über*
e) *auf den PC herunterladen*
f) *eine Veränderung von*
g) *jeder Dritte*
h) *Zunahme an*
i) *eine Vielfalt an*

Translation

7 How do the following participles from the text translate?

a) released ‹L 5›
b) with 39 million reading ‹L 29–30›
c) carried out ‹L 32›
d) found ‹L 36›
e) suggesting ‹L 49›

8 Translate the following paragraphs into German: "Despite much speculation..." ‹L 38› to "... convenience." ‹L 53›.

→ **Translation**
See *skills file* on page 165.

Working with statistics

9 According to the text, 92 million Americans bought a product online in 2005. Note: In 2005 there were 204 million internet users.
a) Analyse the statistics relating to online shoppers in select countries in Western Europe (Fig. 1). How do the figures compare with the US?
b) What do the statistics in Fig. 2 reveal about online advertising spending in select Western European countries?
c) Compare the number of online shoppers and the amount of money invested in online advertising. What strikes you about the statistics?

→ **Statistics**
See *skills file* on page 161.

Fig. 1 Selection of Western European adult internet users who shop online (%)

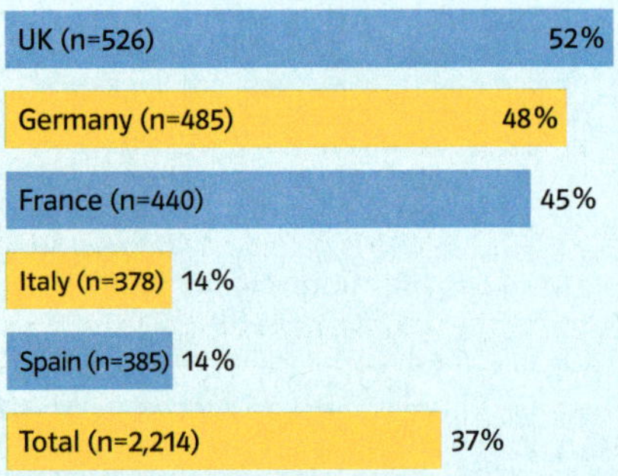

Source: IPSOS Mori (Market & Opinion Research International), November 2006.

Fig. 2 Online advertising spending per user in a selection of Western European countries, 2006, 2007, 2010 (US$)

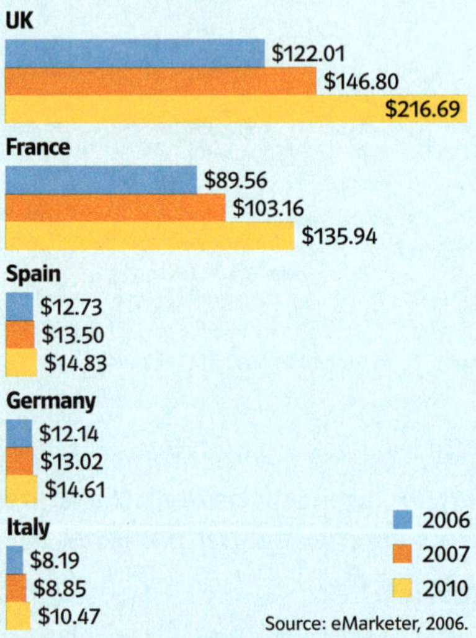

Source: eMarketer, 2006.

Hotspots

a) When carrying out advertising campaigns in the UK, advertisers may come into contact with ASA. Check the web to find out more about ASA and to answer the following questions:

1 What is ASA short for?
2 What does ASA do?
3 What role does ASA play in ad regulation in Europe?

→ **Check the web**
www.asa.org.uk

b) Find out about advertising campaigns that had to be withdrawn. You may use a search engine or the websites of newspapers such as *USA Today* and *The Independent*. You can enter key words such as "ad campaign" and "withdraw". The ASA website also lists controversial ad campaigns.
Present your findings to the class after considering the following points: a description of the campaign – reactions to it – consequences for the advertisers/company.

→ **Presentations**
See *skills file* on page 160.

Advertising standards

VW reviews complaints, pulls ad after all

Caving to pressure from suicide-prevention groups, Volkswagen said Thursday that it would pull a commercial that shows a man who threatens to jump off a building because of concern about the world's troubles.

The ad – in which he decides not to leap after hearing there are three VWs that cost less than $17,000 – was criticized by five mental health groups.

Two – the Suicide Prevention Action Network (SPAN USA) and The American Foundation for Suicide Prevention (AFSP) – sent letters to VW, spokesman Keith Price says. He says VW received no complaints from consumers or its dealers.

VW at first defended the ad, but changed course after reviewing the complaints, he says. The agency that created the ad, Crispin Porter + Bogusky, referred all calls to Volkswagen. AFSP executive director Robert Gebbia says, "We're very happy with (VW's) decision. Suicide is a tragic problem and shouldn't be used ... to sell products."

In addition to no longer airing the ad, VW is trying to get it removed from online video sites such as YouTube.com.

Gebbia says he understands it can't be fully eradicated online. "Obviously, what's out there they have no control over."

This was the latest in a round of commercial controversies. Three ads that ran on the Feb. 4 Super Bowl also drew fire:

- General Motors (GM) is re-editing a commercial to delete a section in which a distraught robot jumps off a bridge.
- Masterfoods USA has dropped an ad in which the reaction of two men to an accidental kiss upset some gay activists.
- Nationwide Mutual Insurance has declined to pull an ad in which Kevin Federline, estranged husband of Britney Spears, plays a fast-food worker dreaming of being a rap star. The National Restaurant Association criticized it for a "demeaning" portrayal of restaurant workers.

The Internet has given advocacy groups immense power to affect ads by letting them vent on a very public stage, agency executive Mark DiMassimo says.

"If sufficiently organized, they can have a major impact, and that's driving fear into the hearts of mass marketers," he says. "Big, conservative companies are used to controlling the media, but that's no longer the case."

Yet, when marketers back down, it creates a "very dangerous" environment for the ad industry, says Drew Neisser, CEO of the Renegade Marketing Group.

"The recent withdrawals will embolden every interest group to push their agenda and complain about any ad that doesn't jibe with their mission," he says.

"To create ads that offend no one is a fruitless endeavor," Neisser says. "To cut through, there must be an element of surprise ... that someone, somewhere, might not like."

By Laura Petrecca, *USA TODAY*, February 15, 2007 – 437 words.

Headline: to pull s.th. *here:* to stop broadcasting s.th.

1 to cave to to finally do what s.o. wants · **6 to leap** to jump · **16 to refer s.th.** *here:* to send s.th. to s.o. else · **21 to air** to broadcast, e.g. on TV · **22 to remove** to take off · **25 to eradicate** to get rid of completely · **29 to draw fire** to be criticized strongly · **31 distraught** [dɪ'strɔːt] out of your mind with unhappiness · **34 accidental** *opposite of* planned · **36 to decline** to refuse · **37 estranged** [ɪ'streɪndʒd] no longer living with your husband or wife · **40 demeaning** disrespectful · **42 advocacy group** ['ædvəkəsɪˌgruːp] interest group · **43 to affect** to influence · **43 to vent** to express strong criticism · **45 sufficiently** enough for a particular purpose · **53 to embolden** *(formal)* to encourage · **55 to jibe with** ['dʒaɪb wɪð] to agree with · **58 endeavor** (*BE* **endeavour**) attempt to do s.th.

Summary: "VW reviews..." on page 39.

1 Summarize the text by answering the questions about it.
a) What was the VW ad about?
b) Who criticized the ad? Who didn't?
c) How did VW react?
d) What arguments do the two marketing experts put forward?

→ **Summaries**
See *skills file* on page 164.

Your opinion: Discussion

2 Discuss the following questions in class: Should adverts be regulated or not? What restrictions, if any, would you place on advertisers?

→ **Discussions**
See *skills file* on page 177.

Further activities

3 Write a mail to VW from one of these viewpoints.
a) Say that you are glad to hear that VW has withdrawn the ad.
b) Say that it is difficult for you to understand why VW has withdrawn the ad. Give reasons.

→ **Mails**
See *skills file* on page 175.

Working with words

4 Find the nouns which correspond to the verbs from the text.

a) threaten ‹L 3›	c) defended ‹L 14›	e) removed ‹L 22›
b) criticize ‹L 8›	d) referred ‹L 16›	f) delete ‹L 31›

5 Find the adjectives which correspond to the words from the text.

a) suicide ‹L 1›	c) addition ‹L 21›	e) environment ‹L 51›
b) prevention ‹L 1›	d) controversies ‹L 28›	f) offend ‹L 57›

6 Write sentences with the verbs and adjectives in tasks 4 and 5.

Targeting the consumer

Before you read: "Teachers' call..." on page 41.

1 Think of different products that are advertised on TV. Which groups of people are often used to advertise them?
Example: Film stars often endorse food products; housewives recommend washing powder.
2 Find examples which illustrate how the respective target group for each product is reached.

Mediation

3 You are an intern in the marketing department of a German company. Your boss asks you to find out what "sexploitation" means based on the text. Find the relevant information in the text and present your findings in a German text (complete sentences).

→ **Mediation**
See *skills file* on page 158.

Understanding the text

4 What has been revealed by the report "Growing up in a Material World" and what courses of action has the NUT called for?
5 Describe the new regulations on advertising.
6 Why is the NUT not satisfied with the new regulations on junk food advertising?

Teachers' call for 'sexploitation' of children to end

Teachers' leaders have demanded an end to the "sexploitation" of children through commercial marketing. They also called for a ban on the advertising of all "unhealthy" food and drink on all TV channels before the 9pm watershed.

A report published by Britain's biggest teachers' union, the National Union of Teachers, warned: "Companies are unashamedly targeting their campaigns to exploit children's 'pester power'."

"Growing up in a Material World"

The report – "Growing up in a Material World" – argued that this included targeting "day to day purchases of food and drink, through treats, such as meals out, to clothes and toys which can include expensive electronic equipment".

The report cited figures from Ofcom, the television regulator, which showed that products with high sugar, salt or fat content accounted for between 82 per cent and 92 per cent of all food and drink advertising before the 9pm watershed.

It also cited examples of what Steve Sinnott, the union's general secretary, described as the "sexploitation of young children" – such as Tesco marketing a pole-dancing kit on the toys section of its website, Asda selling pink and black lace lingerie to children and Next being forced to remove T-shirts for young girls with the slogan "so many young boys, so little time" and BHS selling padded bras with a "Little Miss Naughty" logo.

It also warned teachers "not to be pressurised into using commercial materials in the classroom or take part in schemes such as voucher schemes".

"Parents are collecting vouchers for chocolates with Cadbury's and for crisps with Walkers in return for books," said Mr Sinnott. "We need to change the culture of this country in this regard."

New regulations introduced this week will mean all children's TV channels having to ban advertising for junk food by January 2009. They will also be extended to other channels covering children's programmes by January 2008.

"We need to change the culture of this country in this regard."

However, the NUT said this did not go far enough and demanded a ban on all junk food advertising before the 9pm watershed. It also wants the ban extended to cover "sponsorship, celebrity endorsement, mobile phone, internet, e-mail and publications aimed at children". Asda said it had stopped the sale of its lace knickers, while Tesco said the pole-dancing kit was not sexually orientated and was "clearly aimed at adults who wanted to improve their fitness".

However, Mr Sinnott argued: "All of this sexualisation of childhood is inappropriate for youngsters."

By Richard Garner, *The Independent*, April 7, 2007 – 404 words.

5 watershed time before which certain programmes may not be shown on TV · **9 pester** asking for s.th. over and over again · **12 treat** s.th. you enjoy very much · **15 to cite** [saɪt] to quote · **17 to account for** to make up a figure · **23 pole-dancing** dancing around a metal post, typical of stripper clubs · **23 kit** equipment · **24 lace lingerie** [ˌleɪs ˈlɒnʒəri] *Spitzendessous* · **27 padded bra** *gepolsterter BH* · **27 Little Miss Naughty** [ˌlɪtlˌmɪsˈnɔːti] cartoon character in a series of children's books; **naughty** = cheeky · **29 to pressurise** to force · **31 voucher scheme** [ˈvaʊtʃəˌskiːm] *Rabattcouponaktion* · **35 in this regard** in connection with a certain point · **39 to cover** *here:* to broadcast · **44 celebrity endorsement** *Werbung mit Prominenten* · **47 knickers** [ˈnɪkəz] *Slip* · **51 inappropriate** unsuitable

A step further: Cartoon

7 Describe the cartoon on the right and say how its message relates to the text.

"I think next year I'll go straight to my parents and cut out the middleman."

Working with words: Synonyms

8 Find synonyms for the following words in the text on page 41.

a) demanded ‹L1›
b) published ‹L6›
c) cited ‹L15›
d) need to ‹L34›
e) aimed at ‹L48›
f) improve ‹L49›

Grammar

9 Put the following sentences into the passive.

a) "The report cited figures from Ofcom…" ‹L15›
b) "It also warned teachers 'not to be pressurised into using commercial materials in the classroom.'" ‹L29–30›
c) "Parents are collecting vouchers for chocolates…" ‹L32›
d) "We need to change the culture of this country…" ‹L34–35›

Composition/Essay

10 "Parents are collecting vouchers for chocolates with Cadbury's and for crisps with Walkers in return for books," ‹L32–34› Do you think that it is a good idea to allow companies to sponsor schools in this way, or not? Analyse the pros and cons in an essay of not more than 250 words.

→ **Essays/Compositions**
See *skills file* on page 157.

1|4

Listening comprehension

Consumer's paradise

Listen to the excerpt from the novel *What's eating Gilbert Grape* by Peter Hedges.

Shopping addiction

Understanding the text: "Is shopping…?" on page 43.

1 What are the characteristic traits of compulsive shoppers and how do they behave with regard to shopping?
2 Why do people get addicted to shopping and what do they hope to get out of it?

A step further: Cartoon

3 Describe the cartoon on the right and relate it to the text.

"Due to your lack of discipline and total disregard to your credit limit, you've been chosen customer of the month."

Essay/Composition

4 "The ease with which credit cards are available makes shopping even more difficult to resist." ‹L82–83› Discuss.

Your opinion

5 Do you personally think there is a difference between an addiction to shopping and other addictions, e.g. to drugs, alcohol? Give reasons.
6 In your opinion, what are the key factors that can lead to a shopping addiction? What can you do to overcome such an addiction?

Is shopping your drug of choice?

Must have it, can't afford it, but still buy it? Then you have an addiction, writes Huma Qureshi

In the space of two days, my friend spent £1,199. "I bought a Mulberry handbag (£371) on Friday, and some amazing Bulgari sunglasses (£345) on Saturday," she counts off her fingers. "Oh, and I had to book a flight (£483) as well. Does that count?" Er, yes, it does.

She says she's not a shopaholic – "I'm in control of how much I spend; I know how much is on my credit card, when to pay it off and when to stop" – even though her latest spree makes her look slightly like one. But how can you tell if you are addicted to shopping?

"Just because you like buying clothes, doesn't make you a shopping addict," says Professor Alexander Gardner, a consumer psychologist and member of the British Psychological Association, reassuringly. "Someone like Victoria Beckham can spend a lot, but that doesn't mean she's addicted, it just means she enjoys it – mainly because she can afford everything. Everyone gets a kick out of shopping." True – retail therapy is the ultimate escape. A bad day translates into a new pair of shoes, while a good day justifies treating yourself 'just because'.

But for some people, shopping can spiral out of control. Known unofficially as Madame Bovary syndrome (after Gustave Flaubert's profligate heroine) and officially as oniomania, compulsive shopping is a form of uncontrollable and progressively destructive behaviour that often masks deeper problems of self-esteem. Compulsive shoppers shop routinely and obsessively, not because they need or necessarily even want something, but because the act of buying fills a void and makes them feel better about themselves, even if they can't afford it. Traits of a serious shopping addict, says Dr Robert Lefever, founder of the Promis counselling and recovery centre and a reformed shopping addict himself, include always thinking about it, shopping alone, hiding your purchases, spending more than you planned, shopping to enhance your mood and putting more time and energy into shopping than maintaining relations with family and friends."

"As with all addictions, it emerges when there is a dissatisfaction with the self," says Dr Martin Skinner, a social psychologist at the University of Warwick. "You try and substitute what you need to survive in the world with material goods and can't control your desire any more. Your need becomes so great that you ignore the financial and emotional consequences of consumption."

So, like a drug, shopping becomes a fix. But once the euphoria of a new purchase wears off, you fall back down again – usually when the credit card bills appear.

"It becomes a vicious circle," says Gardner. "Compulsive shoppers are irrevocably, absolutely drawn to shopping, so they want everything even if they can't pay for it. Depression sets in when they see their bills, but they continue spending as a way out of that sadness. Someone in this kind of situation needs to learn that there is a link between the good vibes they get from shopping and the stab in the chest they feel when they see their credit card statement."

The ease with which credit cards are available makes shopping even more difficult to resist. A recent survey reveals nearly a third of Britons, men as well as women, treat themselves when they know they can't afford it. [...]

By Huma Qureshi, *The Guardian*, February 18, 2007 – 570 words.

3 **space** period of time · 12 **spree** *große Einkaufstour* · 24 **reassuringly** making you feel less worried · 33 **to spiral out of control** *here:* to become impossible to limit · 35 **Flaubert** ['fləʊbeə] · 36 **profligate** *(formal, negative)* wasting money · 36 **heroine** main female character in a novel · 37 **compulsive** having an uncontrollable desire · 39 **self-esteem** respect for oneself · 41 **obsessively** being completely fixed on an idea · 43 **void** emptiness · 44 **trait** characteristic · 45 **Lefever** [lə'feɪ:və] · 50 **to enhance** to improve · 53 **to emerge** to appear · 57 **to substitute** to find s.th. of equal value to s.th. else · 68 **euphoria** [ju:'fɔ:rɪə] great happiness · 69 **to wear off** to gradually disappear · 72 **vicious circle** [ˌvɪʃəs‿'sɜ:kl] *Teufelskreis* · 73 **irrevocably** [ˌɪrɪ'vəʊkəblɪ] [ɪ'revəkəblɪ] which cannot be changed · 74 **drawn to** strongly attracted to · 79 **vibe** [vaɪb] feeling · 80 **stab** sudden pain · 80 **chest** *Brust* · 85 **to treat oneself** *sich etwas Gutes tun*

Consumerism and values

Understanding the text

1 Why does the writer say that on the one hand, Christmas and winter sales are different, but that on the other hand, they are similar?
2 What solution does the writer suggest to the conflict between Christmas shopping and traditional values?

Language and style

3 Examine the style which the writer uses in her article.
a) How would you characterize it? Find examples in the text.
b) In your opinion, why does she use this particular style?

→ **Style analysis**
See *skills file* on page 162.

Essay/Composition

4 "Shopping is the true spirit of Christmas." This statement implies a loss of traditional values. In your opinion, which values have been replaced by shopping?

→ **Essays/Compositions**
See *skills file* on page 157.

Shopping is the true spirit of Christmas

I'm not sure which was more irritating, driving to Somerset on Christmas Eve to the strains of some terrible Christmas singles or returning to London yesterday accompanied by incessant adverts for the winter sales. When the choice is between Noddy Holder of Slade and a man offering cut-price sofas from DFS, it's hard not to think that you have finally reached the bottom of the barrel of Western culture. These days, I like to think that the slight air of desperation in the voices of actors urging me to think about a new patio is down to global warming; everything is happening earlier than it used to, and I did most of my shopping for bargains well before the celebrations even started.

Then there's the internet, where you can not only buy cut-price presents before Christmas but "rehome" them – that's what the man from eBay calls it – over the next few days. I'm not sure about the etiquette if, say, you spot the underwear you bought your partner at enormous expense from Agent Provocateur listed as an unwanted gift, but someone will no doubt come up with a guide in due course. [...]

At first sight, it's hard to think of two events more diametrically opposed than Christmas and the winter sales, and there is a palpable sense of release every year when the stores re-open. It may be because we've got used to something approaching 24/7 shopping and the idea of two whole days without sends people into a panic, although I do wonder what possesses anyone to queue at Next at 5am. In fact, it seems to me that the impulses behind the two events are pretty similar, the difference being that before Christmas we have the excuse that we're spending money on other people. In the sales, it's every man and woman for herself, but the net effect – an orgy of over-consumption – is much the same.

2 strains the sound of music · **3 single** *here:* song · **4 incessant** never stopping · **6 Slade** British pop group from the 1970s · **6 cut-price** much reduced in price · **7 DFS** *(GB)* chain of sofa stores · **8 to reach the bottom of the barrel** *(figurative)* to be in the worst possible taste · **10 to urge** to try to persuade · **11 patio** ['pætɪəʊ] terrace · **11 to be down to** to be caused by · **13 bargain** ['bɑːgɪn] *Schnäppchen* · **16 to rehome** *here:* to find a new owner for an unwanted present · **20 Agent Provocateur** *(GB)* luxury underwear label · **22 in due course** at the right time · **24 diametrically opposed** completely different · **25 palpable** noticeable · **25 release** being freed from an unpleasant situation · **29 ...what possesses anyone to do s.th.** what makes s.o. do s.th. strange · **35 orgy** ['ɔːdʒɪ] an extreme amount of one activity

Letter to the editor

5 Do you agree with the writer's description of Christmas? Are your personal experiences similar to hers, or not? Write a letter to the editor expressing your point of view.

Language: adverbs and adjectives

6 Find the adverbs that correspond to the adjectives from the text.
a) true ‹heading› c) global ‹L 11› e) apparent ‹L 55›
b) terrible ‹L 3› d) entire ‹L 44›

7 Write a sentence with each adverb you have come up with in task 6.

8 Find the adjectives that correspond to the adverbs.
a) only ‹L 15› b) diametrically ‹L 24› c) inevitably ‹L 46›

Translation

9 Translate the following paragraph from the text into German: "Whenever I hear…" ‹L 51› to the end.

→ **Translation**
See *skills file* on page 165.

If that sounds cynical, I actually think there's more to it than that, in the sense that this is the time of year when people are positively invited to act out fantasies. It begins with Christmas, which we're all supposed to look forward to with breathless anticipation even though for many people the reality falls quite a long way short of expectation. It isn't often that everyone in the entire country is forced to do the same thing at the same time, and that sense of compulsion – and the absence of alternatives – inevitably grates on the nerves. One of the nicest Christmas mornings I've ever spent was in San Gimignano, where the cafés were open and thronged with people, quite unlike any British town centre on Christmas Day.

"If we were more relaxed about Christmas, we might not need such an extravagant antidote."

Whenever I hear conservative commentators extolling the virtues of the extended family, I wonder whether they've ever experienced a large family gathering at Christmas, when the tensions between generations become apparent. No wonder so many people are eager, after a couple of days, to indulge in a new set of fantasies in the shape of clothes, sofas, computer games and holidays. If we were more relaxed about Christmas, we might not need such an extravagant antidote. And I can't help being amused by the fact that the result of a concentrated dose of family values is to send most of us to the shops to spend as if there's no tomorrow.

By Joan Smith, *The Independent*, December 28, 2006 – 565 words.

41 anticipation looking forward to s.th. · **42 to fall short of expectation** to be disappointing · **46 to grate on one's nerves** to irritate · **49 thronged** [θrɒŋd] crowded · **52 to extol the virtues** [ɪkˌstəʊl ðə ˈvɜːtjuːz] to praise the advantages extravagantly · **52 extended family** *Großfamilie* · **55 apparent** obvious · **56 to indulge in s.th.** to allow oneself a luxury · **60 antidote** [ˈæntɪdəʊt] *Gegengift* · **61 dose** [dəʊs] amount

Too much choice

Bill Bryson was born in the US in 1951. In 1977, he went to England where he lived for many years. He returned to the US with his English wife and four children for some years, but then returned again to the UK.

Bill Bryson has become popular due to his satirical travelogues of everyday life in America.

Understanding the text on page 47

1 Think of a suitable heading for the story.
2 Summarize the events in the story in your own words.
3 What do you personally think of the situation in the story? Is this really consumerism at its best, or not?
4 In your opinion, what message does the writer want to communicate to the reader?

Summaries
See *skills file* on page 164.

Language and style

5 What stylistic devices does the writer use to hold the reader's interest? Give examples from the text.
6 Explain what is meant by the following sentences and phrases from the text.
a) "I really, really needed to get some caffeine into my system." ‹L 4–5›
b) "a galaxy of muffins" ‹L 9›
c) "hours in single figures" ‹L 22›
d) "Anything else is beyond me." ‹L 23›
e) "And so it went." ‹L 44›

Style analysis
See *skills file* on page 162.

Over to you

7 Have you ever been in a situation, similar to the writer, where you found it difficult to get what you wanted because the selection on offer was huge? Summarize what happened to you in that situation in at least ten sentences.

Text

2|14

Lately, […], I have come to realize that you can get too much choice. I had this brought home to me the other week when I was at an airport in Portland, Oregon, standing in a queue of about fifteen people at a coffee stand. It was 5.45 a.m., not my best time of day, and I had just 20 minutes till my flight was to be called, but I really, really needed to get some caffeine into my system. You know how it is.

It used to be if you wanted a cup of coffee that's what you asked for and that's what you got. But this place, being a 1990s coffee stand, offered twenty choices – espresso, latte, caramel latte, breve, macchiato, mocha, espresso mocha, black forest mocha, americano, and goodness knows what else – in four different sizes. There was also a galaxy of muffins, croissants, bagels and pastries. All of these could be had in any number of variations, so that every order went something like this:

"I'll have a caramel latte combo with decaf mocha and a cinnamon twist, and a low-fat cream cheese sourdough bagel, but I'd like the pimiento grated and on the side. Are your poppyseeds roasted in polyunsaturated vegetable oil?"

"No, we use double-extra-lite canola extract."

"Oh, that's no good for me. In that case, I'll have a New York three-cheese pumpernickel fudge croissant. What kind of emulsifiers do you use in that?"

In my mind's eye, I saw myself taking hold of each customer by the ears, shaking his or her head thirty or forty times and saying: "You're just trying to get a cup of coffee and a bread product before your flight. Now ask for something simple and clear off."

Fortunately for all these people, until I have had my first cup of coffee in the morning (and this is particularly true during hours in single figures) all I can do is rise, dress myself (a bit) and ask for a cup of coffee. Anything else is beyond me. So I just stood and waited stoically while fifteen people placed complex, time-consuming and preposterously individualized orders.

When at last my turn came, I stepped up and said: "I'd like a large cup of coffee."

"What kind?"

"Hot and in a cup and very large."

"Yeah, but what kind – mocha, macchiato, what?"

"I want whichever one is a normal cup of coffee."

"You want americano?"

"If that means a normal cup of coffee, then yes."

"Well, they're all coffees."

"I want a normal cup of coffee like millions of people drink every day."

"So you want an americano?"

"Evidently."

"Do you want low-cal whipped cream or regular with that?"

"I don't want whipped cream."

"But it comes with whipped cream."

"Look," I said in a low voice, "it is 6.10 a.m. I have been standing for 25 minutes behind fifteen seriously indecisive people, and my flight is being called. If I don't get some coffee right now, I am going to murder someone, and I think you should know that you are extremely high on my list." (I am not, as you will gather, a morning person.)

"So does that mean you want low-cal whipped cream or regular?"

And so it went. […]

From "Enough already" by Bill Bryson, *Notes from a Big Country*, Reading: Black Swan, 1999 – 541 words.

1 to have s.th. brought home to one to realize s.th. · **10 pastry** a type of sweet cake · **12 decaf** *short for* decaffeinated, i.e. without caffeine · **12 cinnamon twist** type of sweet cake with cinnamon *(= Zimt)* · **13 sourdough** ['saʊədəʊ] *Sauerteig* · **13 pimiento** *(BE* **pimento***)* type of red pepper *(= Paprika)* · **13 grated** *gerieben* · **13 poppyseeds** *Mohn* · **14 polyunsaturated** type of fat associated with low cholesterol · **15 lite** *(informal)* light; low-calorie · **15 canola** rapeseed *(= Raps)* · **16 fudge** a soft, creamy sweet made of sugar, milk and butter · **17 emulsifier** substance used to stop the liquids in food from separating · **18 in my mind's eye** *(figurative)* in my imagination · **24 time-consuming** taking a long time · **24 preposterously** unreasonably · **36 whipped cream** *Schlagsahne* · **43 low-cal** *short for* low-calorie

Unit 4 Multiculturalism

801005-0004

A

B

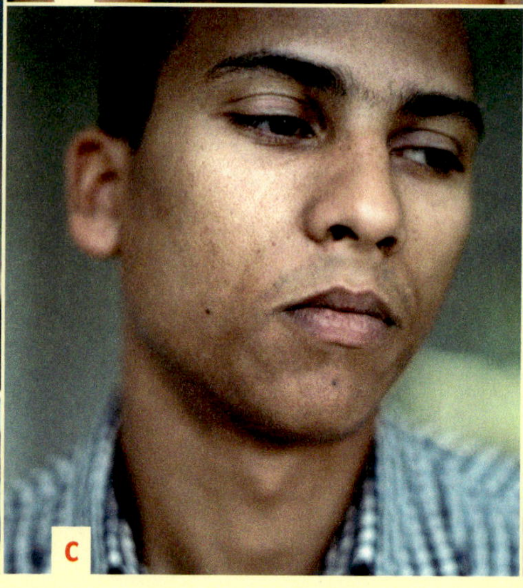
C

D

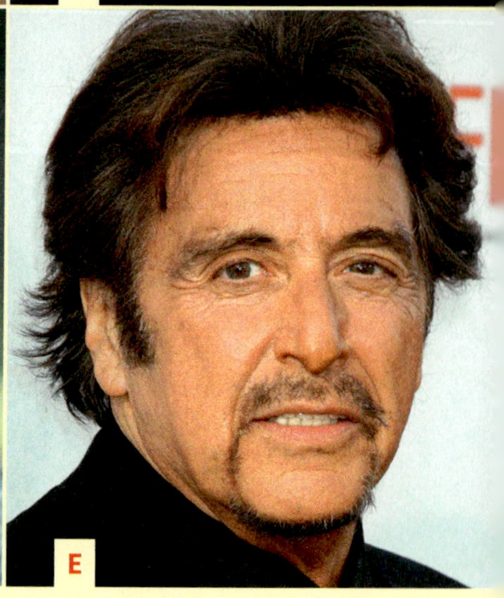
E

Getting started

1 Name the people you see in the pictures. Where do you think they come from?
2 The people in the pictures are immigrants or the descendants of immigrants. For what reasons might they or their parents have left their home country?
3 What problems do you think they or their parents/ancestors might have faced in the new country?

Multicultural USA (1)

The USA consist of five main population groups: the White Americans, the Hispanics, the African Americans, the Asian Americans and the Native Americans, also called Indians. Of all these groups, the Hispanics form the fastest growing immigrant group.

Xtra-File: Hispanics in the USA

Hispanics accounted for almost half (1.4 million) of the national population growth of 2.9 million between July 1, 2005, and July 1, 2006.

California had the largest Hispanic population of any state as of July 1, 2006 (13.1 million), followed by Texas (8.4 million) and Florida (3.6 million). Texas had the largest numerical increase between 2005 and 2006 (305,000), with California (283,000) and Florida (161,000) following. In New Mexico, Hispanics comprised the highest proportion of the total population (44 percent), with California and Texas (36 percent each) next in line.

The Hispanic population in 2006 was much younger, with a median age of 27.4 compared with the population as a whole at 36.4. About a third of the Hispanic population was younger than 18, compared with one-fourth of the total population.

From "Minority Population Tops 100 Million", US Census Bureau News, Public Information Office, online text, www.census.gov, May 17, 2007 – 135 words.

1 to account for to be a particular amount · **10 to comprise** [kəm'praɪz] *here:* to form · **14 median** refers to the middle value

Mediation

1 Summarise the development of the Hispanic population in the USA from 2005 onwards, in German.

Mediation
See *skills file* on page 158.

Over to you

2 In groups, find out current facts and statistics about the other population groups in the US using the internet. Summarise your findings in a short text.

Check the web
Key word: "US Census Bureau"

Multicultural USA (2)

Before you read

1 Look at the map of the USA on the back inside cover and find out which US states are located on the Mexican-American border.

2 a) Think of reasons why people might fear (illegal) immigrants.
b) Think of measures that could be taken to stop illegal immigration.

Understanding the text

3 Describe the scene at the beginning of the article in your own words.

4 Explain who the Minutemen are and what they aim to do.

5 What is meant by the term 'coyote' ‹L 69›?

6 To what extent will the new fence stop illegal immigrants entering the US?

7 Where is the fence being built?

8 According to Al Garza, to what extent can the fence be seen as a symbol?

9 Summarize the different reactions towards the Minutemen's fence.

America's Minutemen build their own fence against Mexican migrants

Activists spend $1m on symbolic wall to demand sealing of the border

Two men stand working in the afternoon sun just yards from the US-Mexico border. Clad in hard hats and work shirts, tool belts slung around their waists, they have been toiling at this spot in the Arizona desert since early October.

One holds an iron stanchion while the other bolts a horizontal bar to it. But before the joint can be tightened, the whole structure starts to sway. A shout goes up: "Watch out!" The five metre pole lurches toward the dry red earth, bringing its neighbour down with it. The latest weapon in the fight against undocumented migrants looks a little shaky.

The iron and steel fence is the latest project from the Minutemen, the volunteer group of anti-immigration activists that has placed itself at the sharp end of the immigration debate since launching a highly publicised series of border watches in 2005. Now, frustrated at what the group sees as the inaction of government, it has taken matters a step further, building its own border fence at a cost of around $1m (€765,000) at one of the busiest points on the line, 90 miles from Tucson.

"It's not only a symbol, although its creation is symbolic of something," says Al Garza, national executive director of the Minuteman Civil Defence Corps. "It's saying: Congress, Mr President, we've pleaded, now we're demanding. You've told us it can't be done, well we're just a handful of people and we're doing it."

Heading: Minutemen *(US)* a volunteer; the term was first used in the War of Independence · **2 to be clad** to wear · **2 hard hat** protection for your head · **3 tool belt** *Werkzeuggürtel* · **3 to sling, slung, slung** to wear on your hips · **4 to toil** to work hard · **6 stanchion** ['stænʃn] a metal post · **7 to bolt** to join two things with bolts (= *Bolzen*) · **7 bar** *Stange* · **8 to sway** [sweɪ] to move gently from side to side · **9 pole** a long thin post · **10 to lurch** to move suddenly in one direction · **12 migrant** ['maɪgrənt] person who moves permanently to another country · **16 to place oneself at the sharp end of s.th.** to take a leading role in s.th. · **18 to launch** to start · **18 highly publicised** widely known · **18 border watch** *(US)* people who observe the US-Mexican border · **20 inaction** remaining passive · **22 m** *short for* million · **24 Tucson** ['tu:sɒn] · **29 to plead** to ask seriously for a favour

Language

10 Examine the article to decide whether the writer is in favour of or against the Minutemen's fence. Give text evidence to support your opinion.

A step further: Cartoon and text

11 a) What is the cartoonist saying about illegal immigration?
b) Would you describe the cartoon as funny, serious or both? Give reasons.
c) Relate the cartoon to the text.

THE FIRST ILLEGAL IMMIGRANTS

Listening comprehension

1|8

Believe in who you are

Listen to Mario talk about his experiences as a Mexican-American.

Wearing a white Stetson and bearing a crisply trimmed white moustache, Mr Garza is the picture of a border activist. A retiree who moved to Arizona from California less than four years ago, he served in the US Marine Corps and worked as a private investigator in California for 35 years.

"We know that the observation won't quash or deter immigration," he says, "so we thought what was the alternative: a fence."

But there is a flaw in the Minutemen's plan. While the US-Mexico border stretches for 1,993 miles, from California to Texas, the Minuteman fence when finished will be just one mile long.

Despite this apparent drawback, Mr Garza is adamant that the fence will have an effect. "It's also deterring traffic from that particular area, which is heavily, heavily travelled. One mile out here is very crucial, so that's one mile the Border Patrol won't have to scout."

Others, however, doubt whether a fence will have any effect. "They'll just go around this fence in the way they go around others," says Daniel Griswold of the Cato Institute think tank in Washington DC. "All a fence will do is direct people to more remote areas and create the likelihood of more deaths." [...]

The Minuteman fence is being built on a private ranch between the towns of Douglas and Naco.

"Until the Minutemen came along and really raised national awareness about this there was nothing like this," says Connie Faust, a Minuteman volunteer who has just taken charge of building the fence. "This was all holes in the fence. Cattle were coming through, illegal aliens were coming through. It's been a real problem for the ranchers out here." [...]

From there the migrants typically head north, to Tucson or Phoenix, having paid a "coyote" – the professional smuggler who brings them across the border – anything between $1,500 and $3,000.

The fence is at the heart of what is known as the Tucson sector, the busiest crossing-point on the border. Of 1.1m arrests made by the Border Patrol in 2005, almost half of them were here. This year the figure, in common with the entire border, has dropped, with 392,000 undocumented migrants held. [...]

"You wonder how many get by," says TJ Bonner, president of the agents' union, the 6,500 member National Border Patrol Council. "Our agents estimate that for every person we catch, two or three get by." Mr Bonner sees the Minutemen fence as a publicity ploy. "I think the impact on day-to-day operations will be really minimal," he says. "The larger impact of groups like the Minutemen is in bringing attention to the problem. The fence project is more of a public demonstration to shame the administration."

By Dan Glaister, *The Guardian*, January 2, 2007 – 711 words.

32 **Stetson** a cowboy's hat · 32 **crisply** sharply · 34 **retiree** [rɪˌtaɪəˈriː] person over a certain age who does not work anymore · 36 **private investigator** *Privatdetektiv(in)* · 38 **to quash** to stop completely · 39 **to deter** to prevent · 41 **flaw** weakness · 45 **drawback** disadvantage · 46 **adamant** [ˈædəmənt] completely sure that one is right · 49 **crucial** [ˈkruːʃəl] very important · 49 **Border Patrol** *(US)* officers who control activity on the border · 50 **to scout** to observe and control · 54 **think tank** *Expertenkommission* · 55 **remote** far away · 56 **likelihood** probability · 64 **cattle** cows and bulls · 65 **alien** foreigner · 76 **entire** [ɪnˈtaɪə] complete · 79 **to get by** to pass · 82 **to estimate** to give an approximate number · 84 **ploy** trick · 84 **impact** effect · 89 **to shame s.o.** to make s.o. feel embarassed

Multicultural USA (3)

2|16

Legal Alien

Bi-lingual, Bi-cultural,
able to slip from "How's life?"
to "Me están volviendo loca,"
able to sit in a paneled office
drafting memos in smooth English,
able to order in fluent Spanish
at a Mexican restaurant,
American but hyphenated,
viewed by Anglos as perhaps exotic,
perhaps inferior; definitely different,
viewed by Mexicans as alien,
(their eyes say, "You may speak
Spanish but you're not like me")
an American to Mexicans
a Mexican to Americans
a handy token
sliding back and forth
between the fringes of both worlds
by smiling
by masking the discomfort
of being pre-judged
Bi-laterally.

"Legal alien" by Pat Mora, *Chants*,
(Houston: Arte Público Press –
University of Houston, 1985) – 97 words.

3 Me están volviendo loca *(Spanish)* They're driving me crazy · **4 paneled** *getäfelt* · **5 to draft** to write · **5 smooth** *here:* fluent · **8 hyphenated** ['haɪfəneɪtɪd] *here:* having two cultural backgrounds (Mexican-American) · **16 handy** useful · **16 token** s.th. that represents a group · **18 fringe** edge · **20 to mask** to hide

Pat Mora (b.1942, El Paso, Texas)
Her family originated from Mexico and she was brought up bilingually (English and Spanish). She writes poetry, children's books and nonfiction, which integrate both languages. Her main topics include Mexican-American culture, family, and being bilingual and bi-cultural in the US.

Understanding the poem

1 a) What do you understand by the term "legal alien"?
b) What connotations does the term have for you?
c) What German equivalent or paraphrase can you think of? What connotations does the German phrase have?

2 Do you think that the speaker feels comfortable living in several worlds, or not? Give reasons.

Style

3 The speaker talks about "sliding back and forth between the fringes of both worlds" ‹L17–18›. How is this idea emphasized by the structure of the poem?

4 Describe the tone of the poem in as much detail as possible.

5 What is the main effect of the use of Spanish?

Tone
See *glossary* on page 203.

Discussion and poem/rap

6 Should minority cultures acculturate (= change in order to fit in) to the majority culture in the host country? Or should the majority culture become more varied by picking up aspects of minority cultures? Discuss.

7 Write a poem or rap about your experiences from one of these viewpoints:
- a bi-cultural/bilingual in a mainly monocultural society;
- a mono-cultural/monolingual in a society that is becoming more bi-cultural.

→ **Discussions**
See *skills file* on page 177.

Multicultural Britain (1)

Xtra-File: Britain's ethnic minorities

Scene in a British shopping centre

The largest ethnic minorities in Britain are those of Caribbean or African descent (1,274,000 people). The next largest ethnic groups are Indians (932,000 people), and Pakistanis and Bangladeshis (639,390 people). Overall, ethnic minority groups represent just about seven per cent of the population of Great Britain. The ethnic population has evolved from the substantial immigration of people from former British colonies in the Caribbean and South Asian subcontinent during the 1950s and 1960s. In addition, in the 1970s Britain admitted some 28,000 Asians expelled from Uganda and some 22,000 refugees from South East Asia. Considerable numbers of Chinese, Italians, Greek and Turkish Cypriots, Poles, Australians, New Zealanders and people from the United States and Canada are also resident in Britain.

Source: British Embassy Berlin, online text, www.britischebotschaft.de – 125 words.

2 **descent** [dɪˈsent] origin · 5 **Bangladeshi** [ˌbæŋɡləˈdeʃɪ] · 8 **to evolve** to develop · 8 **substantial** considerable · 13 **to expel** to throw (out of a country) · 18 **resident** living

Analysts name Britain's most racially diverse areas

Two strangers bumping into each other by accident have a less than 50% chance of belonging to the same racial group in some UK cities, the first official index of diversity revealed yesterday.

The greatest diversity is found in 24 London boroughs as well as Birmingham, Slough, Leicester and Luton. In Manchester, Wolverhampton, Oxford, Blackburn and Bradford the likelihood of bumping into someone of different ethnicity is at least 40%; in Coventry, Watford, Cambridge and Reading it is at least 35%.

[...] The Office for National Statistics said any two people in Brent had an 85% chance of being from different racial groups. In the London borough of Newham the score was 83%, in Westminster 71% and in Kensington and Chelsea, the most prosperous inner-city authority, 68%.

Two hundred local authorities scored below 10%; Carlisle, Hartlepool, Barnsley, St Helens and Berwick upon Tweed were under 5%. The least multicultural was Easington, Co Durham, at 2%.

The report showed the London borough of Harrow was the most religiously diverse, with a 62% chance that a random encounter would be between people declaring a different religion.

The survey found the highest unemployment rates were among black African Muslim men (28%) and women (31%.) The rates among Indian Muslims were lower at 11% for men and 12% for women.

By John Carvel, *The Guardian*, October 6, 2006 – 223 words.

1 **to bump into s.o. by accident** to walk into s.o. without meaning to · 7 **borough** ['bʌrə] *(UK)* part of a city with its own governing council · 8 **Slough** [slaʊ] · 8 **Leicester** ['lestə] · 8 **Luton** ['lu:tən] · 12 **Reading** ['redɪŋ] · 17 **Newham** ['nju:əm] · 17 **score** the number recorded · 19 **prosperous** wealthy · 22 **Carlisle** [kɑ:'laɪl] · 22 **Hartlepool** ['hɑ:tlɪpu:l] · 22 **Barnsley** ['bɑ:nzlɪ] · 23 **Berwick** ['berɪk] · 24 **Co** *short for* county · 28 **random encounter** meeting by chance · 29 **to declare** *here:* to say officially

Understanding the texts

1 Find the cities mentioned in the text "Analysts name…" on a map of Britain.
2 Why, do you think, are some areas of Britain more attractive to immigrants than others?
3 Create bar charts or tables showing Britain's ethnic groups and where they live. Refer to the text above and the Xtra-File on page 53.

Map of Britain
See page 207.
Statistics
See *skills file* on page 161.

Multicultural Britain (2)

Before you read: "Would-be settlers..." on page 56.

1 What do you think a 'Britishness test' might be? Who might have to take it?
2 Think of at least three questions that you would expect to see in a Britishness test.

Understanding the text

3 Who is the Britishness test made for?
4 Which concerns about the test are expressed in the article?
5 Summarize the findings of the Compas study in your own words.
6 Describe the factors that make integration difficult for immigrants.
7 Based on the article, explain what factors can lead to hostility towards immigrants.

Language

8 In small groups, find as many words and expressions related to 'multiculturalism' as you can in the article. Afterwards make a word cluster or mind map, and display your findings in class.

Mind maps
See *skills file* on page 186.

9 Write down the adjective forms of these nouns from the article. (You will find some of the adjectives in the article, too.)
a) protection ‹L 22›
b) minority ‹L 27›
c) anxiety ‹L 34›
d) deprivation ‹L 35›
e) racism ‹L 35›
f) tension ‹L 44›
g) competition ‹L 45›
h) hostility ‹L 54›
i) poverty ‹L 67›

10 Find the noun forms of the following verbs in the text.
a) to exclude
b) to know
c) to immigrate
d) to extend
e) to do research
f) to resent
g) to decide
h) to integrate
i) to cover
j) to arrive

11 Find the opposites of the following words from the text.
a) to settle ‹L 2›
b) indefinite ‹L 8›
c) immigrant ‹L 18›
d) poor ‹L 27›
e) minority ‹L 27›
f) finite ‹L 46›
g) hostile ‹L 62›
h) legal ‹L 63›

A step further: Cartoon

"Well done, you've all passed!"

12 Explain what makes the cartoon funny.
13 Do you think that the immigrants in the cartoon are really British now, or not? Explain your answer.
14 What aspects of the article, "Would-be settlers...", does the cartoon relate to?

Further activity: Research

15 Find out whether similar tests have to be done by immigrants in Germany. If so, bring some sample questions to class for your classmates to answer.

Cartoons
See *skills file* on page 155.

Comment

16 Do you think that a cultural test can help immigrants to integrate, or not? Write a comment of about 150 words giving reasons for your opinion.

Comments
See *skills file* on page 155.

Would-be settlers will have to pass the Britishness test

More than 180,000 people each year who apply to settle in Britain permanently will have to pass tests in the English language and knowledge of life in the UK from next April, the Home Office announced yesterday.

The immigration minister, Liam Byrne, said the extra requirement was being imposed on those applying for indefinite leave to remain because a good grasp of English was essential to play a full role in society and properly integrate into British communities.

The language and Britishness test was first introduced for the 200,000 people who applied for British citizenship last year. The extension to those who want to settle in the UK but retain their own passport is expected to cover a further 180,000. Those over 65 will be exempt.

The Joint Council for the Welfare of Immigrants said it was concerned about the extra hurdle being placed in the way of those seeking indefinite leave to remain, particularly when they had come to Britain to seek human rights protection. It also voiced concern that the decision would only add to the already long queues for courses designed to teach new migrants English.

The decision came as the Home Office published research showing that poor black and minority ethnic groups are just as likely to express resentment towards immigrants as their poor white neighbours.

The findings, from a study by the centre for migration policy and society (Compas) at Oxford University, suggest that the degree of public anxiety over immigration is closely linked to economic deprivation rather than racism.

"People from the lowest social classes are more than twice as likely to express high levels of resentment towards recent migrants receiving public support as people from the highest," the report says.

"White and black minority ethnic [groups] displayed similar attitudes towards recent migrants, which corresponds to reports that tensions do not necessarily arise along racial lines. Rather, where competition over scarce and finite resources is the greatest, relations with newcomers are likely to be negatively affected."

The effect is compounded for asylum seekers dispersed to areas already suffering from poor public services.

The report, edited by Sarah Spencer, says the lack of information about new arrivals in an area, exacerbated by unbalanced media coverage, can create a climate of fear and some overt hostility and violence in which migrants may even hesitate to venture out on to the streets.

It suggests that six key factors limit the integration of new migrants: lack of language skills and recognised qualifications; moving too often from place to place; lack of knowledge about the system, such as how to find a home or a school; hostile public attitudes; public services unable to meet migrants' needs; and legal barriers because of their immigration status.

The Compas research suggests that the challenges faced by refugees and other new migrants are as much to do with poverty, exclusion and racism as with the fact that they have just arrived in the country.

By Alan Travis, *The Guardian*, December 5, 2006 – 491 words.

4 **Home Office** *(GB) Innenministerium* · 6 **Liam Byrne** [ˌliːəm 'bɜːn] · 7 **to impose s.th. on s.o.** to make s.o. do s.th. · 8 **indefinite leave** *here:* permission for an unknown period of time · 8 **to remain** to stay · 9 **grasp** knowledge · 15 **to retain** *(formal)* to keep · 17 **exempt** not having to do s.th. · 19 **hurdle** s.th. that makes it more difficult to do s.th. · 23 **to voice** to express · 24 **queue** [kjuː] group of people waiting for s.th. · 29 **resentment** anger, bitterness · 34 **anxiety** [æŋˌzaɪətɪ] fear, worry · 35 **economic deprivation** not having enough money to live · 42 **to display** to show · 45 **scarce** available in very small amounts · 46 **finite** ['faɪnaɪt] limited · 46 **resource** [rɪ'zɔːs] money available · 48 **to compound** *here:* to make worse · 49 **to disperse** to spread out · 53 **to exacerbate** [ɪg'zæsəbeɪt] to make worse · 54 **overt** [əʊ'vɜːt] obvious · 54 **hostility** [hɒs'tɪlətɪ] *opposite of* friendship · 56 **to venture out** [ˌventʃər‿'aʊt] to dare to go out · 62 **hostile** ['hɒstaɪl] aggressive · 63 **legal barrier** [ˌliːgl'bærɪə] *gesetzmäßiges Hindernis*

Multicultural Germany (1)

Before you read

1 Which ethnic groups does the population of Germany consist of? Make a list.

Xtra-File: Ethnic minorities in Germany

There are few traditional ethnic minorities in Germany. There are the Danish-speaking people in Schleswig-Holstein and Sorbs, a Slavic people, in Brandenburg. However, Germany has about seven million foreign residents, making up almost 9 percent of the total population. Most of these are foreign workers from Mediterranean countries who were originally recruited in the 1950s and 60s and their children and grandchildren.

The largest group of foreign residents is of Turkish origin. Additionally, there are large numbers of people in Germany who have fled their countries and sought asylum in Germany on the basis of its liberal constitutional guarantee of refuge for the politically persecuted. In 2001, they numbered 88,287.

There is also a fairly large number of people from Eastern Europe in Germany who are not considered foreigners even though they might not speak German or have any knowledge of the country. They are the descendants of German farmers and craftsmen who settled in Russia, Romania and other eastern European countries in the 18th century. These people are called "ethnic Germans," and the German constitution gives them the right to German citizenship, if they wish it. In 1999, 205,000 "ethnic Germans" came to Germany. The same right applies to Germans of the Jewish faith who were driven out of Germany by the Nazis, and their descendants. Germany has also accepted about 1.5 million refugees from various crisis spots around the globe.

From the German Embassy, Washington, D.C. website, 2001–2007, www.germany.info – 236 words.

5 Mediterranean [ˌmedɪtərˈeɪnɪən] coming from Southern Europe · **6 to recruit** to employ · **8 origin** *Abstammung* · **10 to seek, sought, sought** to look for, to search for · **11 guarantee of refuge** [ˌgærənˈtiː‿əv ˈrefjuːdʒ] to have the right to be protected and to live in a country · **12 persecuted** treated badly because of one's religious or political beliefs · **16 craftsman** skilled worker, especially who makes things by hand · **22 faith** religion

Understanding the text

2 Write down three questions about the text and ask a partner to answer them.

Mediation

3 Use the information in the text to create a short entry for a German geography book or a German encyclopedia.

→ **Mediation**
See *skills file* on page 158.

Multicultural Germany (2)

Before you read

1 a) Think of problems that members of ethnic minorities might face when they live in Germany.
b) Have you heard about a case of racial injustice in the news lately? Describe the case in a few sentences.

Understanding the text

2 Explain why Lale works in a call-centre although she has studied law.

2|17

Can Germany learn to live with Islam?

Lale is 32 and wears a bright pink headscarf.

She studied law, but has had to take a job in a call-centre – where a woman with a headscarf can be heard but not seen.

She would like a better job, she says, but many employers just don't want to know.

"It's very difficult," she told me. "You never really feel part of society. You feel alienated."

Lale is one of Germany's 3.3 million Muslims – about 4% of the population.

Most are, like her, of Turkish descent.

Look at the German media, and the issues which come up in relation to Muslims are no different to those elsewhere in Europe.

Headscarves. "Honour" killings. Education. Unemployment. Security fears.

German-ness

Yet Germany has its own characteristics which set it apart from its neighbours.

One is a conception of "German-ness" based on blood and ethnicity.

This has meant that, for most of the last 40 years, immigrants from Turkey have found it hard to gain German citizenship.

Another is the *Verfassungsschutz* (Office for the Protection of the Constitution).

This is the rough equivalent of Britain's MI5 and the American FBI.

It monitors extremists, including Islamist groups.

Claudia Schmid, who runs the organisation's Berlin branch, told me why even non-violent Islamists are deemed to be a threat.

"Our task is to inform the public and the state institutions about groups which are trying to change the fundamental values of our constitution."

"These groups can function and promote their ideas. But they can't expect to get money from the state if they want to destroy essential, fundamental elements of our constitution."

The *Verfassungsschutz* – part of the interior ministry – keeps a close eye on Islamist groups such as the Muslim Brotherhood and its Turkish counterpart, Milli Gorus.

To belong to these groups, or even associate with them, is to risk being denied German citizenship or

1 Lale [lɑːlə] · **8 alienated** not feeling as if one is part of a society or community · **18 to set s.th. apart** to make s.th. different · **29 to monitor** to observe · **31 branch** *Zweigstelle* · **32 to deem** *(formal)* to consider · **35 value** principle · **37 to function** to work · **37 to promote** to make public · **44 counterpart** equivalent · **46 to deny s.th.** to refuse to give s.th.

3 Outline the activities of the German Office for the Protection of the Constitution.
4 Explain why even non-violent Islamists are considered to be a threat.
5 According to the writer, how has the German Conference on Islam helped to improve relations between Germany and Islam?

Further activity: Research and poster or leaflet

6 Choose at least one of the following key words from the text: "headscarves, honour killings, education, unemployment, security fears" ‹L15–16›. Find out more about the key word in the context of immigrants in Germany using the internet. Afterwards present your findings to the class in the form of a poster or leaflet.

Check the web
www.google.com
www.excite.com

access to government funding – as Lale discovered to her cost.

When she is not at the call-centre, Lale works as a volunteer with a Muslim youth group.

Because it worked with Arab and Turkish Islamist groups, its state funding was cut off.

"We are doing a good job," says Lale. "The problem is that there is always suspicion from the politicians. They say, 'We like your projects – but can we really trust you?'"

The 'Muslim Test'

Trust, or lack of it, lies at the heart of the problem.

Take, for example, the way some of Germany's provincial states set tests for citizenship.

A test introduced in the state of Baden-Wuerttemberg is popularly known as the "Muslim test".

One sensitive question – says journalist Erkan Arikan, himself a second-generation German of Turkish descent – is about gay rights.

"You've found your son is homosexual and he comes to you and says, 'Dad, I want to marry a German homosexual guy'. So how do you react?

"Do they expect that I will beat up my son, or do a kind of 'honour' killing? This is really ridiculous."

Dialogue

Change is in the air, and not soon enough for young German Muslims like Erkan or Lale.

In September last year, the government organised the German Conference on Islam.

This high-profile event in Berlin was hosted by Interior Minister Wolfgang Schaeuble and brought together state officials and representatives of the main Muslim organisations.

Riem Spielhaus, a young German Muslim academic – daughter of an Egyptian father and a German mother – is a member of one of the working groups which the conference set up.

"I think the conference is very important for Germany and for Germany accepting Muslims as part of the citizens of Germany.

"The interior minister started the conference by proclaiming that Muslims are part of Germany – and I think that was a very, very important signal that we hadn't had for forty years."

The conference set in train a process of dialogue.

It also served to put pressure on Muslim groups to sink their differences.

Four Muslim organisations – including two Turkish groups which for decades have been bitter rivals – are creating a new umbrella body.

Lale wants to believe all this is a step in the right direction. But she is not expecting quick results.

"It needs a new generation to change things. Maybe you need twenty years."

By Roger Hardy for the BBC, March 29, 2007,
news.bbc.co.uk – 715 words.

47 funding financial support · **48 to s.o.'s cost** to s.o.'s disadvantage · **54 suspicion** *opposite of* trust · **64 sensitive** refers to s.th. which one has to be careful when discussing · **89 to proclaim** to say in public · **92 to set in train** to start · **95 to sink** to ignore · **98 umbrella body** organization which is made up of different organizations

Unit 5 Energy and the environment

801005-0005

Second drawing: to go broke to run out of money · **Third drawing: submerged** covered with water · **Fifth drawing: The Sky Is Falling**" refers to the fable, "Chicken Licken" or "Chicken Little", about a chicken that believes that the sky is falling; it characterizes exaggerated warnings of a catastrophe · **poppycock** rubbish

Getting started

1 Summarise the man's complaints to the elderly couple in your own words.
2 How does the couple react?
3 Describe the relationship between the man and the couple. Consider both the situation and the characters' body language.

→ **Cartoons**
See *skills file* on page 155.

An inconvenient truth

2|21

I need to wake up

Have I been sleeping?
I've been so still
Afraid of crumbling
Have I been careless?
Dismissing all the distant
rumblings
Take me where I am
supposed to be
To comprehend the things
that I can't see

Cause I need to move
I need to wake up
I need to change
I need to shake up
I need to speak out
Something's got to break up
I've been asleep
And I need to wake up
Now

And as a child
I danced like it was 1999
My dreams were wild
The promise of this new world
Would be mine
Now I am throwing off the
carelessness of youth
To listen to an inconvenient
truth

That I need to move
I need to wake up
I need to change
I need to shake up
I need to speak out
Something's got to break up
I've been asleep
And I need to wake up
Now

I am not an island
I am not alone
I am my intentions
Trapped here in this flesh
and bone
And I need to move
I need to wake up
I need to change
I need to shake up
I need to speak out
Something's got to break up
I've been asleep
And I need to wake up
Now

I want to change
I need to shake up
I need to speak out
Oh, something's got to
break up
I've been asleep
And I need to wake up
Now

Source: Brook, Michael Brian; Kohaw Music Inc.; Wintrup Musikverlag Walter Holzbauer, Detmold – 246 words.

3 crumbling breaking into small pieces · **5 to dismiss** to regard s.th. as not important · **6 rumbling** low, continuous sound · **14 to shake up** to change things · **27 inconvenient** [ˌɪnkən'viːnɪənt] uncomfortable · **40 intention** plan, purpose · **41 trapped** caught

Working with the song

1 Do you like the song? Say why/why not?
2 Describe in your own words what Melissa Etheridge wants to do.
3 What might the phrase "distant rumblings" ‹L 5–6› refer to?
4 What do you think is meant by "the promise of this new world" ‹L 23›?

Further activity

5 The song is the title song of the film, *An inconvenient truth*. Find out what the film is about and present your findings to the class.

Listening comprehension

1|11

The United Nations Climate Change Conference

Listen to extracts from a statement by Yvo de Boer at the opening of the UN Climate Change Conference on Bali in December 2007.

Climate change

Before you read

1 What do you know about climate change? Make a list of changes and their possible consequences. Present your list in class and discuss it.

Note taking

2 Collect information from the text in note form under the following headings:

a) Climate change
b) Geographical changes
c) Changes in temperature
d) Changes in atmosphere
e) Other predictions for the future

Certainties and uncertainties of climate change

The Earth's climate has varied in the past over many different timescales. Right now we are in an interglacial, a relatively mild period between ice ages. But humans are changing the climate system.

The natural greenhouse effect

Some gases in our atmosphere, for example carbon dioxide, methane, nitrous oxide, and especially water vapour, trap heat emitted from the Earth's surface, keeping the planet about 30 °C warmer than it would otherwise be. This is the 'natural greenhouse effect' and is well understood scientifically.

Human activities, especially burning fossil fuels like coal and oil, have increased the level of these greenhouse gases in our atmosphere. This is throwing the climate system out of balance.

Climate change is the most important environmental issue we face this century. Every one of the hottest 15 years on record has occurred since 1980 – the five hottest since 1997. [...]

Widely accepted facts

- Carbon dioxide and nitrous oxide levels are rising, primarily because of human activities connected with burning fossil fuels.
- Methane levels in the atmosphere more than doubled in the last century. Levels are still rising, though the rise has slowed down.
- Carbon dioxide is responsible for 60 % of human-induced greenhouse warming, methane 20 %, and nitrous oxide and other gases 20 %.
- Carbon dioxide levels in the atmosphere have increased from about 280 parts per million (ppm) in the mid 18th century – the start of the industrial revolution – to around 379 ppm today. You would need to go back millions of years to find another time when carbon dioxide was at such high levels in the atmosphere.
- Nitrous oxide levels are rising by about 0.25 % each year.
- Over the last century, the average global surface temperature rose by around 0.7 °C. Continents in the northern hemisphere have warmed the most.
- 1998 was the warmest year since 1860, the earliest year for which a precise global estimate is possible. 2002 and 2003 tie for second place.
- The majority of the world's mountain glaciers are retreating and Arctic sea-ice appears to be reducing in both extent and thickness.
- Global sea levels have risen 10 – 20 cm over the past 100 years. [...]

6 **carbon dioxide** *Kohlendioxyd* · 7 **methane** *Methan* · 7 **nitrous oxide** *Lachgas, Distickstoffmonoxyd* · 8 **vapour** steam · 8 **to trap s.th.** to stop s.th. escaping · 8 **to emit** to give off · 12 **fossil fuel** material such as coal, gas, oil that is used to produce energy · 17 **issue** [ˈɪʃuː] topic · 27 **human-induced** caused by mankind · 42 **estimate** *(noun)* an approximate number · 43 **to tie for second place** to both come second · 44 **glacier** *Gletscher* · 45 **to retreat** to go back · 46 **extent** size

Paraphrasing

3 With a partner, take turns to paraphrase one of the German terms below in English. See if your partner can guess the English term. (The English terms can be found in the text.)

a) *fossile Brennstoffe*
b) *Durchschnittstemperatur der Erdoberfläche*
c) *Treibhausgase*
d) *beispiellos, noch nie dagewesen*
e) *Eisschicht*
f) *Überschwemmungsgefahr*
g) *Klimawandel*

Global consequences

The IPCC has developed a number of scenarios for future greenhouse gas emissions, and has explored these with a range of climate models. They show that:

- Carbon dioxide levels are likely to at least double from pre-industrial levels by the end of this century. When other factors are added, such as increased water vapour, the estimated average global temperature rise by 2100 is between 1.5–5.8 °C. Though new evidence from climateprediction.net suggests the increase could be as high as 11 °C.
- This rate of warming will be much higher than experienced during the 20th century and is probably unprecedented in the last 10,000 years.
- Global sea level is likely to rise by 10–90 cm over this century. Low-lying coasts will flood, affecting many human settlements, including some major cities. Some habitats will be lost.
- If temperatures over Greenland increase by more than about 3 °C – which appears likely based on current model predictions – the ice sheet there will eventually disappear altogether, raising global sea level by several metres over a period of 1,000 years or more.
- Some regions and seasons will become wetter, others drier. Summer droughts are likely to intensify in the interiors of continents. Tropical cyclones may become more severe. Intense cold weather will become less frequent.
- Many areas will experience more extremely hot weather, like the unprecedented heat in Europe in 2003, and heavier rain, with an increased risk of flooding.
- Food production in mid-latitudes could benefit if climate change is not too severe. However, in tropical and sub-tropical regions, the risk of famine is likely to increase.

- Water availability will become even more of a problem for people in regions where it is already scarce, particularly in the sub-tropics.
- The world's vegetation zones will undergo major changes. In particular, the boundaries between grasslands, forests and scrublands may shift.
- The temperature, flow and level in freshwater systems will change, affecting biodiversity, water supplies and water quality.
- Human and animal diseases, such as malaria, will probably spread to new areas, and deaths related to heat stress are predicted to increase.
- 'Environmental migration' is predicted as many people move from high flood risk areas or arid regions. This could drive conflicts and increase health problems.

Source: National Environment Research Council Brochure, June 2007, www.nerc.ac.uk/publications – 738 words.

50 **IPCC** *short for* Intergovernmental Panel on Climate Change · 54 **pre-industrial** before the industrial revolution · 62 **unprecedented** that has never happened before · 66 **habitat** natural environment for specific plants or animals · 73 **drought** [draʊt] a long period without rainfall · 80 **mid-latitudes** regions around the equator · 85 **scarce** available in very small amounts · 88 **boundary** border between two zones · 89 **scrubland** area covered with small woody plants · 89 **to shift** to move · 91 **biodiversity** *Artenvielfalt* · 97 **arid** [ˈærɪd] very dry

Vocabulary

4 a) Find words and phrases in the text on pp. 62–63 which express that an outcome is probable but not certain.
Example: "Carbon dioxide levels *are likely to* at least double." ‹L 53›
b) Make statements about how the world may be in 2050 using these words and phrases. You can refer to task 1 for ideas.

Discussion in groups

5 a) In groups, discuss and agree on the five most important causes and consequences of global warming. Make a list giving reasons for your choices.
b) Present your list to the other groups using if-clauses and the phrases you found in the vocabulary task.
Example: "We think that carbon dioxide emissions are the most important cause of global warming because if emissions continue, the increase in temperature may be as high as 11 °C by the year 2100." (cf. ‹L 55–59›)
c) Discuss your results in class.

→ **Discussions**
See *skills file* on page 177.

Further activity: Research and leaflet/poster

6 a) Find out more about the causes and effects of climate change.
b) Choose one aspect of climate change and design a leaflet or poster for an environmental organization. Display in your classroom.

Check the web
Key words: "IPCC", "Greenpeace"

Alternative energy sources

Understanding the text: "How mirrors…" on page 65.

1 Explain in your own words how CSP technology works.
2 What does Dr. Knies mean by the "triple use of … energy" ‹L 54›?
3 Outline the advantages of HVDC.
4 According to the writer, what are the advantages of energy generation by CSP compared to energy generation by a fusion reactor?

Language

5 Rewrite the sentences using synonyms or synonymous phrases for the underlined words.
a) "… the easy, efficient transport of electricity from a variety of alternative sources." ‹L 31–32›
b) "There are different forms of CSP but all share in common the use of mirrors…" ‹L 43–45›
c) "It is this triple use of the energy which really boosts the overall energy efficiency of these kinds of plants up to 80 %, to 90 %." ‹L 54–56›
d) "the hot liquid can be stored in large vessels" ‹L 58›

6 Find opposites for the words taken from the text.

a) vast ‹L 2›	c) simple ‹L 17›	e) reduction ‹L 37›
b) underneath ‹L 6›	d) nearby ‹L 27›	f) to heat up ‹L 47›

Surviving without a dictionary

7 List the new words in the text and try to work out their meaning by:
- considering the context as a whole;
- thinking of related words in English;
- thinking of similar words in German or in foreign languages.

→ **Surviving without a dictionary**
See *skills file* on page 187.

How mirrors can light up the world

In the desert, just across the Mediterranean sea, is a vast source of energy that holds the promise of a carbon-free, nuclear-free electrical future for the whole of Europe, if not the world.

We are not talking about the vast oil and gas deposits underneath Algeria and Libya, or uranium for nuclear plants, but something far simpler – the sun. And in vast quantities: every year it pours down the equivalent of 1.5 m barrels of oil of energy for every square kilometre.

Most people in Britain think of solar power as a few panels on the roof of a house producing hot water or a bit of electricity. But according to two reports prepared for the German government, Europe, the Middle East and North Africa should be building vast solar farms in North Africa's deserts using a simple technology that more resembles using a magnifying glass to burn a hole in a piece of paper than any space age technology.

Two German scientists, Dr Gerhard Knies and Dr Franz Trieb, calculate that covering just 0.5 % of the world's hot deserts with a technology called concentrated solar power (CSP) would provide the world's entire electricity needs, with the technology also providing desalinated water to desert regions as a valuable by-product, as well as air conditioning for nearby cities.

Focusing on Europe, North Africa and the Middle East, they say, Europe should build a new high-voltage direct current electricity grid (HVDC) to allow the easy, efficient transport of electricity from a variety of alternative sources. Britain could put in wind power, Norway hydro, and central Europe biomass and geo-thermal. Together, the region could provide all its electricity needs by 2050 with barely any fossil fuels and no nuclear power. This would allow a 70 % reduction in carbon dioxide emissions from electricity production over the period.

CSP technology is not new. There has been a plant in the Mojave desert in California for the past 15 years. Others are being built in Nevada, southern Spain and Australia. There are different forms of CSP but all share in common the use of mirrors to concentrate the sun's rays on a pipe or vessel containing some sort of gas or liquid that heats up to around 400 °C (752 °F) and is used to power conventional steam turbines.

The mirrors are very large and create shaded areas underneath which can be used for horticulture irrigated by desalinated water generated by the plants. The cold water that can also be produced for air conditioning means there are three benefits. "It is this triple use of the energy which really boosts the overall energy efficiency of these kinds of plants up to 80 %, to 90 %," says Dr Knies.

This form of solar power is also attractive because the hot liquid can be stored in large vessels which can keep the turbines running for hours after the sun has gone down, avoiding the problems associated with other forms of solar power. […]

European commission president José Manuel Barroso said […] that he wanted to see the European Union develop a common energy strategy based on low carbon emissions. […]

The outlook is not promising. More than 30 countries last week agreed to spend £7 bn on an experimental fusion reactor in France which critics say will not produce any electricity for 50 years, if at all.

That amount of money would provide a lot of CSP power, a proven, working and simple technology that would work now, not in 2056. […]

Dan Lewis, energy expert at the Economic Research Council, calculates that CSP costs $3–5 m per installed megawatt, one-fifth the cost of fusion. "Fusion is basically a job creation scheme for plasma physicists." […]

By Ashley Seager, *The Guardian*, November 27, 2006 – 616 words.

Disposing of nuclear energy

Before you read

1 Are you in favour of or against the use and production of nuclear power? Give reasons.
2 What are the main arguments used by supporters and opponents of nuclear power? Brainstorm with a partner and draw up a list of ideas.

Understanding the text

3 In your own words explain the difference between 'Low Level Waste', 'Intermediate Level Waste' and 'High Level Waste'.
4 How does the nuclear industry take "full responsibility" ‹L 17› for its waste?
5 What effect does the choice of language have on you, the reader?
6 Do you think BNFL's PR Department did a good job? Why/Why not?
7 Suggest alternatives as if you were a competing advertising company.

Low Level Waste (LLW)

Transportation of spent fuel

radioactive waste:

Nuclear generation may be one of the cleanest forms of large-scale electricity production we have. But doesn't it leave behind hazardous by-products at the same time?

The simple answer is yes. Like all manufacturing processes, waste products do result, and some of ours must be handled with great care and shielded from man and the environment.

But unlike many other toxic metals and chemicals, the behaviour of nuclear wastes is predictable and fully understood. And unlike many other industries, the nuclear industry takes full responsibility, financial and managerial, for its waste.

Waste in context

The treatment and storage of radioactive waste poses no technical or safety problem to either nuclear workers or the general public, because:

It decays naturally. Radioactivity fades away over time. Some toxic substances, for example mercury, remain toxic forever.

It is predictable. We know exactly how long radioactivity takes to decay into a safe state.

It is storable. Even the small amount of High Level Waste in existence is fully containable using existing materials and technology.

It is low in volume. A single tonne of uranium, the nuclear fuel, will deliver as much electricity as 15,000 tonnes of coal. It follows, then, that there is very little radioactive waste left behind to manage. And, its volume is further reduced by reprocessing.

Britain's waste. By volume, by radioactivity

Radioactive waste must, by law, be divided into one of three categories.

Approx. 90% = Low Level Waste (LLW). This comprises routine items such as nuclear worker's gloves and overalls, paper towels and certain plant equipment. Almost all is actually less radioactive than naturally radioactive substances, such as your morning cup of coffee. It is compacted,

Picture: shielded ['ʃi:ldɪd] kept away from s.th. · **Headline: to dispose of s.th.** to get rid of s.th.

4 hazardous dangerous · **5 by-product** s.th. which is produced during the production process of s.th. else · **12 toxic** poisonous · **14 predictable** foreseeable · **21 to pose** *here:* to cause · **25 to decay** to break down · **26 to fade** to disappear slowly · **27 mercury** *Quecksilber* · **42 reprocessing** recycling waste so that it can be used again · **47 to comprise** [kəm'praɪz] to consist of

Further activity

8 BNFL wants to build a nuclear waste disposal site in your area. Not everyone is in favour so there is to be a public hearing.

a) Form the following groups:
- a pressure group of unemployed people from the region you live in
- representatives of BNFL
- representatives of the ruling party of your city council who have not been successful in creating new jobs so far
- representatives of the opposition party of your city council who are strictly against the site
- members of a Greenpeace group
- owners of a huge recreation park next to the planned site
- members of an initiative of farmers whose land surrounds the area.

b) In your groups collect arguments for an open discussion of the plans to build the site. Choose one person to represent your group at the discussion.

→ **Discussions**
See *skills file* on page 177.

Heavily shielded steel containers

Crash test involving flasks

British Nuclear Fuels (plc) = public limited company

disposing of the myths

incinerated, and the ash sealed in drums at the BNFL stores at Drigg in Cumbria. LLW accounts for less than 10% of radioactivity in waste.

Approx. 10% = Intermediate Level Waste (ILW). This includes fuel can debris, filter sludges and ion exchange resins. It must be handled using remotely operated tools and shielding, and is housed at power stations in concrete vaults.

Approx 0.1% = High Level Waste (HLW). This accounts for 90% of all radioactivity in waste, yet less than 0.1% of its volume. HLW comes only from fuel, which is reprocessed at Sellafield. After some forty years of nuclear generation, Britain's total HLW would fill the equivalent of just four double decker buses.

Transporting spent fuel

Nuclear fuel is remarkably recyclable. Ninety-nine percent of Magnox fuel can be recovered, which is why spent fuel is sent from our power stations to the BNFL reprocessing facility in Cumbria.

Its transport is highly regulated and rigid safety guidelines dictate how it is moved.

The fuel is transported in specially designed nuclear 'flasks', each weighing some 50 tonnes and made in forged steel at least 35 cm thick. These flasks have passed a battery of tests to meet the requirements of the International Atomic Energy Agency. The Magnox M2 flask has been shown to withstand fire at a temperature of 800 °C, and is unaffected by water pressure at a depth of 200 metres. They have also survived drop testing and, in one spectacular case, a head-on collision test with a 100mph locomotive. The train was written off, the flask sustained nothing more than scratches and dents.

Since 1962, nuclear flask movements have covered more than 6 million miles on Britain's roads and rails. Not one hazardous incident has ever taken place.

Source: BNFL brochure 2007 – 576 words.

53 to incinerate [ɪnˈsɪnəreɪt] to burn · **53 to seal** to lock up · **59 debris** [ˈdeɪbriː] broken pieces of s.th. big · **59 sludge** mud-like material · **59 ion exchange resin** *Ionenaustauscherharz* · **63 vault** underground room used for storage · **73 spent** used up · **81 rigid** [ˈrɪdʒɪd] strict · **84 flask** container for liquids · **86 forged** *(of metal)* heated and hammered · **87 a battery of s.th.** a large number of · **98 to sustain** *here:* to receive · **99 scratch** mark on a surface · **99 dent** *Delle*

Energy & conservation

Art Buchwald was born in 1925 in Mount Vernon, New York, the son of Austrian immigrants. He became famous as a writer, journalist and humorist. At the height of his career, his columns were published in more than 550 newspapers, although his main work was done for *The Washington Post*. In 1982 Art Buchwald was awarded the Pulitzer Prize. He died on January 17, 2007 in Washington, D.C. On the day following his death *The New York Times* published a video obituary which Buchwald himself had made. In it he greets everyone with the words: "Hi, I'm Art Buchwald, and I just died."

Info-box: obituary [əʊ'bɪtʃʊərɪ] article usually in a newspaper reporting about s.o.'s death and describing his/her life

The following text was written in 1977 between two major oil crises, the first of which was in 1973 and the second in 1979. OPEC (Organization of the Petroleum Exporting Countries) had become increasingly powerful and was able to push up the price of oil thus causing shortages and panic buying in the US and in Europe. The American President, Jimmy Carter (1977–1981), put energy conservation onto the political agenda.

"Let our kids find their own oil."

2|22

WASHINGTON – The argument that President Carter gives for energy conservation is that if we keep using up the petroleum reserves we have now, there won't be any left for our children.

It's probably strong logic with many people, but Clemstone, my gas-guzzling friend, isn't buying it.

"Let the kids find their own oil," he said after the President's address on television.

"How can you say that?"

"We found it, didn't we? We dug in the ground and we brought the stuff up with our own hands. Why should we give the kids our oil on a silver platter?"

"We have to think of future generations who may suffer because of our waste and abuse."

"Why?" Clemstone asked me.

"Because," I said weakly.

"Look, do you think they'll appreciate the oil and gas if we just leave it to them? I know kids. The only things that have any meaning for them are those they worked for themselves. What we should say to them is, 'We're using up whatever petroleum we've found in the ground. You want some for yourselves, go out and find it.' That's the kind of challenge that will grab them."

"But you can't use up all our reserves in ONE generation."

"Sure we can. It's OUR oil and gas. Why should we freeze so some rotten kids can have gas to fool around in their cars 20 years from today?"

"There's something wrong with your argument," I told Clemstone, "but I can't put my finger on it."

4 **guzzling** ['gʌzlɪŋ] consuming a lot of s.th. · 5 **to buy s.th.** *(informal) here:* to believe s.th. · 9 **to give s.o. s.th. on a silver platter** *(figurative)* to give s.o. s.th. for nothing in return · 10 **abuse** [ə'bjuːs] misusing s.th. · 16 **to grab s.o.** *(informal) here:* to catch s.o.'s attention · 18 **rotten** worthless · 19 **to fool around** *(informal)* to act in a silly way

Understanding the text

1 Summarise the arguments for and against saving energy given in the text.
2 Look at the way Clemstone uses personal pronouns. What is the effect on the reader?
3 What characteristic elements of a satire can you find in this text?

→ **Satire**
See *glossary* on page 203.

Your view

4 The text was written in the late seventies. Do you think it is still relevant today, or not? Give reasons for your opinion.

Creative writing and Comment

5 In L 20–21 the narrator is lost for words: "There is something wrong with your argument – but I can't put my finger on it."
a) Think of arguments which the narrator could have used.
b) Write a new dialogue between Clemstone and the narrator starting from L 12 in which the narrator argues back convincingly.

→ **Narrator**
See *glossary* on page 202.

6 Comment on Clemstone's proposals and his attitude towards the younger generation. Say whether you think he could be referring to your generation and whether you agree or disagree with his views, giving reasons.

→ **Comments**
See *skills file* on page 155.

"There is nothing wrong with it. Each generation should fend for itself. Do you think we'd be where we are today if we depended on handouts of oil from our parents? No sir, we worked to get that petroleum. We drilled holes in Texas and Oklahoma. We sweated for it in the Gulf of Mexico and froze our tails off on the northern slopes of Alaska. We kissed the feet of desert sheiks to get our oil. And, by heaven, when we got it we appreciated it." [...]

"You make a strong argument against conservation," I told my friend, "but you forget one thing. You can't take it with you."

"I'm not taking it with me," he yelled. "I'm going to use it up right here, today, tomorrow, next week, next year. When I go there won't be a quart of the stuff left."

"What will your kids think of you? What will they say about a father who doesn't leave his kids a quart of oil after he's gone to that big Exxon station in the sky?"

"They'll bless me. They will eventually say, 'Thanks, Dad, for not making it easy on us. Thanks for having the faith in us so we could find our own Alaskan slope. You found your oil and we found ours, and our kids can find their own.' "

"I'm not sure that was the message the President was trying to get over to the American people," I said.

"Of course, it wasn't," Clemstone said. "But he doesn't have the confidence in the next generation that I do. He doesn't think they have the moral fiber and the pioneer spirit to go out and drill for their own fuel."

"But suppose it's true that there aren't any more reserves of gas and oil left?"

"If my son came to me and said, 'Dad, I can't find any oil,' do you know what I'd do? I'd hand him a shovel and say, 'Okay, go out and dig for coal'."

By Art Buchwald, *The Washington Post*, April 28, 1977 – 591 words.

22 to fend for oneself to take care of oneself · **23 handout** s.th. got for free · **25 to freeze one's tail off** *(slang)* to become very cold · **25 slope** steep side of a hill · **26 sheik** *Scheich* · **26 by heaven** expression used for emphasis · **28 You can't take it with you** *(humorous saying)* One can't bring anything along once one is dead. · **34 to have faith in s.o.** to believe in s.o. · **36 to get s.th. over to s.o.** to communicate an idea to s.o. · **39 moral fiber** *(BE* **fibre***)* strength of character · **43 shovel** tool used for digging holes

Energy user no. 1: the car

Before you read

1 Work with a partner or in a group. Answer Rick Wagoner's question in statement a) and discuss what you think the car of the future will be like. Think about fuel, size, customer requirements, etc. and present your ideas to your class.

→ **Discussions**
See *skills file* on page 177.

Working with the quotes

2 Read the quotes in b) – e) and combine the points made to create a short text with the title "The car in the 21st century". Add further points which you raised in your initial discussion above.

Quotes

A What if we were inventing the automobile today rather than a century ago? What might we do differently?

B The 20th century was the century of the internal combustion engine. The 21st century will be the century of the fuel cell.

Rick Wagoner, President and CEO of General Motors Corp.

C With a hydrogen economy, we have a major opportunity for sustainable economic development, which respects the environment and creates the path to non-petroleum and renewable energy sources without constraining economic growth.

Larry Burns, General Motors Vice President of Research & Development and Planning

D Biofuels are a part of a global strategy to protect our environment.

Brazil's President da Silva

E The motor vehicles of the future will be as different from today's vehicles as the first automobile was from the horse and buggy.

Harry Pearce, General Motors Vice Chairman

Text B: combustion engine engine that works by burning petrol · **fuel cell** *Brennstoffzelle*; **Text C: sustainable** which can be kept at a constant level · **renewable** which can be replaced · **to constrain** to restrict; **Text E: buggy** carriage drawn by a horse

Alternative fuels for cars

Before you read

1 a) Make a list of the alternative fuels that you know.
b) Which fuel is the most, and which is the least, environmentally friendly?

Understanding the text

2 Explain the three "impact categories" ‹L 38–39› in your own words.
3 What does the author mean by a "well-to-wheel approach" ‹L 3›?
4 If necessary, add to the list of alternative fuels you started in exercise one.

Comparing Alternative Fuels For Cars

Norwegian scientists have drawn up a league table of alternative fuels for cars. Their analysis is based on a well-to-wheel approach that takes into account manufacturing, energy use, greenhouse gas emissions, and local and regional pollutants.

Bottom of the table, unsurprisingly, are petrol vehicles, but coming in a close second last are hybrid vehicles that can run on compressed natural gas or petrol. Top of their league are fuel-cell powered vehicles using hydrogen gas obtained from natural gas methane.

Karl Høyer of Oslo University College and Erling Holden of Western Norway Research Institute, Norway, reported [...] their analysis of fuel chains including petrol, natural gas, and alternative fuel sources such as methanol and ethanol, hydrogen and biofuels.

"Alternative fuels are not in themselves a road towards sustainable mobility," the researchers say. However, their analysis places petrol and hybrid vehicles firmly at the bottom of the league table when all energy factors from source to consumer use are taken into account. "Any alternative fuel we considered is better than the cars that are used mostly today," they add.

Currently, there is no consensus regarding sustainable transport development. Even if a particular energy reduction goal is set for the transport sector there is no agreement on actions that should be taken to achieve this goal. Different lobbying groups have different approaches to the problem and opponents of any particular approach can usually find evidence to suggest a particular approach is not sustainable. The ongoing biofuel debate is a case in point.

Nevertheless, there are several factors that must be considered in assessing a particular alternative fuel: the efficiency route, the substitution route and the reduction route. Each has its strong defenders, say Høyer and Holden, but in reality there are substantial grey areas between them. One important facet of the debate that is often overlooked, is to ensure the three impact categories – energy use, carbon emissions, and nitrogen oxide pollution – are considered together. "This is a highly problematic task and should only be carried out with great care," the team adds.

They used a simple ranking system to create their league table, based on giving each energy form a weight from 1 to 16 depending on its impact in these three areas. When the weights are added up from well to wheel, they provide an overall value for each energy chain. For example, extraction of natural gas, processing into liquefied hydrogen, storage, and end use in a fuel cell car. The energy chains giving the lowest sum-figures are the highest in the league table and those with largest figures are considered potentially the most environmentally harmful.

Interestingly, the team's analysis puts a fossil-based alternative, natural gas conversion into hydrogen for fuel cells at the top of the list. In contrast the direct use of natural gas in hybrid cars is lower down the list in terms of efficiency, energy, and pollution. Biological methanol for use in fuel cell vehicles is way down the list despite biomethanol being a potentially renewable resource unlike natural gas. "It must be emphasised that no single chain comes out with the best score on all impact categories," the researchers say, "There are always some sorts of trade offs involved. Thus, there are no obvious winners; only good or bad trade offs between different impact categories."

Source: *Inderscience Publishers*, April 29, 2007, adapted by *Science Daily*, www.sciencedaily.com – 555 words.

1 league table comparison of features in a table · **3 well-to-wheel** refers to fossil fuel production from the source to its use in a vehicle · **8 compressed natural gas** *komprimiertes Erdgas* · **17 sustainable** which can be kept in its present form · **25 goal** target · **27 lobbying group** interest group which tries to influence politicians · **31 a case in point** a good example · **32 nevertheless** in spite of all that · **33 to assess** to consider the good and bad points · **34 substitution** replacement · **36 substantial** [səbˈstænʃl] considerable · **39 impact** effect · **40 nitrogen oxide** *Stickstoffoxid* · **48 extraction** bringing raw materials out of the ground · **49 liquefied** [ˈlɪkwɪfaɪd] made into liquid · **64 trade off** compromise

Car-sharing

Before you read

1 What do you know about car-sharing?
2 a) Where might car-sharing clubs be the most/least successful?
b) What kind of services could they offer in order to attract more members?

Understanding the text

3 Retell in your own words the writer's experience on her first trip to Berkshire in a car-club vehicle.
4 Describe what a CCC member must do when he or she wants to use one of their cars.
5 Why does the writer own a car? Find reasons in the text.

Further activity

6 a) Imagine you plan to do a number of trips in a car-club vehicle starting from Brighton:
- a seven-day trip to Cornwall (total distance: 480 miles)
- a shopping trip to a furniture store (total distance: 16 miles; time: 4 hours)
- a two-week holiday in Scotland (total distance: 1,100 miles).

Calculate how much the three trips would cost with each of the three car-sharing firms in Brighton (CITY CAR CLUB, WHIZZ GO and STREETCAR).
b) Add two further trips per month for twelve months (time: an average of four hours; average distance: 50 miles). Decide which car-sharing club you would join for a year to get the best deal.

Brighton car clubs

CITY CAR CLUB

MEMBERSHIP: £75 for life
HOURLY RATE: £4.50
SEVEN-DAY RATE: £180
FREE DAILY MILES: 50, then 20p per mile
CURRENT FLEET SIZE: 17

WHIZZ GO

MEMBERSHIP: no membership if you spend less than £25 a month, or various packages from £25 to £100 a month.
HOURLY RATE: £4.95
SEVEN-DAY RATE: £189
FREE DAILY MILES: 30, then 20p per mile
CURRENT FLEET SIZE: 4

STREETCAR

MEMBERSHIP: £49.50 a year
HOURLY RATE: £4.95
SEVEN-DAY RATE: £195
FREE DAILY MILES: 30, then 19p per mile
CURRENT FLEET SIZE: 5

Comment

7 Would you be prepared to take part in a car-sharing scheme? Write an essay in the form of a formal comment saying why or why not.

Comments
See *skills file* on page 155.

Creative writing: Family drama

8 The 10-year-old car owned by the Fisher family has broken down yet again! Having the car repaired will be very expensive. The family is sitting at the dinner table discussing the possibilities of repairing the car, buying a new one or joining a car club.
Write a short scene with the following characters: Herman Fisher, 45 years old / Elizabeth Fisher, 44 years old / Thomas, 16 / Michael, 11 / Ruth, 18.
Try to make your scene as lively and dramatic as possible.

Join the car club

Cars, eh? The bête noir of environmentalists. I have a confession to make, though. I've got one.

Modern life sometimes deems it utterly impractical to get everywhere you are going in a green style – especially if you have years of experience relying on petrol power. Saying we shouldn't drive because of the environment is one thing, coming up with practical alternatives is quite another.

Enter car clubs: nicely branded hire companies that, for a small membership fee, allow people to use a car as regularly or irregularly as they like and without the hassle or expense of actually owning one.

As for the environment, it may seem odd to encourage car use, but car club members generally reduce their annual mileage by about a half, as well as increase their use of alternative, greener methods of transport.

I hung up my car keys and signed up for a month with City Car Club to see if it really did cut down my driving or whether it was just complicated conscience salving.

My first mission was to get [...] to my mother's wedding, somewhere in the middle of Berkshire. [...]

Logging on to the website is simple enough and, even without reading the instructions it doesn't take much effort to click a few buttons and book a car. [...]

We picked up the Toyota Yaris from our preferred handy location with no problem. [...]

The tank was nearly empty but a card in the glove box meant filling it up was done courtesy of City Car Club and not my wallet.

It costs £67.50 for two days' hire, including insurance, plus you get 50 miles a day free, 20p a mile thereafter.

Our 160-mile round trip cost us £12 in mileage, making the weekend car use total £79.50.

It might sound like a lot of money to pay in one go. But remember a full tank of petrol would normally set you back the best part of £50 anyway, plus there is no tax, no annual insurance, no wear and tear to worry about. [...]

If truth be told, I cling on to my four-wheeled friend not because of practicality or necessity but, like many other people I suspect, because I struggle desperately with the thought of not being able to jump in it at a moment's notice and take off dramatically into the sunset – not that I have ever actually done this.

The brilliant thing about City Car Club is you don't lose that sense of independence at all. In fact, you gain plenty more freedom through financial savings, not having to worry about maintenance or long-term parking, and in losing that nagging eco-guilt for owning an evil gas-guzzling car in the first place.

There are three car clubs in Brighton and Hove and they all work in a similar way.

You book online or at their call centre – even a few minutes before you need the car – and then pick it up at your nearest car club parking space.

You swipe your membership card across the windscreen, locate the keys in the secret key hiding place, punch your PIN into a little onboard computer and pootle off. Hourly charges can vary between £4 and £5 and you get between 30 and 50 miles free a day, paying about 20p a mile thereafter.

Having to book your car in advance might sound like a hassle but it is just a slightly different way of thinking.

You do have to plan your journeys and, to a certain extent, commit to a time frame. You are forced into analysing each trip you make – how long will it take? How many miles are you going?

Is there a better way of getting there?

And that is really the essence of what being green is about: asking yourself "Do I really need this?" [...]

By Sarah Lewis, *The Argus*, August 4, 2007 – 638 words.

1 **bête noir** s.th. that s.o. dislikes · 3 **to deem** *(formal)* to make · 3 **utterly** completely · 12 **hassle** trouble · 17 **I hung up my car keys** I put my keys away for a time. · 19 **conscience salving** s.th. that makes one feel less guilty · 21 **Berkshire** ['bɜːkʃə] · 26 **handy** *here:* easiest to reach · 28 **courtesy of** paid for by · 35 **to set s.o. back** to cost X amount of money · 37 **wear and tear** damage through ordinary use · 39 **to cling on to s.th.** to have an emotional dependence on s.th. · 48 **maintenance** having a car checked in the garage · 49 **nagging** annoying · 50 **gas-guzzling** consuming a lot of petrol · 56 **to swipe a card** to move a card across or through s.th. that reads the information on its magnetic strip · 59 **to pootle off** *(informal)* to drive away when you are ready

Talking about the cartoon

9 Describe the four pictures of the cartoon above in detail.
10 Point out at least three details which underline the message of the cartoon.
11 a) Paraphrase the arguments the driver uses in the first three pictures.
b) Which is the least convincing argument for not changing his lifestyle?
12 Think of other arguments that he might have used. Discuss your ideas.
13 Which of the ideas presented in this unit might have helped to convince the driver to change his lifestyle earlier?
14 How important, do you think, will a car be for you ten years from now?

→ **Cartoons**
See *skills file* on page 155.

Hotspot

Research and report – local action
Work in groups of three or four. Choose a topic dealt with in the unit. Research and prepare a report on how the topic is dealt with (or not) in your area. You can use the ideas below when you check the web.
- **Global warming & climate change:** heating systems · changing weather: flooding, heatwaves, etc.
- **Forms of energy:** types of electricity produced: nuclear, solar, wind, fossil fuel, etc. · recent changes · problems, dangers
- **Energy & conservation:** Environmental groups and activists · environmental problems and solutions · measures taken, planned and/or necessary at local level
- **Cars & fuel:** traffic · infrastructure · public transport · car-sharing clubs
- **Ecology & the economy:** businesses involved in recycling · businesses involved in producing ecological goods (e.g. solar panels)

→ **Reports**
See *skills file* on page 182.

Check the web
www.google.com
www.excite.com

Using energy – saving energy

Quiz

1 Complete the sentences by choosing the correct words and figures.

Quiz

A Turning your thermostat down by 1 °C could cut your heating bills by ? per year.

2% | 7% | 10% | 13%

B Your thermostat should not be set higher than ? .

60 °C | 65 °C | 70 °C | 75 °C

C Energy-saving light bulbs last up to ? longer than old-style light bulbs.

2 times | 5 times | 8 times | 12 times

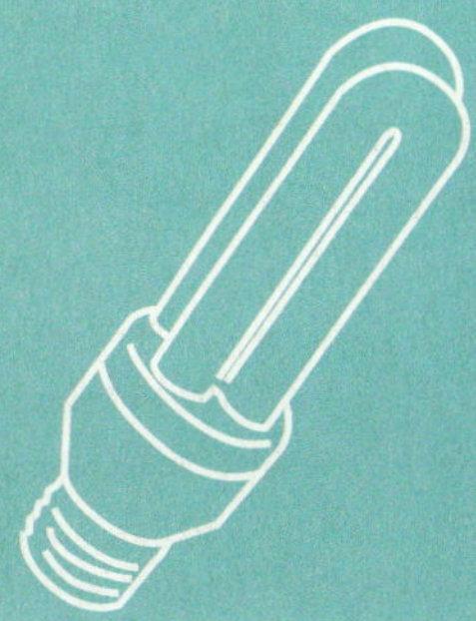

D Just one energy-saving light bulb can reduce your lighting costs by up to ? over the lifetime of the bulb.

£10 | £50 | £100 | £150

E When driving a petrol car, check the revolutions per minute (rpm) and change to a higher gear ? .

before 1,000 rpm | before 2,500 rpm | before 2,000 rpm | before 3,000 rpm

F If you want to increase fuel efficiency, you should use the ? sparingly.

air conditioning | brakes | radio | lights

G The most efficient speed depends on the car but it is typically around ? mph.

45–55 | 55–65 | 65–75 | 75–85

5: **revolutions per minute** number of revolutions *(= Umdrehungen)* of a motor

2 Find the correct answers to the questions and more examples of how to save energy.

Check the web
Key word: "Energy Saving Trust"

Unit 6 Technology and futurology

801005-0006

A new form of transport

Cordless telephone and television

A spaceship landing on the moon

Getting started

The three pictures above originate from the 1930s and show technical developments in the future. The pictures appeared on margarine packets, and could be collected and put into an album.

1 Describe the developments that the three pictures predict in detail.

2 Imagine creating a similar collection of "pictures of 2060". What three predictions would you make? Make a drawing or collage with your ideas.

→ **Illustrations and photos**
See *skills file* on page 158.

Futurology (1)

Before you read

1 Imagine you had the subject 'Futurology' at school. What could it cover?

2 a) Write a definition of 'futurology'. Compare your definition with a partner's.
b) Look the term up in a dictionary and correct your definition if necessary.

Understanding the texts

3 What do the predictions below tell you about futurology?

2|24

Oops! They got it horribly wrong

A But what is it (an early version of the microchip) good for?

Engineer, advanced computing systems division of IBM, 1968

B Every home will have a robot servant.

Scientists' predictions from the 1960s to the mid-1980s

C Spiro Agnew declared that the nation's next major space goal should be a manned landing on Mars by the end of the century.

Time Magazine, September 26, 1969

D Drill for oil? You mean drill into the ground to try and find oil? You're crazy.

Drillers to Edwin L. Drake, 1859, after he had tried to enlist them for the first project to drill for oil

E This telephone has too many shortcomings to be seriously considered as a means of communication. The device is inherently of no value to us.

Western Union internal memo, 1876

F Heavier-than-air flying machines are impossible. [and] Radio has no future.

Statements made in 1895 and 1897 respectively by Lord Kelvin, president of the Royal Society

G Computers in future may weigh no more than 1.5 tons.

Popular Mechanics, 1949

H I think there is a world market for maybe five computers.

Thomas Watson, chairman of IBM, 1943

I Who the hell wants to hear actors talk?

H.M. Warner, Warner Brothers, 1927

Text A: **to enlist s.o.** to hire s.o.; **Text E:** **shortcoming** fault · **device** [dɪ'vaɪs] object used for a certain purpose · **inherently** by its nature

4 a) Which incorrect predictions on page 77 do you consider to be the least important mistakes?
b) In your opinion, which prediction is the most important mistake? Give reasons for your choice.

Further activity

5 Which of the following predictions for the future do you find interesting? Give reasons for your answer.

Predictions that will change the world and when they'll happen

First commercial application	earliest	most likely	latest
Prevention of cancer	2009	2013	2017
Robotic exercise companion	2015	2020	2025
Cities built deep underground in Japan	2015	2020	2025
Extension of average life span to 100+	2015	2020	2025
Human knowledge exceeded by machine knowledge	2012	2017	2022
Artificial intelligence imitating thinking processes of the brain	2013	2018	2023
Intelligence enhancement by external means	2025	2030	2035
Artificial brains	2030	2035	2040
Use of unlimited nuclear fusion as power source	2035	2040	2045

From the articles by Simon Reeve, *The European*, February 23 – March 1, 1998.

1 application use · **6 extension** lengthening of s.th. · **6 life span** number of years s.o. lives · **8 to be exceeded by s.th.** *here:* to be overtaken by s.th. · **11 to imitate** to copy · **13 enhancement** *here:* improvement in the function of s.th.

1|15

Listening comprehension

The next fifty years

Listen to predictions for the next fifty years as made by experts from different areas of science.

Futurology (2)

Instant futures

When the sci-fi thriller *Minority Report* was released in 2002, its holographic computers were dismissed as Hollywood fantasy. Now they are about to become reality. With technology moving so rapidly, what else can we expect in the next five years?

With a sweep of his hand, in the film *Minority Report*, Tom Cruise effortlessly moved, enlarged and shrank pictures displayed on a massive screen in front of him. His movements allowed him to manipulate the holographic computer without need of mouse or keyboard.

When the movie was released in cinemas in 2002, this bit of futuristic technology was purely Hollywood fantasy. Five years later, however, electronics engineers have developed a computer that brings this vision to real life. [...]

Steve Prentice, chief of research at the consumer technology analysis firm Gartner, said: [...] "There is a whole generation now who expect wireless access wherever they go. A mobile phone is a basic human right. This is the way they have grown up."

The number of personal computers in the world is this year expected to pass the one billion mark. Already, however, there are more than 40 billion microprocessors, the chips that control computers, in use every day globally. Technology has become less and less obvious, with microchips hidden inside devices quietly performing tasks that make our lives easier without us even knowing it.

Computing power has crept into everyday appliances to such a degree that it is almost impossible to avoid using it. The average modern family car has more than 50 computers on board, controlling everything from the assisted braking to ensuring the car starts every time the key is turned.

"We are going to see more and more computing," said Professor Nigel Shadbolt, president of the British Computer Society. "In some ways, as technology becomes increasingly commonplace and invisible, it will become unremarkable. Home robots, for example, are unlikely to become common as we have had vacuum robots for a while but they have never really taken off. It is much more likely the intelligence used in robots is going to be put into your boiler and other white goods products."

A vacuum robot

Householders could soon be using washing machines and the like that turn themselves on in the middle of the night, when electricity is cheapest. Manufacturers have already revealed prototype fridges that can alert their owners to when they need to be restocked or cleaned. A digital display can list items inside without the fridge needing to be opened and even flash up messages for the rest of the family. [...]

Experts also predict that the capacity of computer memory will continue to soar, providing disks capable of storing 1,000 gigabytes and an unprecedented ability to record our lives.

The unanswered question is what we will do with it. "What this massive increase in memory means is that people will have continuous records of their daily activities," explained Professor Shadbolt. "Everything from live home videos to the continuous monitoring of your health will be possible. Whether this is a good thing or not remains to be seen."

By Richard Gray, *The Sunday Telegraph*, January 7, 2007 – 512 words.

6 sweep movement · **34 assisted braking** device which controls a car's brakes · **39 commonplace** everyday · **42 to take off** *here:* to become popular · **44 white goods** household machines, e.g. fridges, washing machines, etc. · **49 to alert** to warn · **55 to soar** to rise fast · **56 unprecedented** s.th. that has never happened before · **63 this remains to be seen** we will have to wait and see

Understanding the text: "Instant futures" on page 79.

1 What was Hollywood's "fantasy" in 2002 and what has changed since then?
2 Explain the significance of the latest developments in computers.
3 What does Professor Shadbolt predict for the near future?

Comment

4 "The unanswered question is what we will do with it (the massive increase in computer memory)", ‹L 58–59›. Try to answer the question.
5 Which of the future developments mentioned in the text do you find most important? Which ones do you find least important? Give reasons for your opinion.

→ **Comments**
See *skills file* on page 155.

Language

6 Paraphrase the underlined parts of the sentences in your own words.
a) "Tom Cruise effortlessly moved, enlarged and shrank pictures" ‹L 7–8›
b) "controlling everything from the assisted braking to ensuring the car starts every time the key is turned." ‹L 33–35›
c) "washing machines and the like that turn themselves on in the middle of the night" ‹L 46–48›
d) "fridges that can alert their owners to when they need to be restocked" ‹L 49–50›
e) "Everything from live home videos to the continuous monitoring of your health will be possible." ‹L 61–63›

Style

7 Identify the dominant text type in the article. Give reasons and examples to support your choice.

→ **Style analysis**
See *skills file* on page 162.

Teleportation

Before you read: "Beam me up ..." on page 81.

1 If you saw the newspaper headline on page 81 would you read the article, or not? Give reasons.
2 In the TV series and film, *Star Trek*, people are teleported from one place to another. Describe how teleportation works.

Understanding the text

3 Describe the "teleportation" success that took place in Australia and its possible value.
4 Outline the writer's view of the likelihood of beaming humans to different locations.

Mediation

5 Imagine a friend is organizing a meeting of German, *Star Trek* fans. He/she knows that the other fans would be very interested in the content of the *Independent* article and he/she has asked you to summarise the main points in German.

→ **Mediation**
See *skills file* on page 158.

Beam me up, Scotty
– one laser-beam encoded stream of information at a time

It's teleportation, Jim, but not as *Star Trek* fans know it. A team of scientists in Australia have managed to "teleport" a stream of information encoded in one laser beam and made it reappear in another beam a metre away using quantum physics.

The true value of the work will probably lie in creating super-secure communications channels for governments and financial institutions, as it is impossible to tap such quantum communications.

But Trekkies can still live in hope: the team leader, Dr Ping Koy Lam of the Australian National University in Canberra, reckons that in "the next three to five years" someone will manage to teleport an atom. After that, teleporting an entire person such as Kirk or Spock would only be a question of repeating that feat with a billion billion billion atoms at once – and creating their copies exactly correctly.

The Australian breakthrough was achieved using a process called "quantum entanglement", which has been the object of repeated experiments around the world for the past few years since its theoretical feasibility was demonstrated nearly a decade ago. Since then about 40 laboratories globally have been experimenting in this area.

In 1998, scientists in California demonstrated that it was possible to "teleport" a single photon, or particle of light. Using a bizarre property of subatomic physics, scientists generate two photons at the same point whose internal properties – called their "spin" – are exactly complementary. This is called "entanglement"; the photons can be sent in different directions from their source, and will keep that spin until they are destroyed by being detected. By finding out the spin of an entangled photon at any point, one automatically knows the spin of the other.

In the Australian experiment, two entangled beams were created. One of the beams was then encoded with radio data and sent over an optical fibre link, while the other was sent to another location in the laboratory. At the far end of the optical fibre, the laser beam was destroyed – and then the other beam was monitored to read the values of its entangled photons. They turned out to contain the data which had been included in the first beam – meaning that the information, and in effect the photons, had been teleported from one place to the other.

The ANU team of scientists from Australia, Germany, France, China and New Zealand is the first to achieve a successful trial with 100 percent reliability.

Teleportation of objects would rely on the fact that if two atoms have the same subatomic properties, such as spin and atomic weight, then they are practically identical. But it would require destroying the object to be teleported at its departure point so that an "identical" one could be created – by giving it the properties of the original – at another location.

That is the unspoken mechanism of the *Star Trek* transporter – and it's one which might give even the most eager fans a pause.

By Charles Arthur, *The Independent*, June 18, 2002 – 501 words.

Heading: beam ray; **Text: 9 to tap** to get information secretly · **12 to reckon** to guess · **14 entire** [ɪnˈtaɪə] complete · **15 feat** [fiːt] achievement · **19 quantum entanglement** *(in quantum mechanics)* description of two or more objects with reference to one another · **22 feasibility** possibility of doing s.th. · **27 property** feature · **30 complementary** which combine well with one another · **33 to detect** to find · **35 spin** quantum property *(= Eigenschaft)* of photons · **44 in effect** in fact · **49 reliability** dependability · **58 to give s.o. a pause** to make s.o. stop and think

Robotics

Tracked and wheeled versions of the Gladiator Tactical Unmanned Ground Vehicles (TUGV) determine security of an area

Asimo, the humanoid robot created by Honda

Remote Ordnance Neutralization System (RONS) robot inspects a suspicious package during a bomb threat scenario

Robots could be babysitters of the future

The human population of the world is at risk of striding like automata into a future dominated by robots, scientists have warned.

Unheralded advances in automation mean that robots are in development that will be able to look after children and the elderly, do routine housework, guard criminals and fight wars, although not all at the same time.

Prof Noel Sharkey, a senior fellow of the Engineering and Physical Science Research Council, said he was concerned that once robots had been used for urban warfare it would be a logical progression to use them for policing.

"Is this a good thing or a bad thing?" he asked. "I don't know, but we need more informed public debate."

Scientists envisage a future in which the elderly are cared for not by expensive human beings, but by mobile machines programmed to respond to human commands.

A learned discussion in central London, under the heading "Rights for Robots", drew attention to the possibility that robots would have a form of consciousness recognisable to human beings within 50 years.

Prof Sharkey said: "The problem is that robots may be required to make decisions that affect our lives much sooner than that."

"While some governments are beginning to draw up ethical guidelines, we need to initiate proper consultation and informed public debate now." The electronics company Samsung has already designed robots that it says would be able to police the highly-sensitive frontier between North and South Korea, with a policy of shooting to kill intruders at a range of 500 yards or more. Within a decade, a third of American military transport is expected to be driverless, the scientists said.

But they expressed concern that studies on safety and reliability of robot technology were lagging far behind the development of new and far-ranging applications.

By Ben Fenton, *The Daily Telegraph*, April 25, 2007 – 335 words.

2 to stride to walk in a particular direction · **2 automata** [ɔːˈtɒmətə] (*singular* **automaton**) machines, robots · **4 unheralded** unexpected · **13 progression** (further) development · **22 learned** [ˈlɜːnɪd] academic, scientific · **25 consciousness** [ˈkɒnʃəsnəs] knowing what is happening around one · **32 consultation** discussion with experts · **37 intruder** [ɪnˈtruːdə] *here:* s.o. who crosses the border illegally · **43 to lag behind** to develop more slowly than the others · **44 far-ranging** *here:* which can be used in many different areas

Understanding the text

1 a) Work in groups. Make a list of the areas in which robots can – or will be able to – work. Rank the examples in a table from the most desirable to the least desirable. Give reasons for your choice.
b) Compare your table with the other groups' tables.

Comment

2 Professor Sharkey "was concerned that once robots had been used for urban warfare it would be a logical progression to use them for policing. 'Is this a good thing or a bad thing?'" ‹L11–14› Try to answer Professor Sharkey's question giving reasons for your opinion.

→ **Comments**
See *skills file* on page 155.

Translation

3 Find at least two ways of translating the following phrases/parts of sentences into German.
a) " … the world is at risk …" ‹L1›
b) " … once robots had been used …" ‹L11–12›
c) " … mobile machines programmed to respond to human commands." ‹L20–21›
d) " … robots may be required …" ‹L27–28›
e) " … military transport is expected to be driverless …" ‹L39–40›

→ **Translation**
See *skills file* on page 165.

A step further: Cartoons

4 a) Describe the situations in the two cartoons in your own words.
b) Outline the similarities and differences between the robot shown in cartoon A and the robots described in the text, "Robots could be babysitters of the future".
c) At the beginning of this unit, on page 76, you were asked to make a collage of your predictions for the year 2060. Would you include these two cartoons in your collage, or not? Give reasons for your answer.

→ **Cartoons**
See *skills file* on page 155.

A

"Bad news. You're being outsourced by robots from a Third World country."

B

Stem cell therapy

Understanding the text

1 What information does the reader get about Dr. Hwang and Dr. Moon?
2 Explain in your own words the difference between reproductive cloning and therapeutic cloning.
3 What are Dr. Hwang's reasons for cloning human cells?

2 Friends, 242 Eggs and a Breakthrough

[...] Dr. Hwang, 51, and Dr. Moon, 56, faculty members at Seoul National University in South Korea, had announced at a news conference here at a meeting of the American Association for the Advancement of Science that they had successfully cloned a human embryo and extracted a stem cell line from it. [...]

The men say they are close friends. For years, Dr. Hwang (rhymes with song) has been making headlines in South Korea by cloning cows and pigs. Eighteen months ago, he approached Dr. Moon and asked him to join his research team; Dr. Moon's work in *in vitro* fertilization, he said, would greatly aid his efforts at human cell cloning.

"Therapeutic cloning is not really a medical doctor's job; it's a research doctor's job," Dr. Moon said. "Professor Hwang's lab is really fantastic. It's known as the 'cloning academy' or 'the power plant for cloning'."

Dr. Hwang added: "It's a power plant where we want to help solve some incurable human diseases."

Question: Leon R. Kass, the bioethics adviser to President Bush, said that he would like to see your type of research banned in the United States. What is your reaction?

Hwang: Our goal has never been to create cloned human babies, but to find the causes of incurable diseases and to offer a new window for cures. [...]

Do you have problems with your own government over your work?

Hwang: I can answer your question like this: If Korea were to prohibit therapeutic cloning research, we would have to go to other countries where it is permitted – Singapore, mainland China, maybe Great Britain. But my hope is that the Korean government will give us the license to do this kind of research. If they don't, we will move. [...]
You know, almost half of our research team is Christian, including Dr. Moon, who is Methodist. At the lab, we have discussed why we have to do this work. We have asked ourselves, is there any way to achieve the treatment of some incurable diseases without therapeutic cloning? The

1 faculty university department · **6 to extract** to remove · **6 stem cell** *Stammzelle* · **21 incurable** that cannot be healed · **33 to prohibit** [prəˈhɪbɪt] to forbid

Further activities: Letter to the editor and Interview

4 Write a letter to the editor of the *New York Times* commenting on the cloning of human cells.

5 Two years after the interview took place it was revealed that Dr. Hwang had faked the stem cell research and had never created the stem cell lines he mentioned in the interview. He was fired from Seoul National University. Write down questions you would ask him in a second interview and justify your questions.

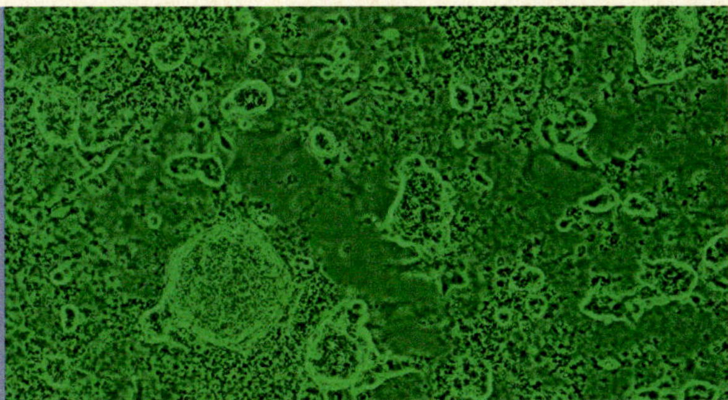

Stem cells under a microscope

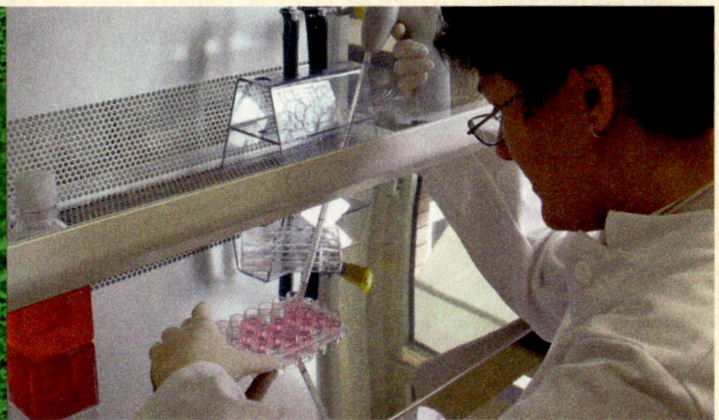

Stem cell research

answer is, it is a scientist's responsibility to do this research because it is for a good purpose.

What is the religious tradition you come from, Professor Hwang?

Hwang: I am a Buddhist, and I have no philosophical problem with cloning. And as you know, the basis of Buddhism is that life is recycled through reincarnation. In some ways, I think, therapeutic cloning restarts the circle of life. [...]

To create this cloned embryo that was used for a new stem cell line, 16 Korean women donated 242 human eggs to your project. How did you find these remarkable volunteers?

Hwang: In Korea like everywhere else there are young ladies who are curious about therapeutic cloning. Some heard about us and they contacted us with e-mail. Also, we sometimes gave lectures about our work. After we spoke, we received inquiries and we arranged meetings and discussed fully what egg donation meant. If they said yes, we enlisted them. We did physical and mental examinations. We asked if they understood what we were trying to do. We gave them a chance to change their minds. [...]

What are the economics of this? Will you become rich?

Hwang: We have applied for a worldwide P.C.T. [Patent Cooperation Treaty] patent for the technique we developed and also the cloned human embryo stem cells. Sixty percent of the patent will be owned by the university. The remaining 40 percent will go to the other collaborators. Dr. Moon and I will not be participating because we are professors.

Are you refusing money so that your motives can never be questioned?

Moon: That's right. Korea is a country where respect for the professorship is a little bit different than in the West. Professor Hwang takes the honor, not the money.

Do you think you'll get a Nobel Prize?

Hwang: Not now. The way I understand it, if the younger generation accomplishes its task and takes what we have done further, then maybe. What we've done is a beginning step.

From "A Conversation With Woo Suk Hwang and Shin Yong Moon; 2 Friends, 242 Eggs and a Breakthrough" by Claudia Dreifus, *The New York Times*, February 17, 2004 – 691 words.

53 **reincarnation** state of being born again · 67 **to enlist s.o.** *here:* to use s.o. in an experiment · 79 **collaborator** colleague · 89 **to accomplish** *here:* to fulfil

Human "spare parts"

Understanding the text

1 Describe in your own words what the narrator thought of babies when she "was little" ‹L1›.
2 Compare the narrator's attitude towards babies to the interests of "other kids" ‹L3›.
3 Make a list of the reasons the narrator gives why people have babies.
4 Outline briefly the circumstances surrounding the narrator's own birth.
5 Explain the line: "… we practically set a place for Death at the dinner table." ‹L34–35›

Creative writing

6 Write the dialogue between the narrator and her parents when they explain to her why she was born ‹L19–22›.
7 a) Write a diary entry for the day when the narrator found out why she was born. Choose from the point of view of one of the following characters: the narrator • Kate • Jesse • the narrator's father • the narrator's mother.
b) Compare the different viewpoints in class.

Jodi Picoult was born in 1966 on Long Island, New York. Her writing has included novels, short stories and a comedy series. Jodi Picoult's novels mainly concentrate on complex human relationships.

Info-box: Picoult [pɪ'kəʊ]

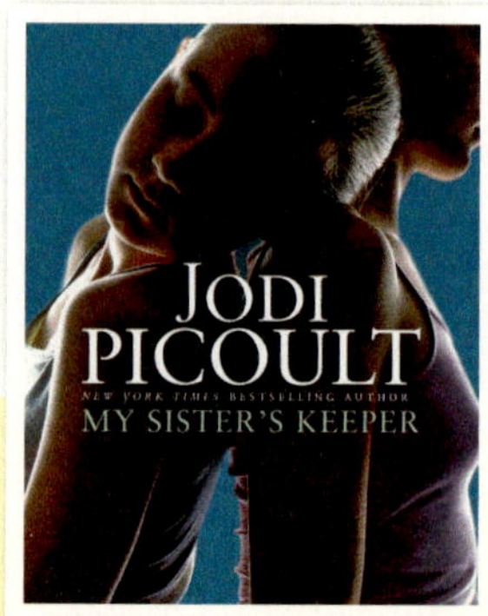

Anna

When I was little, the great mystery to me wasn't *how* babies were made, but *why*.

The mechanics I understood – my older brother Jesse had filled me in – although at the time I was sure he'd heard half of it wrong. Other kids my age were busy looking up the words *penis* and *vagina* in the classroom dictionary when the teacher had her back turned, but I paid attention to different details. Like why some mothers only had one child, while other families seemed to multiply before your eyes. Or how the new girl in school, Sedona, told anyone who'd listen that she was named for the place where her parents were vacationing when they made her (*"Good thing they weren't staying in Jersey City,"* my father used to say).

Now that I am thirteen, these distinctions are only more complicated: the eighth grader who dropped out of school because she *got into trouble*; a neighbor who *got herself pregnant* in the hopes it would keep her husband from filing for divorce. I'm telling you, if aliens landed on earth today and took a good hard look at why babies get born, they'd conclude that most people have children by accident, or because they drink too much on a certain night, or because birth control isn't one hundred percent, or for a thousand other reasons that really aren't very flattering.

On the other hand, I was born for a very specific purpose. I wasn't the result of a cheap bottle of wine or a full moon or the heat of the moment. I was born because a scientist managed to hook up my mother's eggs and my father's sperm to create a specific combination of precious genetic material. In fact, when Jesse told me how babies get made and I, the great disbeliever, decided to ask my parents the truth, I got more than I bargained for. They sat me down and told

Text: 7 **to vacation** *(AE)* to go on holiday · 9 **distinction** difference (from s.th. else) · 11 **to file for divorce** to officially ask for a divorce · 14 **flattering** making s.o. look good · 17 **to hook up** *here:* to put together · 19 **I got more than I bargained for** [aɪgɒtˌmɔːðənaɪ'bɑːgɪndfɔː] *here:* The answer was worse than I had expected.

Hotspot

a) Do research into the legal, scientific, ethical and religious issues that are linked to organ donation. Compare the situation in the UK with the one in Germany and the US. You could check the websites of the following organizations and institutions:
- Deutsche Stiftung Organtransplantation,
- Organspende (Bundeszentrale für gesundliche Aufklärung),
- UK Transplant,
- The BBC (Health section),
- The US Government on Organ & Tissue Donation and Transplantation.

b) Discuss the results in class.

→ **Discussions**
See *skills file* on page 177.

me all the usual stuff, of course – but they also explained that they chose little embryonic me, specifically, because I could save my sister Kate. "We loved you even more," my mother made sure to say, "because we knew what exactly we were getting."

It made me wonder, though, what would have happened if Kate had been healthy. Chances are, I'd still be floating up in Heaven or wherever, waiting to be attached to a body to spend some time on Earth. Certainly I would not be part of this family. See, unlike the rest of the free world, I didn't get here by accident. And if your parents have you for a reason, then that reason better exist. Because once it's gone, so are you. [...]

My parents tried to make things normal, but that's a relative term. The truth is, I was never really a kid. To be honest, neither were Kate and Jesse. I guess maybe my brother had his moment in the sun for the four years he was alive before Kate got diagnosed, but ever since then, we've been too busy looking over our shoulders to run headlong into growing up. You know how most little kids think they're like cartoon characters – if an anvil drops on their heads they can peel themselves off the sidewalk and keep going?

Well, I never once believed that. How could I, when we practically set a place for Death at the dinner table?

Kate has acute promyelocytic leukemia. Actually, that's not quite true – right now she doesn't have it, but it's hibernating under her skin like a bear, until it decides to roar again. She was diagnosed when she was two; she's sixteen now. *Molecular relapse* and *granulocyte* and *portacath* – these words are part of my vocabulary, even though I'll never find them on any SAT. I'm an allogeneic donor – a perfect sibling match. When Kate needs leukocytes or stem cells or bone marrow to fool her body into thinking it's healthy, I'm the one who provides them. Nearly every time Kate's hospitalized, I wind up there too.

From *My Sister's Keeper* by Jodi Picoult, London: Hodder & Stoughton, 2004, pp. 7–8, pp. 9–10 – 676 words.

31 **to run headlong** to rush towards s.th. without thinking · 32 **anvil** *Amboss* · 36 **promyelocytic leukemia** [prəˌmaɪələˌsɪtɪkljuːˈkiːmɪə] *(AE) Promyelozytenleukämie* · 37 **to hibernate** *(figurative)* to be inactive for a time · 38 **relapse** return of an illness · 38 **granulocyte** type of white blood cell · 38 **portacath** *short for* portable catheter; it allows medicines to be given internally at any time · 39 **SAT** *(US) short for* scholastic aptitude test; students must pass this to go to college · 40 **allogeneic donor** donor whose genes are similar, but not identical to, those of the person receiving their blood, cells, etc. · 40 **bone marrow** the inside part of a bone

Unit 7 Space – the final frontier?

801005-0007

astronaut

cosmonaut

Apollo

ISS

taikonaut

Galileo Galilei (1564–1642)

Columbia Feb 1, 2003

Star Trek

space tourism

NASA

Getting started

1 The words, dates and illustrations above are all related to the topics in this chapter and are also significant in terms of the history of space travel. What do you know about them or associate with them?

2 a) Make your own list of words that are related to space travel.
b) Exchange lists with a partner and make a mind map or word cluster based on his/her list.

→ **Illustrations and photos**
See *skills file* on page 158.
Mind maps
See *skills file* on page 186.

Space travel (1)

Before reading/listening

1 What difficulties, do you think, do astronauts face in space?

2|33

David Bowie
Space Oddity

Ground Control to Major Tom
Ground Control to Major Tom
Take your protein pills and put your helmet on

Ground Control to Major Tom
Commencing countdown, engines on
Check ignition and may God's love be with you

Ten, Nine, Eight, Seven, Six, Five, Four, Three, Two, One,
Lift-off

This is Ground Control to Major Tom
You've really made the grade
And the papers want to know whose shirts you wear
Now it's time to leave the capsule if you dare

"This is Major Tom to Ground Control
I'm stepping through the door
And I'm floating in a most peculiar way
And the stars look very different today
For here
Am I sitting in a tin can
Far above the world
Planet Earth is blue
And there's nothing I can do.

Though I'm past one hundred thousand miles
I'm feeling very still
And I think my spaceship knows which way to go
Tell my wife I love her very much she knows"
Ground Control to Major Tom
Your circuit's dead, there's something wrong
Can you hear me, Major Tom?
Can you hear me, Major Tom?
Can you hear me, Major Tom?
Can you …

"Here am I floating round my tin can
Far above the Moon
Planet Earth is blue
And there's nothing I can do."

6 **ignition** *Zündung* · 27 **circuit** *here:* connection

Working with the song

2 Describe what happens in the song in a few sentences using the phrases: at the beginning/end · then · at first · suddenly.

3 In your own words, describe how Major Tom feels about being in space, physically and emotionally.

Language

4 Explain line 10: "You've really made the grade".

5 a) Find the metaphor used by Major Tom to describe his spaceship.
b) Think of metaphors to describe: a car, your house, your school and your classroom.

6 Find words in the song relating to 'space travel' and explain them. Add more examples to the list you started on page 88 as you work through this chapter.

Metaphor
See *glossary* on page 202.

Your opinion

7 Comment on the melody, the instrumentation and the text by:
a) describing how David Bowie differentiates between "Ground Control" and "Major Tom" in the song.
b) saying whether or not you like the song. Give reasons.

Creative writing

8 Imagine you work at Ground Control and have to break the news to Major Tom's wife about what has happened. Choose one of the following tasks.
a) Write another verse.
b) Write the scene in the form of a screenplay. (The screenplay extracts of *Independence Day* on pp. 101–102 may help you.)

→ **Film analysis**
See *skills file* on page 184.

9 Write a newspaper article about the events described in the song. Give your article a suitable headline. You could include "quotes" from Ground Control, Major Tom's wife and family, ex-astronauts, opponents of space travel, etc.

1|20

Listening comprehension

The moon landing

Listen to excerpts of the live recording of the Apollo 11 moon landing.

Space travel (2)

Before you read: "We must travel . . ." on page 91.

1 Collect as many reasons as you can why mankind wants to explore space.

Understanding the text

2 What reasons does Stephen Hawking give as to why space exploration should be continued?
3 a) What is the main problem with space travel according to Stephen Hawking?
b) How might this problem be solved?
4 Why does Stephen Hawking dream of travelling into space one day?

Language

5 a) Find as many words as you can in the text that are related to 'space exploration' and 'space travel' and come up with appropriate definitions.
b) Present your definitions in class and let your classmates guess which words you are trying to explain.

Comment

6 Stephen Hawking warns that humankind can only survive by moving into outer space. Comment on this warning giving reasons for your opinion.

→ **Comments**
See *skills file* on page 155.

Research and presentation

7 Find out about Stephen Hawking's life and work. Prepare and give a short presentation.

→ **Presentations**
See *skills file* on page 160.

We must travel to the stars to save the human race, says Hawking

Stephen Hawking warned that future generations would need to leave the planet to ensure the survival of the species as he picked up a prestigious scientific accolade yesterday.

Professor Hawking, 64, a mathematics professor at the University of Cambridge, said space rockets using the kind of technology seen in *Star Trek* would be needed to colonise hospitable planets.

His warning came as he collected Britain's highest scientific award, the Royal Society's Copley Medal, previously granted to Charles Darwin, Michael Faraday and Captain James Cook. Professor Hawking, who suffers from motor neurone disease, said he was "honoured" to be in the company of such esteemed men.

The society's president, Lord Rees, said he had contributed "as much as anyone since Einstein to our understanding of gravity".

Professor Hawking also spoke of his desire to go into space, and appealed to the Virgin tycoon, Sir Richard Branson, who is planning a "space tourism" venture, to realise his ambition. "My next goal is to go into space. Maybe Richard Branson will help me," he said.

In an interview with BBC Radio 4, he said scientists may be within 20 years of reaching the prediction in his book, *A Brief History of Time*, that mankind would one day "know the mind of God" by understanding the laws governing the universe.

He added that this knowledge may be vital to the human race's continued existence. "The long-term survival of the human race is at risk as long as it is confined to a single planet.

"Sooner or later, disasters such as an asteroid collision or nuclear war could wipe us all out. But once we spread out into space and establish independent colonies, our future should be safe. There isn't anywhere like the Earth in the solar system, so we would have to go to another star.

"If we used chemical fuel rockets like the Apollo mission to the moon, the journey to the nearest star would take 50,000 years. This is obviously far too long to be practical, so science fiction has developed the idea of warp drive, which takes you instantly to your destination. Unfortunately, this would violate the scientific law which says that nothing can travel faster than light.

"My next goal is to go into space. Maybe Richard Branson will help me."
Stephen Hawking

"However, we can still within the law, by using matter/antimatter annihilation, at least reach just below the speed of light. With that, it would be possible to reach the next star in about six years, though it wouldn't seem so long for those on board," he said.

The cult science-fiction series, *Star Trek*, has featured matter/antimatter annihilation as an explanation for the warp drive which powers spaceships like the Enterprise through vast distances in short periods.

But in reality, some scientists believe the radiation produced when matter and antimatter are brought together could one day be used to accelerate aircraft close to the speed of light.

Meanwhile, to recognise Professor Hawking's achievements, the British astronaut Piers Sellers carried his medal into space on the July shuttle mission.

"Stephen Hawking is a hero to all of us involved in exploring the cosmos. It was an honour for the crew of the STS-121 mission to fly his medal into space," he said.

By Arifa Akbar, *The Independent*, December 1, 2006, news.independent.co.uk – 527 words.

3 prestigious [pres'tɪdʒəs] *here:* important · **4 accolade** ['ækəleɪd] award · **8 hospitable** *here:* which supports human life · **11 to grant s.th.** to give s.th. · **13 motor neurone disease** *eine Nervenkrankheit* · **14 esteemed** admired and respected · **21 venture** ['ventʃə] a new business · **25 prediction** forecast for the future · **29 vital** ['vaɪtl] necessary · **43 warp drive** *(in science fiction)* travelling faster than light · **53 annihilation** [ə,naɪɪ'leɪʃn] destruction · **56 radiation** *Strahlung* · **58 to accelerate** to go faster

Xtra-File: The International Space Station

The International Space Station (ISS) is probably the most important contemporary space project and it is also the biggest space station ever built! Here are some facts about the ISS:

- weight: 471,444 pounds;
- habitable volume: 15,000 cubic feet;
- span of solar arrays: 240 feet;
- length: 146 feet;
- height: 90 feet.

An international crew of three astronauts lives and works on the ISS. The participating countries are: The United States, Russia, Japan, Canada, and 11 European countries (Belgium, Denmark, France, Germany, Italy, the Netherlands, Norway, Spain, Sweden, Switzerland and the United Kingdom).

The purpose of the station is to:

- give private industry the opportunity to develop products in space for use on earth;
- perform long-term observation of earth and space;
- study the long-term effects of weightlessness on the human body and to use that knowledge in the exploration of space and to better the health of humans on earth;

- bring together the world community through governmental, academic, and industrial cooperation;
- develop new processes and products to benefit life on earth;
- test new technologies for the next step in the human exploration of the solar system;
- carry out experiments in the absence of gravity's effects.

Source: www.space.gc.ca and www.nasa.gov

7 **solar array** *Solarmodul*

Mediation

8 Create a leaflet or flier about the ISS in German based on the main points in the Xtra-File.

→ **Mediation**
See *skills file* on page 158.

Space travel (3)

Before you read: "The Big Question ..." on page 93.

1 Draw up a table listing the pros and cons of manned space travel.

Understanding the text

2 Outline the biggest disadvantage of manned space flight.
3 Explain why robots are still unsuitable substitutes for human astronauts.
4 How do most people regard manned space flights?
5 Compare your list of pros and cons of manned space flights with the arguments in the text. Which ones could be added to your list?

Vocabulary

6 Continue your glossary of space travel terms, adding words or phrases from the text that are not on your list yet.

7 Add the verb and adjective forms of each noun.

a) safety <L 6>
b) exploration <L 22>
c) life <L 32>
d) advances <L 37>
e) fascination <L 46>
f) colonisation <L 50>

Example:

noun	verb	adjective
safety	to save	saving

Over to you

8 What do you think are the "more pressing problems on Earth" ‹L 49›?

9 Explain why space tourism is bad for the planet.

Discussion

10 Look at your list from exercise 1. Form groups of supporters and opponents and have a class discussion about the necessity of manned space flight.

→ **Discussions**
See *skills file* on page 177.

The Big Question: Do we need to send people into space, or could robots do it better?

Is it not better to send robots to explore space?

Many intelligent people believe this is the case, given that a robot mission costs between 10 and 100 times less than a manned mission. Safety in space can be incredibly expensive, and to send people aloft means that three or four levels of safety precautions have to be built in to minimise risks.

Robots are a long way from being able to substitute humans. A robot geologist, for instance, might take weeks analysing a Martian landscape or a piece of lunar rock that a human specialist could evaluate in minutes. Steve Squyres, the principle scientist on the Nasa mission to explore Mars, pointed out that for all their apparent sophistication, space robots are still relatively primitive machines. "We are many decades away from robots that can match humans even in the lab. And laboratory robotics is about 20 years ahead of space robotics," he said.

So who is in favour of manned space flight?

Most of us, apparently. A recent BBC poll found that 61 per cent of the public is in favour of Britain playing a leading role in human space exploration. The proportion is even higher in America.

A recent report by scientists at the Royal Astronomical Society, in London, also came out in favour of manned space flight. "We find that profound scientific questions relating to the history of the solar system and the existence of life beyond Earth can best, perhaps only, be achieved by human exploration on the Moon or Mars, supported by appropriate automated systems," the report said.

Perhaps the argument for manned space flight is best summed up by Lord Rees of Ludlow, the Astronomer Royal Martin Rees: "My view about manned space flight is that, as a scientist and practical man, I'm against it, but as a human being I'm in favour of it."

Advances in robotics is making the case for manned space flight weaker, but there is still a need for it in terms of human adventure.

Should we send people into space?

Yes...

- It is the ultimate adventure to 'boldly go' where no man has gone before.
- Robots, despite all their apparent sophistication, will never be as adept in space as humans.
- Rich people with a fascination for space travel need something to spend their money on.

No...

- There are more pressing problems on Earth to solve before we dream of space colonisation.
- Space robots, though relatively primitive machines, are cheap and dispensable, people are not.
- The rich must learn that space tourism is bad for the planet we all have to live on.

By Steve Connor, *The Independent*, May 8, 2007, news.independent.co.uk – 441 words.

5 incredibly unbelievably · **5 aloft** into the air · **6 safety precaution** *Sicherheitsvorkehrung* · **11 lunar** from the moon · **11 to evaluate** to examine · **12 Squyres** [skwaɪəz] · **14 apparent** obvious · **14 sophistication** complex level of development · **17 lab** *short for* **laboratory** · **20 poll** *Meinungsumfrage* · **25 to come out in favour** to prefer · **26 profound** *here:* which requires a lot of study · **30 appropriate** suitable · **33 Astronomer Royal** important post in the Royal Astronomical Society in London · **37 advances** progress · **42 ultimate** greatest · **42 boldly** bravely · **45 adept** skilful · **49 pressing** urgent · **52 dispensable** not needed much

Space tourism

Before you read

1 If you had the chance to travel into space as a tourist, would you like to do so? Say why, or why not.

Understanding the text

2 What kind of people want to travel into space as tourists and why do they want to go there?
3 How much does a space flight with Virgin cost and how does it work?
4 What precautions have been taken to ensure passengers' safety?
5 What do you get to know about Virgin's spaceport location and how it is being financed?
6 What benefits might the spaceport have for the people living nearby?

Richard Branson *(right)* with Governor Bill Richardson of New Mexico

Who's paying $200,000 for a few minutes in space?

The next space race is on, and this time it's for the masses.

Well, not exactly the masses. More like the actors, real estate magnates, hedge fund managers and well-off adventurers who can afford $200,000 or so for a quick jaunt beyond the Earth's atmosphere and several minutes of zero-gravity weightlessness.

They include actress and skin-care entrepreneur Victoria Principal, 57, who wonders what color her spacesuit will be, and Hollywood director Bryan Singer, 41, who got turned on to the idea while planning a shuttle disaster scene for his movie *Superman Returns*.

Among the not-so-famous is Soviet émigré Lina Borozdina-Birch, 38, who took out a second mortgage on her house to fulfill her extraterrestrial dream – despite her fear of flying. Space junkies George and Loretta Whitesides, both 33, plan to celebrate their honeymoon more than 70 miles above Earth.

"There's a wide range of scientists, entrepreneurs, business people and people who really have a vision of wanting to go into space and always have," says Will Whitehorn, president of Virgin Galactic, one of several private companies trying to kick-start the space tourism industry, democratize the astronaut corps and

4 estate magnate [ɪ'steɪtˌmæɡneɪt] owner of land on which houses are built · **4 hedge fund manager** *Hedge-Fonds Manager(in)* · **6 jaunt** trip · **8 skin-care** refers to lotion and make-up for your face and body · **8 entrepreneur** [ˌɒntrəprə'nɜː] businessman or woman · **13 émigré** emigrant who leaves for political reasons · **14 mortgage** ['mɔːɡɪdʒ] *Hypothek* · **15 to fulfill** *(BE* **fulfil***)* to make s.th. happen · **18 honeymoon** journey after one's wedding · **23 to kick-start** to get s.th. moving · **24 corps** [kɔː] *here:* crews from different countries

Language and grammar

7 Add words and phrases from the text to your glossary on 'space travel'.

8 Find examples of as many different tenses in the text as you can and explain their meaning. Check the *Online-Link* for help.

801005-0011

Role play

9 Work in pairs. One of you is a journalist, the other takes the role of a space tourist mentioned in the article. Write an interview with the space tourist after their trip into space. Then act out the interview in class.

Check the web

10 How has the Virgin Galactic project progressed since the article was written? Find out up-to-date information about space tourism and create a poster or brochure. Afterwards present your findings in class.

→ **Presentations**
See *skills file* on page 160.

turn a profit doing so. Principal and the others have signed up with Virgin.

The company, part of flamboyant businessman Richard Branson's Virgin Group, has recruited about 200 people for 2½-hour suborbital flights aboard an eight-seat spacecraft. It hopes to start offering the flights in 2009.

Customers have put down $21 million in deposits, Whitehorn says. Those who want to be among the first 100 to fly had to pay the full $200,000 fare up front; the rest put down a minimum deposit of $20,000.

Recent space tourists have paid much more to take Russian rockets into orbit. Software pioneer Charles Simonyi spent more than $20 million for his trip to the International Space Station last month.

Virgin, which plans to eventually offer two spaceflights a day, is trying to appeal to a broader audience. In its quest to become the first commercial "spaceline," however, it has several competitors. […]

Virgin plans to operate five spaceships and offer flights from California initially, then New Mexico, as well as spaceports in other countries.

Each Virgin spaceship, built by renowned aerospace designer Burt Rutan's company, Scaled Composites, will seat six passengers and two pilots.

The spaceship will be attached to the belly of a jet carrier that will take off like a regular plane and then release the spaceship at about 50,000 feet.

There, a rocket will ignite and hurl the ship toward space at more than 3,000 mph.

The ship will peak at about 400,000 feet, and passengers will experience four to five minutes of weightlessness, Whitehorn says. They will be encouraged to somersault through the cabin. […]

Rutan says the ship, called SpaceShipTwo, will be safe.

If, for instance, the rocket engine were to malfunction, it could be shut off and the fuel dumped, and the spacecraft could glide back to land, Rutan says.

The Virgin spacecraft's design also accounts for some of the risks that contributed to the breakup of NASA's space shuttle Columbia, which disintegrated when it re-entered the atmosphere in 2003, Rutan says.

The Virgin ship will straighten itself into a stable position for re-entry by having its tails and part of the wing folded into a "feathered" position, Rutan says.

"That greatly increases the safety for atmospheric re-entry," he says. […]

Initially, Virgin Galactic will take off from a spaceport in the Mojave Desert, then will move to New Mexico when Spaceport America opens in late 2009 or early 2010.

The $198 million spaceport, about 45 miles northeast of Las Cruces, will be built with about $140 million from the state and about $60 million from local taxes, says Rick Homans, executive director of the New Mexico Spaceport Authority.

Supporters believe the spaceport and the commercial aerospace industry will attract jobs and businesses to the area. "There's already more hotels. There's going to be more businesses and restaurants," says Doña Ana County Commissioner D. Kent Evans. […]

By Emily Bazar, *USA TODAY*, May 7, 2007,
www.usatoday.com – 665 words.

25 **to turn a profit** to make money · 27 **flamboyant** [flæm'bɔɪənt] showy · 29 **suborbital** approx. 100 km above sea level · 31 **deposit** *Anzahlung* · 33 **to pay up front** to pay beforehand · 40 **quest** *here:* attempt · 42 **competitor** rival · 44 **initially** at first · 46 **renowned** famous · 52 **to ignite** to start the rocket's engine · 52 **to hurl** to shoot into the air · 54 **to peak** to reach the highest point · 56 **to somersault** ['sʌməsɔ:lt] ['sʌməsɒlt] to turn upside down · 63 **to account for** to consider problems and find solutions · 73 **Mojave** [məʊ'hɑ:vɪ] · 77 **Las Cruces** [ˌlæs'kru:sez]

Satellites

Before you read

For many years satellites were exotic, top-secret devices, which were used primarily by the military for navigation and espionage. Now satellites are an essential – if invisible – part of our daily lives.

→ **Presentations**
See *skills file* on page 160.

1 Work with a partner or in small groups and find out more about satellites using the internet. Prepare a short presentation about satellite use in at least one of the following areas:
- weather reports,
- television transmission,
- telephone calls and the internet,
- newspaper and magazine printing & distribution,
- navigation via Global Positioning System (GPS).

2 What are the advantages of geo-synchronous orbit (= moving at the same speed as the earth)? The illustration on the right may give you some ideas.

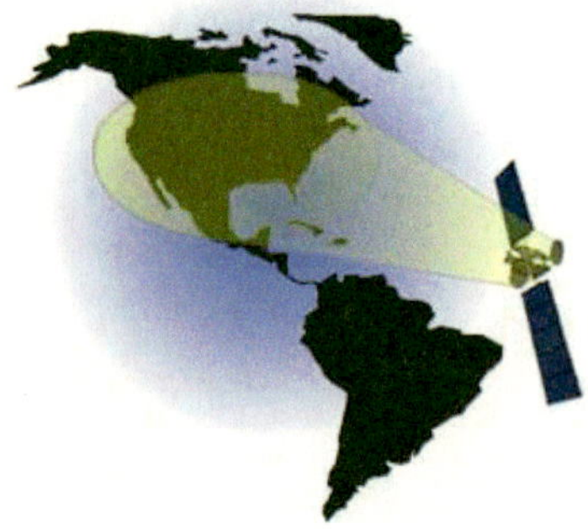

Understanding the text

3 a) Outline the recent findings of the Nasa satellites.
b) According to Dr. Famiglietti are these findings something to worry about?

4 Summarize the reasons for the trend mentioned in the article.

5 Describe the Grace mission in your own words.

Further activity: Research and report

6 Read the information in the Xtra-File below and find out more about the U.S. space programme, past and present. Write a report giving your opinion on the possibility of an extended arms race in space.

→ **Reports**
See *skills file* on page 182.

Xtra-File:
Star Wars – the military use of satellites and space technology

Under the Bush administration the U.S. military space programme increased in importance. Some groups believe that more should be done to develop a technology to protect U.S. satellites in space (and possibly to attack enemy satellites). Other groups speak of establishing a Space Force similar to the Air Force. Greenpeace and similar organizations are against an extension of the arms race into space.

Satellites weigh Africa's water

Africa has experienced a significant drying in the past three years, new satellite data reveals.

The volume of water lost from the land amounts to 334 cubic km, which is almost as much as all Africans have consumed over the period.

The data comes from Nasa spacecraft that can detect changes in gravity caused by water as it cycles between the sea, the atmosphere and the land.

Experts stress no firm conclusions should be drawn from the short study.

Professor Jay Famiglietti from the University of California, Irvine said much longer time series were needed to detect real trends and any signal that might indicate a significant shift in climate.

"There are natural climate variations, the natural ups and downs," he explained.

"Another big factor is human control of the water cycle – reservoir management, the storage of water on continents.

"Groundwater mining leads to heavy depletions of water. Wetland drainage, river diversion projects – all of those factors contribute to these storage variations that we see and we'll be working on trying to sort those out over the next few years," he told the BBC. [...]

The information was obtained by the Grace (Gravity Recovery and Climate Experiment) mission, a pair of satellites that observe changes in mass by monitoring tiny fluctuations in the pull of gravity as they fly over the Earth.

The huge volumes of water that are shifted around the globe in the hydrological cycle result in anomalies in the gravity field that Grace can map and monitor over time.

The variations will reflect changes in water stored in rivers, lakes, reservoirs; in floodplains as snow and ice; and underground in soils and aquifers.

Grace scientists have been doing this for more than 50 major drainage basins that cover most of Earth's land area. [...]

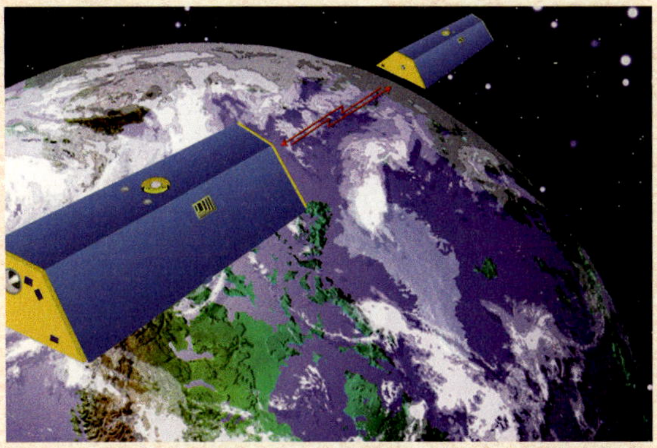

Grace (Gravity Recovery and Climate Experiment)

The Grace mission is a joint venture between Nasa and the German Aerospace Centre (DLR). It has already been used to weigh the ice sitting on the Greenland and Antarctic landmasses and demonstrate the billions of tonnes lost to melting each year.

The gravity data returned from the spacecraft is also being used to study ocean circulation to improve climate models.

The satellites obtain their data by executing a carefully calibrated pursuit in orbit.

As one spacecraft lurches and drags through the Earth's uneven gravity field, the second follows 210 km behind, measuring changes in their separation to the nearest micron (a thousandth of a millimetre).

It is the size of those changes detected by the twins that describes the nature and scale of the gravity anomalies over which they pass.

"You can think of them as two automobile-sized objects, one of them in Los Angeles and the other in San Diego, and they're measuring the distance between each other to about the size of a red blood cell," said Dr Michael Watkins, the Grace project scientist at Nasa's Jet Propulsion Laboratory.

By Jonathan Amos, *BBC News*, December 13, 2006, news.bbc.co.uk – 477 words.

9 to detect to find out · **10 to cycle** *here:* to go through a series of changes · **14 Famiglietti** [ˌfæmɪl'jetɪ] · **17 shift** change · **24 depletion** decrease · **25 wetland drainage** [ˌwetlænd‿'dreɪnɪdʒ] system which removes water from wetland · **25 diversion** *here:* changing the direction of s.th. · **30 to obtain** to get · **33 tiny** ['taɪnɪ] little · **37 anomaly** s.th. that is not normal · **38 to map** to measure and to record · **38 to monitor** to observe · **40 floodplain** area beside a river; it is covered during flooding · **42 aquifer** ['ækwɪfə] *Grundwasserleiter* · **46 joint venture** project shared by two or more groups · **55 to execute** to make · **56 calibrated** *geeicht* · **56 pursuit** [pə'sjuːt] [pə'suːt] *here:* study · **57 to lurch** to move unsteadily · **57 to drag** to pull itself · **60 micron** *Mikrometer, ein tausendstel Millimeter* · **70 jet propulsion** *Düsen-, Strahlantrieb*

Utopian short fiction

Kurt Vonnegut (1922–2007)

Before you read

1 Which science-fiction writers, novels, stories or movies do you know? Make a class survey.

2 Before you start reading the extract from a short story by Kurt Vonnegut, find out more about his life and works.

Tomorrow and tomorrow and tomorrow...

2|34

The year was 2158 A.D. and Lou and Emerald Schwartz were whispering on the balcony outside Lou's family's apartment on the seventy-sixth floor of Building 257 in Alden Village, a New York housing development that covered what had once been known as Southern Connecticut. When Lou and Emerald had married, Em's parents had tearfully described the marriage as being between May and December; but now, with Lou one hundred and twelve and Em ninety-three, Em's parents had to admit that the match had worked out well.

But Em and Lou weren't without their troubles, and they were out in the nippy air of the balcony because of them.

"Sometimes I get so mad, I feel like just up and diluting his anti-gerasone," said Em.

"That'd be against Nature, Em," said Lou, "it'd be murder. Besides, if he caught us tinkering with his anti-gerasone, not only would he disinherit us, he'd bust my neck. Just because he's one hundred and seventy-two doesn't mean Gramps isn't strong as a bull."

"Against Nature," said Em. "Who knows what Nature's like anymore? Ohhhhh – I don't guess I could ever bring myself to dilute his anti-gerasone or anything like that, but, gosh, Lou, a body can't help thinking Gramps is never going to leave if somebody doesn't help him along a little. Golly – we're so crowded a person can hardly turn around, and Verna's dying for a baby, and Melissa's gone thirty years without one." She stamped her feet. "I get so sick of seeing his wrinkled old face, watching him take the only private room and the best chair and the best food, and getting to pick out what to watch on TV, and running everybody's life by changing his will all the time."

"Well, after all," said Lou bleakly, "Gramps *is* head of the family. And he can't help being wrinkled like he is. He was seventy before anti-gerasone was invented. He's going to leave, Em. Just give him time. It's his business. I know he's tough to live with, but be patient. It wouldn't do to do anything that'd rile him. After all, we've got it better'n anybody else, there on the daybed."

"How much longer do you think we'll get to sleep on the daybed before he picks another pet? The world's record's two months, isn't it?"

"Mom and Pop had it that long once, I guess."

"When *is* he going to leave, Lou?" said Emerald.

"Well, he's talking about giving up anti-gerasone right after the five-hundred-mile Speedway Race."

"Yes – and before that it was the Olympics, and before that the World's Series, and before that the Presidential Elections, and before that I-don't-know-what. It's been just one excuse after another for fifty years now. I don't think we're ever going to get a room to ourselves or an egg or anything."

5 **to be between May and December** to be short-lived · 7 **nippy** *(informal)* cold · 9 **to feel like just up and** *(informal)* to want to do s.th. suddenly · 9 **to dilute** to add water · 9 **anti-gerasone** fictional liquid which makes you live forever · 10 **to tinker with** to manipulate · 11 **to disinherit** to change your mind about leaving s.th. to s.o. when you die · 11 **to bust** *(informal)* to break · 14 **gosh** exclamation · 16 **golly** exclamation · 18 **wrinkled** *opposite of* smooth · 21 **bleakly** in a frustrated way · 23 **it would not do to...** *(informal)* there is no sense in doing s.th. · 24 **to rile** to provoke · 25 **daybed** sofa · 26 **to pick a pet** to choose a favourite person · 32 **World's Series** *(US)* baseball final

Utopias and dystopias
A utopia (from Greek; meaning "place that does not exist") refers to a society that is socially, legally, and politically perfect, and free of evils such as poverty and war. A utopia may also be used to refer to a society that is unrealistic and impossible to achieve. A dystopia is a negative utopia: a world that is repressive and totalitarian, e.g. George Orwell's *1984*, Aldous Huxley's *Brave New World*. Source: en.wikipedia.org

"All right – call me a failure!" said Lou. "What can I do? I work hard and make good money, but the whole thing, practically, is taxed away for defense and old age pensions. And if it wasn't taxed away, where do you think we'd find a vacant room to rent? Iowa, maybe? Well, who wants to live on the outskirts of Chicago?"

Em put her arms around his neck. "Lou, hon, I'm not calling you a failure. The Lord knows you're not. You just haven't had a chance to be anything or have anything because Gramps and the rest of his generation won't leave and let somebody else take over."

"Yeah, yeah," said Lou gloomily. "You can't exactly blame 'em, though, can you? I mean, I wonder how quick we'll knock off the anti-gerasone when we get to Gramps' age."

"Sometimes I wish there wasn't any such thing as anti-gerasone!" said Emerald passionately. "Or I wish it was made out of something real expensive and hard-to-get instead of mud and dandelions. Sometimes I wish folks just up and died regular as clockwork, without anything to say about it, instead of deciding themselves how long they're going to stay around. There ought to be a law against selling the stuff to anybody over one hundred and fifty."

"Fat chance of that," said Lou, "with all the money and votes the old people've got." He looked at her closely. "You ready to up and die, Em?"

"Well, for heaven's sakes, what a thing to say to your wife. Hon! I'm not even one hundred yet." She ran her hands lightly over her firm, youthful figure, as though for confirmation. "The best years of my life are still ahead of me. But you can bet that when one hundred and fifty rolls around, old Em's going to pour her anti-gerasone down the sink, and quit taking up room, and she'll do it smiling."

"Sure, sure," said Lou, "you bet. That's what they all say. How many you heard of doing it?"

"There was that man in Delaware."

"Aren't you getting kind of tired of talking about him, Em? That was five months ago."

"All right, then – Gramma Winkler, right here in the same building."

"She got smeared by a subway."

"That's just the way she picked to go," said Em.

"Then what was she doing carrying a six-pack of anti-gerasone when she got it?"

Emerald shook her head wearily and covered her eyes. "I dunno, I dunno, I dunno. All I know is, something's just got to be done." She sighed. "Sometimes I wish they'd left a couple of diseases kicking around somewhere, so I could get one and go to bed for a little while. Too many people!" she cried, and her words cackled and gabbled and died in a thousand asphalt-paved, skyscraper-walled courtyards. [...]

From the short story, "Tomorrow and tomorrow and tomorrow" by Kurt Vonnegut, Jr. published first in 1953 and later republished in: Kurt Vonnegut, Jr: *Welcome to the Monkey House*. Vintage, 1994, pp. 284–287 – 947 words.

38 **to tax away** to make s.o. pay so much tax they have nothing left · 38 **vacant** free · 40 **hon** *short for* honey · 43 **gloomily** unhappily · 47 **dandelion** *Löwenzahn* · 55 **to quit** to stop · 61 **to get smeared** *(informal) here:* to be run over · 64 **wearily** tiredly · 64 **I dunno** *short for* I don't know · 67 **to cackle, to gabble** to be loud and unclear

Understanding the text

3 Summarize the differences in everyday life in 2158 compared to now.
4 Who are the members of the Schwartz family? What do you get to know about them?
5 What problems do they suffer from?

Analysis

6 Analyze how the relationships between the family members are affected by their taking anti-gerasone.
7 Refer to the information in the box on page 99 and explain to what extent the term 'utopia' applies to the world portrayed in the short story.
8 To what extent can the story be identified as a piece of 'social science fiction'? Read the information below and refer to examples in the text to support your answer.

Science fiction
Science-fiction writer, Issac Asimov (1920–1992) once distinguished between 'adventure science fiction' and 'social science fiction'. Adventure science fiction is based on action, gadgets and technical developments. Social science fiction makes the reader aware of social problems that already exist or could arise in future.

Language

9 a) Find ten colloquial expressions in the text. Re-write them in formal English.
b) What effect do these expressions have on the reader?

→ **Style analysis**
See *skills file* on page 162.

Over to you

10 Imagine you are Gramps. Write a diary entry in which you talk about your relationship with and feelings towards the other family members.
11 Think of an appropriate ending for the story and write it down.

UFOs and aliens (1)

Note taking: "Independence Day" on page 101.

1 While reading the extracts from the screenplay of *Independence Day* note down what the following abbreviations and words mean.

a) INT.	c) CONTINUOUS	e) super up	g) cut to
b) EXT.	d) widen	f) super	h) same

The photo shows David Levinson (Jeff Goldblum), Captain Steve Hiller (Will Smith) and President Whitmore (Bill Pullman).

INDEPENDENCE DAY
SCREENPLAY EXTRACTS

Extract 1

AN AMERICAN FLAG

Oddly still, posted in gray dusty sand.

WIDEN TO REVEAL:

EXT. LUNAR SURFACE – THE MOON

One small step for man, one large pile of garbage for moon-kind. Untouched for years, the flag stands next to the cast off remains of the Apollo mission. Slowly the discarded equipment begins to RATTLE and SHAKE.

AN ENORMOUS SHADOW creeps towards us blotting out the horizon, a loud RUMBLE is heard.

Suddenly we are covered in DARKNESS as the SHADOW engulfs us.

Only the lonely image of our EARTH hangs in the air, until a huge silhouetted OBJECT suddenly blocks our view.

CUT TO:

EXT. NEW MEXICO – RADIO TELESCOPE VALLEY – NIGHT

A field of large satellite dishes scan the skies.

Super up: S.E.T.I. INSTITUTE, NEW MEXICO

INT. INSTITUTE – MONITORING CONTROL CENTER – SAME

A lone TECHNICIAN works on his putting skills. Behind him, wall-to-wall technical equipment quietly sifts through data. A RED LIGHT begins to flash.

The Technician turns and slowly walks towards the source. One by one a series of LIGHTS turn on. The Technician (TECH ONE) grabs a pair of headphones. His eyes widen.

INT. SLEEPING QUARTERS – SAME

Sleepily a SUPERVISOR picks up the phone.

SUPERVISOR: If this isn't an insanely beautiful woman, I'm hanging up.

INT. CONTROL CENTER – SAME

TECH ONE: Shut up and listen.

He holds the phone up to a speaker, increases the volume. A strange FLUCTUATING TONE plays out in sequential patterns.

INT. SLEEPING QUARTERS – SAME

HEARING it, the Supervisor BOLTS UP, banging his head on the bunk above him.

INT CONTROL CENTER – MOMENTS LATER

A pajama party on acid. Five other technicians, in various states of undress, hover anxiously around the main console. The Supervisor enters, tying his robe.

SUPERVISOR: God, I hope it's not just another damned Russian spy job.

TECH THREE: (overlapping) Negative. Computer affirms the signal is unidentified.

TECH TWO: (hanging up the phone) The boy from Air Res Traffic says the skies are clear. No terrestrial launches.

TECH ONE: It's the real thing. A radio signal from another world.

The room becomes quiet as they realize that after years of searching the heavens, they might have finally found something.

Extract 1: 4 **lunar surface** the topmost layer of the moon · **7 cast off** which is no longer wanted · **7 remains** *Überreste* · **8 discarded** thrown away · **10 enormous** [ɪ'nɔːməs] very large · **10 to creep** to move very slowly · **10 to blot out** to hide · **13 to engulf** [ɪn'gʌlf] to surround and cover completely · **19 to scan** to search · **20 S.E.T.I. Institute** *short for* Search for Extra-Terrestrial Intelligence Institute; its focus: the study of life in the universe · **22 to putt** [pʌt] to hit a golf ball into the hole · **24 to sift through** to sort through carefully · **36 fluctuating** ['flʌktʃʊeɪtɪŋ] rising and falling · **37 sequential** [sɪ'kwenʃl] characterized by a sequence · **39 to bolt up** to sit up very suddenly · **40 bunk** *Etagenbett* · **42 acid** *(slang)* LSD · **43 to hover** ['hɒvə] to stand in one place making small nervous movements · **48 to affirm** to show that s.th. is true · **51 Air Res Traffic** *short for* Naval Air Reserve Traffic Control; armed forces which monitor flight activity

Extract 2

INT. SPACE COMMAND – THE PENTAGON – CONTINUOUS

Banks of computers, Technicians and assistants working feverishly through the night. The Officers cross the room.

Super: SPACE COMMAND – THE PENTAGON

COMMANDING OFFICER: Satellite reception has been impaired but we were able to get these.

They arrive at a glass table. The surrounding officers snap to attention as a SECOND OFFICER quickly brings over a large transparency. We SEE a grainy image of a large vague OBJECT.

GENERAL GREY: Looks like a big turd.

The two officers exchange a glance.

COMMANDING OFFICER: We estimate it has a diameter of over five hundred and fifty kilometers and a mass roughly one fourth the size of our moon.

The General turns to the Second Officer, concerned.

GENERAL GREY: A meteor?

SECOND OFFICER: No Sir. Definitely not.

GENERAL GREY: How do you know?

SECOND OFFICER: Well, er ... it's slowing down.

GENERAL GREY: It's doing what?

SECOND OFFICER: It's ... slowing down, Sir.

The General walks over to a phone, picks it up.

GENERAL GREY: Get me the Secretary of Defense. (pause) Then wake him up.

Extract 3

INT. AIR FORCE ONE – SAME

Back in the passenger section, the President sits with General Grey and Chief of Staff Nimziki. The Technician from the command module is briefing them.

TECHNICIAN: They must be targeting our satellites. We've lost all satellite communication, tracking and mapping.

GENERAL GREY: Have NORAD relayed intelligence to our on-board computers?

The Technician nods and exits. Defeated, the President slumps sullenly.

GENERAL GREY: We've moved as many of our forces away from the bases as possible but we've already sustained heavy losses.

The President nods his approval absently. Coming out of the bathroom, David overhears.

NIMZIKI: I spoke with the Joint Chiefs when they arrived at NORAD. They agree, we must launch a counter offensive with a full nuclear strike. Hit 'em with everything we've got.

PRESIDENT: Above American soil?

NIMZIKI: If we don't strike soon, there may not be much of an America left to defend.

The Technician returns, his face is white with fear.

GENERAL GREY: What's the latest from NORAD?

OFFICER: It's gone, sir. They've taken out NORAD.

NIMZIKI: That's impossible ...

GENERAL GREY: My God, the Vice President and the Joint Chiefs ...

NIMZIKI: Mr. President, we must launch. A delay now would be more costly than when you waited to evacuate the cities!

Extract 2: 60 feverishly with a lot of activity · **64 to impair** to stop s.th. from functioning optimally · **67 to snap to attention** to stand up suddenly and salute · **68 transparency** *Folie* · **68 grainy** unclear · **70 turd** *(vulgar) Scheißhaufen* · **71 to exchange a glance** *(figurative)* to look at each other meaningfully · **Extract 3: 92 Chief of Staff** officer with the highest rank in the armed forces · **93 to brief s.o.** to tell s.o. the details of s.th. · **97 NORAD** *short for* North American Aerospace Defense Command · **101 to slump** to sit down heavily · **101 sullenly** in a bad mood · **104 to sustain** to experience · **105 heavy losses** a large number of deaths · **106 absently** doing one thing while thinking about s.th. else · **107 to overhear** to hear a conversation by chance

That stings the President. He considers the option. David is shocked.

DAVID: You can't be seriously considering firing nuclear weapons?

CONSTANCE: David, don't ...

David pushes past her.

DAVID: If you fire nukes, so will the rest of the world. Do you know what that kind of fallout will do? How many innocent people ...

The General gets up running interference. Constance tries to pull David back.

GENERAL GREY: (stern) Sir, I remind you that you are just a guest here ...

CONSTANCE: (overlapping) David, please ...

DAVID: This is insanity! You'll kill us and them at the same time. There'll be nothing left!

NIMZIKI: (interrupting) Sit down and shut up!

Suddenly Moishe is on his feet, interrupting.

MOISHE: Don't tell him to shut up! You'd all be dead, were it not for my David. You didn't do anything to prevent this!

As everyone is about to besiege Moishe, the President tries to calm him down.

PRESIDENT: Sir, there wasn't much more we could have done. We were totally unprepared for this.

MOISHE: Don't give me unprepared! Since nineteen fifty whatever you guys have had that space ship, the thing you found in New Mexico.

DAVID: (embarrassed) Dad, please ...

MOISHE: What was it, Roswell? You had the space ship, the bodies, everything locked up in a bunker, the what is it, Area fifty one. That's it! Area fifty one. You knew and you didn't do nothing!

For the first time in a long time, President Whitmore smiles.

PRESIDENT: Regardless of what the tabloids have said, there were never any space crafts recovered by the government. Take my word for it, there is no Area 51 and no recovered space ship.

Chief of Staff Nimziki suddenly clears his throat.

NIMZIKI: Uh, excuse me, Mr. President, but that's not entirely accurate.

The President and General Grey turn to Nimziki, shocked.

From the screenplay "Independence Day"
by Dean Devlin and Roland Emmerich.

129 to sting s.o. *here:* to make s.o. feel bad · **137 fallout** shower of radioactive particles after an explosion · **139 to run interference** *(AE)* to turn attention away from s.th. · **141 stern** very serious · **145 insanity** craziness · **155 to besiege** [bɪ'si:dʒ] *here:* to attack verbally

Understanding the text

2 Find out as much as you can about the spacecraft in each of the extracts and write as detailed a description of it as possible.

3 a) What is the original version of the line "One small step for man, one large pile of garbage for moon-kind." ‹L 5–6›? When and where was it used, and by whom?
b) Write a narrative version of extract 1 as if you were turning the screenplay into a science-fiction novel.

4 Decribe the relationship between the General and the officers in extract 2.

5 a) Outline the problem that the President is facing in extract 3 and the options that are available to him.
b) Where and what is Area 51?
c) At the end of the third extract why is David embarrassed and the President shocked?

→ **Listening comprehension**
See page 90.

Style

6 Describe the atmosphere in one of the extracts. Consider stage directions, choice of words, sentence structure and the characters' behaviour.

Atmosphere
See *glossary* on page 201.

Your opinion

7 Consider these two points of view and answer the questions a)–c).

> NIMZIKI: "Mr. President, we must launch. A delay now would be more costly than when you waited to evacuate the cities!" ‹L 125–128›
>
> DAVID: "If you fire nukes, so will the rest of the world. Do you know what that kind of fallout will do? How many innocent people ..." ‹L 135–138›

a) Who do you think is right?
b) What should the President do?
c) Can you think of any other options?

8 In the film the President has not been fully informed about Area 51. How likely do you think this is in a real-life context?

Film analysis
See *skills file* on page 184.

UFOs and aliens (2)

Before you read: "So much space ..." on page 104.

1 Do you believe that extraterrestrial life forms could exist somewhere out in the universe, or not?

Understanding the text

2 Explain why aliens could not have found us yet according to the text.
3 What is meant by the term "galactic habitable zone" ‹L 22–23›?

A step further

4 Describe the cartoon. Explain what makes it funny, referring to the text on page 105 in your answer.

Cartoons
See *skills file* on page 155.

"Scrub that previous message Houston. There is no, I repeat no intelligent life on Mars."

So much space, so little time: why aliens haven't found us yet

It ranks among the most enduring mysteries of the cosmos. Physicists call it the Fermi paradox after the Italian Nobel laureate Enrico Fermi, who, in 1950, pointed out the glaring conflict between predictions that life was elsewhere in the universe – and the conspicuous lack of aliens who have come to visit.

Now a Danish researcher believes he may have solved the paradox. Extra-terrestrials have yet to find us because they haven't had enough time to look.

Using a computer simulation of our own galaxy, the Milky Way, Rasmus Bjork, a physicist at the Niels Bohr institute in Copenhagen, proposed that a single civilisation might build eight intergalactic probes and launch them on missions to search for life. Once on their way each probe would send out eight more mini-probes, which would head for the nearest stars and look for habitable planets.

Mr Bjork confined the probes to search only solar systems in what is called the "galactic habitable zone" of the Milky Way, where solar systems are close enough to the centre to have the right elements necessary to form rocky, life-sustaining planets, but are far enough out to avoid being struck by asteroids, seared by stars or frazzled by bursts of radiation.

He found that even if the alien ships could hurtle through space at a tenth of the speed of light, or 30,000 km a second, – Nasa's current Cassini mission to Saturn is plodding along at 32 km a second – it would take 10 bn years, roughly half the age of the universe, to explore just 4% of the galaxy. His study is reported in *New Scientist* today.

Artist's impression of the separation of the Huygens probe *(bottom right)* from the Cassini orbiter *(top left)*

Like humans, alien civilisations could shorten the time to find extra-terrestrials by picking up television and radio broadcasts that might leak from colonised planets. "Even then, unless they can develop an exotic form of transport that gets them across the galaxy in two weeks it's still going to take millions of years to find us," said Mr Bjork. "There are so many stars in the galaxy that probably life could exist elsewhere, but will we ever get in contact with them? Not in our lifetime," he added.

By Ian Sample, *The Guardian*, January 18, 2007, www.guardian.co.uk – 357 words.

1 to endure [ɪnˈdjʊə] to last · **3 Nobel laureate** winner of a Nobel prize · **4 glaring** obvious · **6 conspicuous** [kənˈspɪkjʊəs] striking · **20 habitable** where humans can live · **21 to confine** to limit · **26 life-sustaining** which can support life · **27 to sear** to burn · **28 to frazzle** to burn · **30 to hurtle** to fly at great speed · **32 to plod along** to move slowly · **40 to leak** *here*: to come through by accident

Unit 8 USA: People, politics, perspectives

801005-0008

Pledge of allegiance

Presidential inauguration

Saluting the flag

Naturalization ceremony

Getting started

1 Describe the situations in the photos.

2 a) Describe the people's facial expressions, their body language and their postures.
b) Make a mind map with words that describe people's feelings.
Examples: to look bored, to be serious …

→ **Illustrations and photos**
See *skills file* on page 158.
Mind maps
See *skills file* on page 186.

The American dream

Before you read

1 Would you ever acquire a new citizenship? Which circumstances would:
a) make you do this and which citizenship would you then choose, and why?
b) prevent you from changing your present citizenship?

2 For what reasons do people leave their home countries?

2|37

Schwarzenegger Welcomes New U.S. Citizens

I have been fortunate enough to receive many wonderful titles, like Bodybuilding Champion, Mr. Olympia, action hero, and now even Governor. But I have to tell you honestly that the title that I treasure most of all is the title American.

Not because of the name alone, but just because of what it meant. What it means is to be part of the greatest country in the world, of the most generous country in the world. America was always the place that I dreamt about coming to. Even when I was 10 years old I always dreamt about coming to America, because it was always known as the Promised Land, the place of freedom and unlimited opportunity, the place where if you worked hard and if you played by the rules and did the right thing, you could make your dreams become a reality.

But it is important to not just think about what America can do for us, but it is also important to say and to think about what can we do for America? What can we give back to America? So I came here and I studied the language, I studied English. Not that I'm perfect yet, but I studied English, nevertheless.

And I went to college and I studied business, I studied how the American economy and the political system really worked, so that I could become part of the American fabric, so I could take advantage of all the great opportunities that are available here in America, but also so I'm able to give something back. My dreams came true beyond my wildest imagination, and I really believe that the same can be true for all of you right in here.

I will never forget the actual day when I became a citizen in 1983, 15 years after arriving here in America. Of course I felt like being an American all along, way before I ever came here with my gym bag and with 20 dollars in my pocket. But I got so excited on the actual day of my swearing in, I remember raising my hand and repeating the oath, and I had chills. I had kind of like goosebumps all over my body, I was so excited about it. And then after that

4 to treasure to mean a lot · **18 nevertheless** all the same · **21 fabric** *(figurative)* society · **28 gym bag** ['dʒɪm,bæg] bag you use for your sports clothes · **31 chills** cold feeling when you are excited · **31 goosebumps** *(AE) Gänsehaut*

ceremony I went home and I wrapped myself in the American flag, and I put on an American flag hat, and I put on an American flag tie around my neck, and I was smiling from ear to ear because I was so excited about now being officially called an American.

It meant that I could vote, I could go and travel around now with my American passport, and I could even run for office. [...]

I know some of the hardships that many of you have gone through to get here. Some of you are political refugees, some are seeking asylum from dangerous and life threatening situations in your own country. Some of you had it much easier, you applied for a green card, and you got your green card, came over here with a green card, and there was already a job waiting for you, and you already had a sponsor ready to sponsor you. But however hard it was to get here, and how much difficulties that you went through to get here, the bottom line is, it was worth it.

And I want to just remind you of how many, how many people in the history of California that were successful and have contributed here, that were immigrants. America gets some of the best doctors, engineers, scientists, inventors, from nations like those represented here today. As a matter of fact, when you hear these days so much about the immigrants, the cost of immigrants in this country, let's not forget all the great things that immigrants contribute to this country.

I mean, who knows? [...] I know there are some of you out there that maybe will entertain millions of people worldwide. I know there are some of you out there that will make billions of dollars. I know there are a lot of best-selling authors out there. I know there are some out there that even maybe one day will become Governor of the great State of California. Hey, how about that? [...]

And I can tell you firsthand, with all the jobs that I have ever had, but this job that I'm doing today is the greatest one of all, being Governor of the great State of California, because now I have a chance to give something back to this great state that has given me absolutely everything, every success that I've ever had. [...]

Extract from a speech held by Arnold Schwarzenegger, Governor of California, at the Naturalization Ceremony, May 23, 2006, gov.ca.gov – 784 words.

41 asylum [ə'saɪləm] a safe place to live · **47 the bottom line is...** the fact is...

Understanding the text

3 a) How does Governor Schwarzenegger define the American dream?
b) Compare his statement with a definition of the American dream you find on the internet.

4 How is Governor Schwarzenegger a good example of the American dream?

5 How does Governor Schwarzenegger describe the new American citizens' path to the naturalization ceremony?

6 Summarize his expectations of the new citizens in the future.

7 Why does Governor Schwarzenegger stress his position as Governor of the State of California? Describe his own path to naturalization.

Language

8 Governor Schwarzenegger uses different expressions to describe his feelings on the day of his naturalization.
Example: "I was smiling from ear to ear." ‹L35›
Find other expressions in the text that describe feelings and add them to your mind map from page 106.

Mediation

9 You are listening to Governor Schwarzenegger's speech on the internet when a friend calls. He/she wants to know what you are doing and what is so interesting in the speech. You say that you will mail him/her the most important points. Find the relevant information in the speech and write the mail.

→ **Mediation**
See *skills file* on page 158.

Research and report

10 Find out where new American citizens come from and what positive and negative effects immigration has on the USA. Make a list of the effects.

11 In another part of his speech Governor Schwarzenegger lists some famous immigrants such as Henry Kissinger, Madeleine Albright, Isaac Stern and Carlos Santana, and their influence on America.
a) Think of other famous immigrants to the US.
b) Choose one immigrant and report on her/his life to your class.

A step further: Compare two texts

12 a) Read the "Oath of Allegiance" which applicants for American citizenship swear before becoming American citizens. Use a dictionary to look up words you don't know and then summarize the oath in your own words.
b) Analyse the language used in the oath and compare with the language in Governor Schwarzenegger's speech.

→ **Style analysis**
See *skills file* on page 162.

UNITED STATES OF AMERICA OATH OF ALLEGIANCE

"I hereby declare, on oath, that I absolutely and entirely renounce and abjure all allegiance and fidelity to any foreign prince, potentate, state, or sovereignty of whom or which I have heretofore been a subject or citizen; that I will support and defend the Constitution and the laws of the United States of America against all enemies, foreign and domestic; that I will bear true faith and allegiance to the same; that I will bear arms on behalf of the United States when required by the law; that I will perform noncombatant service in the Armed Forces of the United States when required by the law; that I will perform work of national importance under civilian direction when required by the law; and that I take this obligation freely without any mental reservation or purpose of evasion; so help me God."

Source: Immigration and Naturalization Service (INS), www.ins.gov

Americans about America

Before you read

1 What is an American? Collect ideas in class and discuss them.

Understanding the texts

2 Summarize each person's statement about being American/living in America and record the positive and negative aspects in a table.

2|42

My America

A For me, [being American] means the freedom to be me. You know, like, if I wanna dance, I can just dance. You know, there's no one tellin' me that I have to be a dancer, that I have to be [a] gymnast or anything like that. It's not dictated, you know. You basically have the opportunity to be whatever you want as long as you can find something or somebody to help you along the way.

Kenye, Sierra Leonian/Indian/Scottish American, teenager, born in the U.S.

B I want to say that I think the best part about being American is getting to learn about the entire world without actually leaving this country. Because, you know, I live here, I get to watch Jamihlah perform African dance, I get to listen to Omar tell me about Malcolm X and all the great African American leaders and about Egypt, and because I have a lot of Hispanic friends, I know a lot of Spanish slang. You're exposed to a lot of different cultures, and it keeps you from being really narrow.

Heather Petersen, Irish/Norwegian American, teenager, born in the U.S.

Christina, Ecuadorian American, teenager, born in the U.S.

C I have seen negative sides to being an American. I think that as people become Americanized and generations stay here, we [...] lose the backgrounds, we lose the dialect, first of all, because we're Americanizing. Like we change the words. I know my family has. [...] I know like, in my house, we've changed a lot of traditions. And I think that that's the sad part. I think that we should keep up with those traditions. That's like the down side of being an American.

Text A: **Kenye** ['kenjeɪ]; **Text B:** **entire** [ɪn'taɪə] whole · **to be exposed to** to get to know about · **narrow** *here:* narrow-minded

3 a) The statements A–D are made by U.S.-born teens, whereas the last three statements are from adults who were born elsewhere. Compare the comments made by the two groups.
b) What reasons can you think of for these differences?

Style

4 a) Find typical examples of colloquial English in the statements.
b) Rewrite the examples you find using formal English.

→ **Style analysis**
See *skills file* on page 162.

Jaime, Mexican American, teenager, born in the U.S.

D I consider myself a Mexican-American but you can't say that in front of [Latino] people sometimes … because they think you're a sell-out or something. … I mean, right now, we're well-off. … I don't speak a lot of Spanish, and sometimes I say Spanish words that sound like English-Spanglish words and they say 'you're not really Mexican,' or something. 'You're too white to be Mexican.' It makes me feel real horrible, you know, because I'm proud of my parents and the country they came from … I want to spend my life here. I love the United States; I don't know why. I consider myself a Mexican-American, but not just American, and that's it.

E It's my dream. The American dream, to me, is if you really try hard you can do well. You have more chances. I do feel free.

Tseng Tan-Kiang, 36, born in the People's Republic of China

Gilbert Sigua, 41, born in the Philippines

F There are a lot of positive aspects to this country. The right to vote, respect for human rights and more opportunities, especially for children.

G It was a child's dream to come to America. America is freedom – of speech, movement, religion, and you can vote. I was born in South Africa, but because I was a non-white, I had none of that freedom.

Nazam Bashid Adam, 54, born in South Africa

Text D: sell-out s.o. who is disloyal to his/her origins · **well-off** doing well financially; **Text E: Tseng Tan-Kiang** [ˌtseŋˌtænkɪˈæŋ]

The melting pot

Before you read: "Out of many ..." on page 113.

1 a) Which of the following terms – melting pot • salad bowl • orchestra • mosaic • pizza – best describes American multicultural society, and why?
b) What words would you use to describe your own society? Give reasons.

Understanding the text

2 Explain the message of Israel Zangwill's play "The Melting Pot".

3 a) Which groups of immigrants does the writer of the article talk about? When did they come to the U.S.?
b) In view of current demographic trends, what are experts certain will happen as a result of this immigrant influx?
c) What are the likely results of these trends?

4 Explain why many historians argue that those who lived in the U.S. in the past had a more unified idea of what it means to be American.

Language and style

5 Find the meaning of the words below without using a dictionary. Rewrite the sentences in which the words occur using synonyms.

a) to pour ‹L 2›	e) incoming ‹L 14›	i) rapid ‹L 27›
b) central ‹L 5›	f) far-reaching ‹L 20›	j) descent ‹L 29›
c) tremendous ‹L 7›	g) overwhelmingly ‹L 25›	k) to evolve ‹L 40›
d) to transform ‹L 9›	h) shift ‹L 27›	

6 Analyse the style of the text giving specific examples.

Discussion

7 "Today ... there is more emphasis on preserving one's ethnic identity, of finding ways to highlight and defend one's cultural roots." ‹L 61–64›. Do you think that this is a positive or a negative trend in the U.S.? Discuss and compare with your own country.

Further activity

8 What issues are immigrants confronted with nowadays when they enter the U.S. compared to the past? Refer to the picture and advert below.

→ **Surviving without a dictionary**
See *skills file* on page 187.

→ **Style analysis**
See *skills file* on page 162.

→ **Discussions**
See *skills file* on page 177.

"Welcome to the Land of Freedom", 1887.
Drawing by a passenger aboard the "Germanic".

Out of many, one

By William Booth

AT THE BEGINNING of this century, as steamers filled with European immigrants poured into American ports, a Jew from England named Israel Zangwill wrote a play whose story line has long been forgotten, but whose central theme has not. His production was entitled "The Melting Pot" and its message still holds a tremendous power on the national imagination – the promise that all immigrants can be transformed into Americans, a new alloy forged in a crucible of democracy, freedom and civic responsibility.

In 1908, when the play opened in Washington, the United States was in the middle of absorbing the largest incoming group of immigrants in its history – Irish and Germans, followed by Italians and East Europeans, Catholics and Jews – some 18 million new citizens between 1890 and 1920.

Today, the United States is experiencing its second wave of immigration, a movement of people that has far-reaching implications for a society that by tradition pays homage to its immigrant roots at the same time it confronts complex and deeply ingrained ethnic and racial divisions.

The immigrants of today come not from Europe but overwhelmingly from the still developing world of Asia and Latin America. They are driving a demographic shift so rapid that within the lifetimes of today's teenagers, no one ethnic group – including whites of European descent – will make up a majority of the nation's population.

This shift, according to social historians, demographers and others studying the trends, will severely test the premise of the legendary melting pot, the idea, so central to national identity, that this country can transform people of every color and background into "one America".

Just as possible, they say, is that the nation will continue to split into many separate, disconnected communities with no shared sense of commonality or purpose. Or perhaps it will evolve into something in between, a pluralistic society that will hold on to some core ideas about citizenship and capitalism, but with little meaningful interaction among groups.

The demographic changes raise other questions about political and economic power. Will that power, now held disproportionately by whites, be shared in the new America? What will happen now that Hispanics have overtaken blacks as the nation's single largest minority?

[…] Fear of strangers, of course, is nothing new in American history. The last great immigration wave produced a bitter backlash, epitomized by the Chinese Exclusion Act of 1882 and the return, in the 1920s, of the Ku Klux Klan, which not only targeted blacks, but Catholics, Jews and immigrants as well.

But despite this strife, many historians argue that there was a greater consensus in the past on what it meant to be an American, a yearning for a common language and culture, and a desire – encouraged, if not forced by members of the dominant white Protestant culture – to assimilate. Today, they say, there is more emphasis on preserving one's ethnic identity, of finding ways to highlight and defend one's cultural roots.

Adapted from "One Nation Indivisible: Is it History?" by William Booth, *The Washington Post*, February 22, 1998 – 493 words.

1 **steamer** ship driven by a steam engine · 4 **story line** plot · 7 **message** ['mesɪdʒ] main point · 10 **alloy** ['ælɔɪ] *(figurative) here:* person with at least two nationalities · 10 **to forge** [fɔ:dʒ] *(figurative) here:* to shape · 10 **crucible** ['kru:sɪbl] *(lit.) here:* melting pot · 11 **civic** ['sɪvɪk] relating to the citizens · 21 **to pay homage** ['hɒmɪdʒ] to show respect · 21 **root** origin · 22 **ingrained** [ɪn'greɪnd] difficult to change · 26 **to drive** *here:* to cause · 33 **severely** [sə'vɪəlɪ] greatly · 33 **premise** ['premɪs] idea · 38 **to split** to come apart · 39 **commonality** sharing the same ideas · 42 **core** key · 43 **interaction** communicating and working together · 46 **disproportionately** to a comparatively large degree · 52 **backlash** strong reaction to s.th. · 52 **to epitomize** [ɪ'pɪtəmaɪz] to be a typical example · 56 **despite** in spite of · 56 **strife** [straɪf] conflict · 58 **yearning** strong desire

Fighting for the homeland (1)

Before you read

1 Judging by the title of the novel, *Born on the Fourth of July*, what do you expect the text extract to be about?

Understanding the text

2 Summarize each paragraph in one sentence.

3 a) Explain why Ron Kovic is bothered by the men helping him.
b) How do the men treat him?

4 a) Why does the commander refer to Korea and World War II?
b) Explain what the commander means in ‹L 45–46›: "We have to win … because of them!"

→ **Summaries**
See *skills file* on page 164.

In the excerpt from *Born on the Fourth of July*, Ron and his friend Eddie Dugan have been asked by people in their hometown to be the grand marshals in the Memorial Day parade.

2|49

Born on the Fourth of July

The street was a sea of red, white, and blue. He remembered how he and all the rest of the kids on the block had put on their cub scout uniforms and marched every Memorial Day down these same streets. He remembered the hundreds of people lining the sidewalks, everyone standing and cheering and waving their small flags, his mother standing with the other mothers on the block shouting for him to keep in step. "There's my Yankee Doodle boy!" he'd hear her shouting, and he'd feel embarrassed, pulling his cap over his eyes like he always did.

There were scouts decorating the Cadillac now with red, white, and blue crêpe paper and long paper banners that read *welcome home Ron Kovic and Eddie Dugan* and *support our boys in Vietnam.* There was a small sign, too, that read: OUR WOUNDED VIETNAM VETS … EDDIE DUGAN AND RON KOVIC.

When the scouts were finished, the commander came running over to the car with a can of beer in his hand. "Let's go!" he shouted, jumping back in with the heavy guy.

They drove slowly through the crowd until they were all the way up in the front of the parade. He could hear the horns and drums behind him and he looked out and watched the pretty drum majorettes and clowns dancing in the street. He looked out onto the sidewalks where the people from his town had gathered just like when he was a kid.

But it was different. He couldn't tell at first exactly what it was, but something was not the same, they weren't waving and they just seemed to be standing staring at Eddie Dugan and himself like they weren't even there. […]

Introduction: **grand marshal** person in charge of a parade · **Memorial Day** *(US)* holiday (May 30) honouring those who have been killed in combat

Text: 2 **cub scout** *junger Pfadfinder* · **5** **to keep in step** *(figurative)* to walk as fast as s.o. else · **5** **Yankee Doodle** Revolutionary War song, *here:* patriotic · **8** **crêpe paper** ['kreɪp‿peɪpə] long, coloured paper strips used for decoration · **10** **vet** *short for* veteran · **15** **drum majorette** [ˌdrʌm‿meɪdʒər'et] girl in uniform who leads the band

Ron Kovic Born on July 4, 1946, Ron Kovic grew up as an all-American boy with a dream to serve his country. He became a Marine, and experienced the horrors of Vietnam (see p. 122). His combat time ended when he was severely wounded – paralysed from the waist down. Ron spent months in hospitals, before returning to a life that would never be the same. He later became famous for his anti-war activism, his fight for veteran rights, and for his memoirs, *Born on the Fourth of July*, which describe the experiences that made him into a soldier, a veteran and an activist.

Ron Kovic: Kovic ['kəʊvɪk] · **3 Marine** member of a special part of the American Navy · **6 waist** [weɪst] *Taille*

When they came to where the speakers' platform had been erected, he watched Eddie push himself out of the back seat, then up on his crutches while the heavy guy helped him with the door. The commander was opening the trunk, bringing the wheelchair to the side of the car. He was lifted out by the heavy guy and he saw the people around him watching, and it bothered him because he didn't want them to see how badly he had been hurt and how helpless he was, having to be carried out of the car into the chair like a baby. [...]

He pushed himself to the back of the platform where two strong members of the Legion were waiting to lift him up in the chair. "How do you lift this goddamn thing?" shouted one of the men, suddenly staggering, almost dropping him. He tried to tell them how to lift it properly, the way they had shown him in the hospital, but they wanted to do it their own way and almost dropped him a second time.

They finally carried him up the steps of the stage where he was wheeled up front next to Eddie, who sat with his crutches by his side. They sat together watching the big crowd and listening to one speaker after the other, including the mayor and all the town's dignitaries; each one spoke very beautiful words about *sacrifice and patriotism and God*, crying out to the crowd to support the boys in the war so that their brave sacrifices would not have to be in vain.

And then it was the tall commander's turn to speak. He walked up to the microphone slowly, measuring his steps carefully, then jutted his head up and looked directly at the crowd. *"I believe in America!"* shouted the commander, shaking his fist in the air. *"And I believe in Americanism!"* The crowd was cheering now. *"And most of all ... most of all, I believe in victory for America!"* He was very emotional. Then he shouted that the whole country had to come together and support the boys in the war. He told how he and the boys' fathers before them had fought in Korea and World War II, and how the whole country had been behind them back then and how they had won a great victory for freedom. Almost crying now, he shouted to the crowd that they couldn't give up in Vietnam. *"We have to win ..."* he said, his voice still shaking; then pausing, he pointed his finger at him and Eddie Dugan, *"... because of them!"*

Suddenly it was very quiet and he could feel them looking right at him, sitting there in his wheelchair with Eddie all alone. It seemed everyone – the cub scouts, the boy scouts, the mothers, the fathers, the whole town – had their eyes on them and now he bent his head and stared into his lap. [...]

From *Born on the Fourth of July* by Ron Kovic, New York: McGraw-Hill Book Company, © 1976, pp. 89–93 – 785 words.

21 platform a small stage · **22 crutch** *Krücke* · **23 trunk** *(AE)* part of a car where you store luggage · **27 Legion** *(US) short for* American Legion, U.S. veterans' association · **29 to stagger** ['stægə] to walk unsteadily · **34 dignitary** important person of high rank · **35 sacrifice** s.th. one gives up for the good of s.o. else · **38 to measure one's steps** *(figurative)* to take steps in an exact way · **38 to jut** to move suddenly · **41 to support** [sə'pɔːt] to help

Language

5 Explain the examples of figurative speech in your own words.
a) to be behind someone ‹L 43›
b) to have one's eyes on someone ‹L 49›

6 Replace the underlined words with synonyms/synonymous phrases.
a) "where the people from his town had gathered" ‹L 16–17›
b) "where the speakers' platform had been erected" ‹L 21›
c) "so that their brave sacrifices would not have to be in vain" ‹L 36›

→ **Figurative language**
See *glossary* on page 202.

Style

7 Where is the literary technique 'flashback' used in the text, and what purpose does it have?

8 Characterize the commander using examples from the text.

9 Describe the atmosphere of the text. Give examples.

→ **Flashback & atmosphere**
See *glossary* on pages 201–202.

Discussion

10 During the speeches, Kovic and Dugan were not asked to speak about their experiences and feelings. Why do you think that this is the case? Discuss.

A step further: Photos and film scene

11 The picture on the right shows a scene from the film version of the book. The setting is the Republican Convention of 1972.
a) What do you think is happening?
b) What do you think the veterans are yelling?
c) What might the Convention delegates be thinking?

12 a) Compare the way Ron Kovic is portrayed in the novel extract with the character in the film still (figure seated third from the left).
b) Watch the scenes in the film which correspond to the extract. Did the film makers transform the text into suitable movie scenes, or not? Give reasons.

→ **Film analysis**
See *skills file* on page 184.

1|23

Listening comprehension

For America

Listen to the song *For America* by Jackson Browne.

Fighting for the homeland (2)

Understanding the text: "The triumph ..." on page 117.

1 Outline the ways in which the suicide bombing has changed Ty's life.

2 What is his attitude nowadays to being a soldier?

3 Compare Ron Kovic and Ty Ziegel's experiences of war, and the way they cope with their changed lives.

Further activity: Letter to the editor

4 Write a letter to the editor of *The Sunday Times* giving your arguments for or against sending young people to fight in wars.

→ **Formal letters**
See *skills file* on page 170.

The triumph of love

The US marine Ty Ziegel suffered horrific burns in a suicide bomb attack in Iraq. After months in hospital, he was eventually able to return home – and marry his childhood sweetheart.

US soldier on guard duty in Iraq

[...] Ty gets headaches sometimes, but he just takes an aspirin and gets on with it. In hospital he saw soldiers and marines with fewer injuries than him behave more self-pityingly. "Anger has a lot to do with the person," he says. "I've seen guys, who had no complaints really, act pretty pissed off."

Ty has a plastic skull now, and the old one is still stuck in his insides. He taps the side of his waist, where there is a slight bulge. The lump of bone will be removed one day but he is in no hurry to undergo another operation. There will be plenty of those ahead: he hopes the sight in his blind eye can be restored, though he doubts he is going to rebuild his nose – it involves too many awkward skin grafts.

In Metamora, people know him well enough not to stare a lot, but he gets plenty of looks elsewhere. Mostly he shrugs it off. "I give people the benefit of the doubt. If you were me, I might look at you." If they are particularly rude, he will turn and say: "So what were you going to ask me?"

On the plus side, Ty claims: "I can be a lot more of an ass and get away with it." It is also a long time since he has bought dinner. "I tried to take Renee out on her birthday and somebody paid for it. People know you are in the military and they want to thank you."

He did not join the marines to get thanks and he does not feel strongly about the war one way or the other.

"I'm not political and I don't complain." His younger brother is also in the marines and may be deployed in Iraq. Sometimes it bothers Ty, but they both signed up, so that's that, he says stoically. At one stage he hoped to remain in the marines, but when he thought seriously about it for 10 minutes, he decided to quit. He is living on his pension now while Renee works part-time in a bar. In the spring, he hopes to build a house on a plot of land near his family: "When that's done, it will be the last house I'll live in."

Renee and Ty are thinking about having children soon. "We want to be young, cool parents," says Renee.

By Sarah Baxter, *The Sunday Times*, January 21, 2007 – 432 words.

7 to get on with it to keep going despite problems · **11 to act pissed off** *(slang)* to show that one is angry about s.th. · **14 bulge** s.th. that sticks out from under the surface · **20 skin graft** moving skin from one part of the body to another · **21 Metamora** ['metəmɔ:rə] farming town in Illinois, Midwest USA · **23 to shrug s.th. off** to treat s.th. as if it is not important · **23 to give s.o. the benefit of the doubt** not to think the worst of s.o. · **27 to be an ass** *(slang)* to behave stupidly · **28 to get away with s.th.** to do s.th. bad and not be punished · **38 to deploy** to send soldiers to a position where they must fight · **40 stoically** ['stəʊɪkəlɪ] without bitterness

The right to bear arms

Before you read: "Lax gun laws ..." on page 119.

1 Should ordinary citizens be allowed to carry firearms, or not? Collect arguments for and against in a table and discuss them in class.

Understanding the text

2 Which questions will be of interest for the investigation into the shooting? Which question(s) will be left out? Make two lists and discuss why some questions are asked and some are not.
3 How is the aggressor characterized in the text?
4 Outline the regulations which apply when a person wants to buy a gun in Virginia.
5 Describe people's reactions to the shooting in Virginia.

Language and translation

6 Explain and translate the grammatical forms in a)–e). Then find more forms with '-ing' in the text and translate them.
a) engineering ‹L2›
b) introducing ‹L8›
c) going ‹L10›
d) shooting ‹L14›
e) warning ‹L30›

→ **Translation**
See *skills file* on page 165.

A step further: Quotations

7 "America has a long history of firearm rights" ‹L9›. What does Alec Calhoon mean by this? Take both the Oath of Allegiance on p. 109 and the Second Amendment below into consideration in your answer.

→ **Quotation**
See *glossary* on page 203.

SECOND AMENDMENT TO THE CONSTITUTION OF THE UNITED STATES OF AMERICA

A well regulated Militia, being necessary to the security of a free State, the right of the people to keep and bear Arms, shall not be infringed.

to infringe to limit (s.o.'s legal rights)

Translation

8 Translate from ‹L61› "There was little serious discussion" to the end of the text.

→ **Translation**
See *skills file* on page 165.

Hotspot

a) Work in groups. Find out what regulations pupils and staff at your school have to follow in the event of violence. Also find out about the regulations neighbouring schools have and compare with the rules at your school.
b) Design a poster outlining your findings and present your work in class.
c) Discuss possible improvements to the regulations at your school.

→ **Projects and group work**
See *skills file* on page 167.
Presentations
See *skills file* on page 160.

Lax gun laws sure to get off scot-free

By Ewen MacAskill

Alec Calhoon was one of the lucky ones in the Virginia Tech massacre. The 20-year-old engineering student was the last to jump out of a classroom window without being shot. The students behind him were wounded and his professor, who tried to bar the door, was shot dead.

In spite of all this Calhoon does not necessarily favour introducing tough new laws to control guns. "America has a long history of firearm rights. In a society like this, things like this are going to happen," he said. "It is safety versus freedom. I do not know where to draw the line."

Calhoon's comment, made only a few hours after the shooting, offers a telling insight into the likely outcome of an investigation to be held into the shooting, which claimed the lives of 32 students and academic staff plus the killer. It was ordered by the governor of Virginia at the request of the university. Among the questions it will examine are whether the campus police and university officials made the wrong decision after the first shooting. The killer, Cho Seunghui, shot two dead in their dormitory at about seven in the morning [...] but the police assumed that it was the result of a domestic row [...]. Two hours later Cho emerged in a classroom block and killed 30 more.

The investigation will consider whether the police and university authorities should have cancelled classes after the first shooting, sealed off the campus and issued a warning to students to be on their guard.

There are other questions, too. Given Cho's erratic behavior in the preceding two years – stalking female students, trying to take indecent pictures, his total silence in class, his admission to a mental hospital – should academic staff have long before thrown him off campus?

But the obvious question for investigation, from a European point of view and from that of many Americans, will hardly be addressed, if at all: the lax gun control laws. Virginia is one of the easiest states in which to buy a gun. There are restrictions, but of a kind that would make most Europeans laugh or shake their heads in wonder: customers are allowed to buy only one gun a month. That is why Cho bought one in February and a second in March.

To buy a firearm in Virginia, which has 1,700 registered gun-dealers, you need only to be over 21, to show two pieces of ID and have no criminal record. Non-US citizens must also prove at least 90-day residency in the state. Virginia state police carry out background checks, although these are far from thorough.

In the days after the killings there was confusion about the law. Neither the police nor lawyers were totally sure whether having been in a mental hospital was a bar to buying a gun. In the end the consensus was that having a record of mental illness was not a bar. [...]

There was little serious discussion on radio, television or in print, or even on the campus, about gun laws. Both sides of the debate have become so fixed in their positions that further argument is regarded as largely pointless. On the few occasions when there was discussion, usually on talk radio, both sides saw Virginia Tech as vindicating their positions. The anti-gun lobby argued that, without easy access to guns, Cho could not have carried out the killings. The pro-gun lobby countered that, if one of the professors or one of the other students had had a gun that day, they could have stopped Cho.

Reform of the gun laws is not likely any time in the near future. None of the candidates in the 2008 presidential race is advocating tighter controls; they regard it as a vote-loser.

The investigation may conclude that police and university officials on the day made a tactical mistake in not closing down the campus. It is almost certain to propose a more efficient warning system for students. What it is unlikely to do is blame America's gun laws.

By Ewen MacAskill, *The Guardian Weekly*, April 27-May 3, 2007 – 679 words.

Headline: **lax** *opposite of* strict · **to get off scot-free** to get away without punishment

Text: 6 **to bar** to block · 22 **Seunghui** [ˌsʌŋ'hiː] · 25 **to emerge** to appear · 29 **to seal off** to close off an area · 32 **erratic** unpredictable, moody · 33 **preceding** beforehand · 34 **indecent** not appropriate or correct · 54 **thorough** complete, detailed · 58 **bar** s.th. that stops s.o. from doing s.th. · 66 **talk radio** radio station which concentrates on chat shows and call-ins · 67 **to vindicate** to prove that s.th. you are saying is right · 70 **to counter** to argue, to reply · 76 **to advocate** to support

Xtra-File: U.S. history and foreign policy

A sense of mission

In the 17th century, the Puritans who settled in the New World were inspired by a mission to set an example for all others, to establish a model community, or a 'city upon a hill' for everyone else to see and copy. Over the course of American history, Americans have defined their role in the world in terms of this 'mission'. Over time, this sense of mission has gone back and forth between two extremes: a) setting an example for the rest of the world from a distance by concentrating on challenges and improvements in the U.S. itself, b) active involvement to promote democracy and the American way in the world outside the U.S. The phases when the focus was more on setting an example and less on U.S. world involvement are called isolationist phases. The periods of active involvement are called internationalist (or interventionist) phases.

"The First Thanksgiving" (1914), Jennie Augusta Brownscombe (1850–1936)

From isolationism to internationalism

At the beginning of the republic, the USA was so weakened by the War of Independence with the British (1775–1783) that George Washington advised his successors to follow the policy of 'no entangling alliances' (1796). However, with another American victory against Britain in the War of 1812, President Monroe declared the whole of the Western hemisphere as the U.S. special sphere of interest, and with his Monroe Doctrine (1823) warned the European powers against interference. For most of the 19th century, Americans concentrated primarily on settling the great stretches of land that had become part of the country, and on developing their industries and resources.

Once the continent was almost settled, the U.S. gradually turned towards the outside world, and pursued a more active internationalist policy. The U.S. won a massive piece of territory, including California, as a result of the Mexican War (1846–1848). Negotiations between America and Japan resulted in Japan opening its harbours to foreign trade in 1853–1854. From 1861–1865 America concentrated on its affairs at home because of a bloody Civil War. The 1880s, however, ushered in the period of imperialism, when the U.S. sought more territory and influence abroad. With its victory in the Spanish American War (1898), the U.S. extended its power to Puerto Rico, Guam, and the Philippines.

3 model ideal · **20 to advise** to suggest what s.o. could do · **21 successor** [sək'sesə] s.o. who takes over a position from s.o. else · **21 entangling alliance** [ɪnˌtæŋglɪŋə'laɪəns] relations with countries which would require (e.g. military) involvement · **25 interference** getting involved in s.th. against the wishes of those affected · **31 massive** ['mæsɪv] very large · **32 negotiation** [nɪˌgəʊʃɪ'eɪʃn] a formal discussion to reach agreement · **33 harbour** *Hafen* · **35 to usher in** to introduce

Making the world safe for democracy

In the first half of the 20th century the U.S. was torn twice between isolationism and internationalism. Twice the Americans had to decide whether they should intervene in a war between the European powers. And twice, after long deliberation, they decided to become involved "to make the world safe for democracy" (President Woodrow Wilson, 1917). After World War I there was a sharp reaction against such entanglement when the idealistic notions of the U.S. for a peace settlement could not be realized. The U.S. never signed the Treaty of Versailles and did not join the League of Nations. The resulting disillusionment combined with the Great Depression, which started in 1929, resulted in a period of isolationism that would last well into the 1930s.

The majority of Americans wanted to stay out of World War II, but this attitude changed fundamentally after Japan bombed Pearl Harbor on December 7, 1941. After this, the U.S. became directly involved in the fighting in both the European and Asian theatres. By the end of the war and thereafter, the U.S. had established factual dominance in the spheres of business, trade, technology and popular culture, and was in a position to set the agenda for the greater part of the world. The nation's self-image was put in a nutshell by media czar Henry Luce when he proclaimed the 20th century the "American Century".

The Cold War

After 1945, the Americans waged a campaign against communism, which they considered to be the major threat to the world. Economically, they tried to include as many countries as possible in the sphere of the free market; politically, they promoted democracy; militarily, they guaranteed security to countries within their sphere of influence. Ideologically, the containment of communism was considered a fight between good and evil. During the Cold War, the threat of nuclear war became very real. In the Cuban Missile Crisis (1962), when American spy planes found Soviet missiles in Cuba, a miracle of diplomacy prevented what might have been world destruction. Many Americans believed that the nuclear stand-off prevented direct confrontation with the Soviet Union.

41 to intervene [ˌɪntəˈviːn] to become involved in s.th. in order to change it · **42 deliberation** [dɪˌlɪbəˈreɪʃn] thinking about s.th. carefully · **45 notion** idea · **45 settlement** agreement · **53 theatre** *here:* place where there is a war · **56 to put s.th. in a nutshell** *(figurative)* to express s.th. in a short, clear way · **59 to wage** to start · **66 influence** power · **67 containment** [kənˈteɪnmənt] keeping s.th. from spreading · **74 stand-off** where two powers do not enter a conflict as neither could win

1960s: the over-extension of power

In the Cold War era, world politics were dominated by the two superpowers, the U.S. and the Soviet Union. In this bipolar world, political action did not always have the result of creating a better world. The U.S. became involved in other campaigns to defend the free world that, in hindsight, were ill-advised, and finally overextended its power in the Vietnam War (approximately 1964–1973).

1970s: detente

The end of the Vietnam War brought U.S. withdrawal, humiliation and greater reluctance to get involved actively in other foreign engagements. America's faith in itself was shaken, and its isolationist tendencies increased as it focused more on its economic problems and the repercussions of the Watergate scandal (1973–1974) on the political system. This was also an age of attempted de-escalation of tensions between the superpowers, an age of detente. Internationally, the U.S. was considered rather weak – a situation which may have contributed to the events in Iran 1979–1981, when over fifty Americans were held hostage in the American Embassy. The military operation to rescue these hostages failed miserably, humiliating the U.S. even further.

1980s: a new confidence

The 1980s, however, were more confident years. Many believed that the economy was becoming strong (although the national debt skyrocketed), and there was renewed international activism. For example, arms were supplied to Afghanistan to fight a Soviet invasion, and, also illegally, to Iran and Nicaragua (Iran Contra Scandal of 1986) under the Reagan government. There were military interventions against communism in Grenada (1983) and against international terrorism in Libya (1986). In 1987 Ronald Reagan and Michail Gorbachev signed the INF Treaty, which eliminated all intermediate-range missiles from Europe.

1990s: the lonely superpower

With the fall of the Berlin Wall in 1989 (see photo on page 123) and the breaking apart of the Soviet Union, the U.S. became the sole remaining global power, and the Cold War was over. Nevertheless, the U.S. and its global partners still face many dangers. The U.S. tries to stem the threat from hostile Third-World countries with nuclear and/or chemical weapon arsenals.

For some, the U.S.'s actions have earned it a reputation as global bully, for example during the Gulf War (1991) when it took military action to end Saddam Hussein's invasion of Kuwait. Still, many countries expect, and even demand, U.S. aid in trouble spots such as the Balkans (1993–1998).

79 hindsight looking back on s.th. · **80 ill-advised** not having received good advice · **80 to overextend** to go beyond a reasonable limit · **82 withdrawal** pulling back after losing a conflict · **82 humiliation** [hjuːˌmɪlɪ'eɪʃn] great embarrassment · **83 reluctance** [rɪ'lʌktəns] not wanting to do s.th. · **85 repercussion** [ˌriːpə'kʌʃn] a negative effect · **90 hostage** *Geisel* · **94 to skyrocket** to rise quickly · **95 renewed** further · **105 to stem** *(formal)* to stop · **105 hostile** threatening

Berlin, 1989

2000s – today: Fight against the "axis of evil"

After the terrorist attacks on the World Trade Center on September 11, 2001, the U.S. launched a war with its allies to fight the terrorist threat in today's world – Afghanistan (2001), Iraq (2003).

Indeed, Americans in general still see it as their mission to promote peace and democracy in the world, yet some are also concerned that the U.S. expends too much of its power abroad and too little at home. The U.S. continues to work to define the boundaries of its new role between the two extremes: that of key global ally, for example, at the G8 summit of 2007, and of lonely superpower who keeps the option open, if necessary, to act in its own interests.

116 **to expend** *(formal)* to use

Presentation and discussion

Prepare a 10-minute presentation on one of the following topics. You should also be ready to take questions in a discussion after your presentation.

a) In 1917 US President Woodrow Wilson justified his country's involvement in World War I as a way "to make the world safe for democracy". Show how this path has been followed by his successors and what steps they took to fulfil this legacy.

b) Media czar Henry Luce proclaimed the 20th century to be the "American Century". Present arguments and examples which prove him right or wrong.

c) Present the role that the U.S. played in German politics after World War II, from Germany's division into four political and economic zones to the fall of the Berlin Wall.

→ **Presentations**
See *skills file* on page 160.
Discussions
See *skills file* on page 177.

Unit 9 British politics – past and present

801005-0009

The Queen's title in the UK is "Elizabeth the Second, by the Grace of God of the United Kingdom of Great Britain and Northern Ireland and of Her other Realms and Territories Queen, Head of the Commonwealth, Defender of the Faith".

Source: www.royal.gov.uk

realm [relm] country that is ruled by a monarch

Getting started

1 Analyse the different parts of the Queen's title and explain what they mean.

2 Find out what other titles the Queen has, and what these titles refer to and/or why she is entitled to them. For example: How does the Queen sign official documents? Present your findings in class.

The Monarchy

The next 50 years of monarchy

As part of a live debate, "Our monarchy: the next 50 years", the BBC gave the British public the opportunity to have a say about their monarchy.

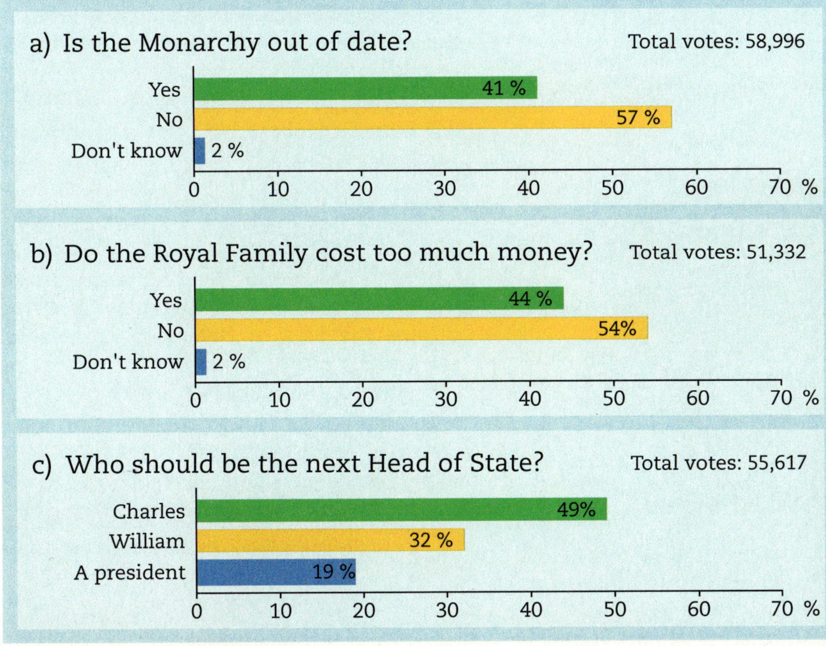

Source: BBC News, www.bbc.co.uk, June 12, 2002.

Understanding statistics

1 Analyse attitudes in Britain towards the monarchy as shown by the statistics.
2 How would you have answered the questions in a)–c)?
3 Find out how your classmates answered and make new bar charts with the answers from your whole class.

Language

4 There are different ways of presenting statistics. Describe the following in your own words:
a) a bar or column chart b) a pie chart c) a graph.
5 Make a table with phrases that describe the different movements of graphs. Your table could look like the one below.

→ **Statistics**
See *skills file* on page 161.

↗	↘	→

Further activities

6 Choose one set of findings from the debate and write a short report for your school magazine.
7 As Heads of State, Queen Elizabeth II and the German President both have certain functions and powers. Compare their functions and powers, and present your results in class.

→ **Presentations**
See *skills files* on page 160.

Britishness

Debating race, identity, citizenship and culture

As tests for immigrants who want to become British were introduced and a lot of people started to think and talk about identities, the *Catalyst Magazine* asked people to contribute their opinions about 'Britishness', what they think it is and how it is evolving.

A We need an inclusive British identity that can meet our needs in the 21st century. Most attempts to do so start from the assumption that there is a real "core Britishness" that we need to discover, articulate and require everyone – particularly newer communities – to share. But historical Britishness cannot deny the strong strands of racism, exploitation, and class division that have been interwoven with the more amenable parts of our history.

The other problem with "discovered Britishness" is that it seems to place all the obligation to change on the newer communities and none on the majority. While incomers will always have the greatest adjustment to make, those of us who grew up in a Britain that was overwhelmingly white and confident in its imperial history need to know that Britain has gone for ever. The question cannot be "who we are" but "who we want to be".

John Denham MP, Secretary of State for Innovation, Universities and Skills – 148 words.

B What is Britishness? It has several dimensions. It is a technical legal-political term referring to the possession of British citizenship. It might also be taken to refer to the past (since 1707), present and future of the British state – that English dominated collaboration of nations and peoples – and everything that has been done and said in its name. [...]

Britishness is historically associated with the protestant religion, and empire, and the unity forged in two world wars. As those things are fading or in the past for the majority of today's citizens the idea of Britishness is also fading – especially, since devolution, for the Scots and Welsh. But as Britishness is also one of the most open and flexible of categories – that transcends narrower, ethnic or racial or regional or social class identities – it is important to keep it alive and, if possible, to give it new content.

David Goodhart, Editor, *Prospect* magazine – 147 words.

C There are times when I wish we would stop this obsessive navel-gazing about our identity – reminiscent of patients addicted to psychoanalysis – but yet I believe it is vital for us all to buy into a new British identity, a collective that can connect us and, in time, deepen our cultural and emotional bonds.

'There is a modern British identity we must strive to make, although much of it will happen in any event and cannot be invented. The story we tell of ourselves should be both honest and accurate. We should refrain from the embarrassing habit of declaring ourselves the best at everything, yet also delight in the many things we are good at.

Yasmin Alibhai-Brown, author and journalist – 114 words.

Introduction: 6 to evolve to develop; **Text A: 9 assumption** belief · **9 core** the most important part of s.th. · **12 to deny** to say that s.th. is not true · **13 a strand of racism** *(figurative)* a racist element · **14 interwoven** *(figurative)* closely connected · **15 amenable** easy to control · **20 adjustment** *here:* change made to one's behaviour · **21 overwhelmingly** *here:* almost completely; **Text B: 30 collaboration** the act of working with others · **33 associated with** connected to · **35 to forge** [fɔːdʒ] *here:* to make a strong relationship · **36 to fade** to become weaker · **38 devolution** the act of handing over power from central to local government · **40 to transcend** to go beyond the usual limits; **Text C: 45 navel-gazing** *(negative)* concentrating on one thing only · **46 reminiscent** reminding s.o. of s.th. else · **48 to buy into s.th.** *(informal)* to take part in s.th. · **50 bond** s.th. that holds people together · **51 to strive, strove, striven** to try hard to achieve s.th. · **55 to refrain from** to stop doing s.th. · **57 to delight in s.th.** to enjoy doing s.th. · **Yasmin Alibhai-Brown** [jæzmɪn ˌælɪbaɪˈbraʊn]

D Britishness is not a static, backward-looking set of symbols. It is about how we all live together in the same shared space. Finding ways to promote this idea of Britishness and common citizenship are important. As new communities arrive and existing communities become more fluid, so the British identity will be enriched and will evolve, but the inclusive, polite, tolerant heart of Britishness should remain the same. I don't think it needs to be discovered or created but it needs to be appreciated and encouraged. Whereas in the past British behaviour was instinctively derived from, and promoted and reinforced by, the tea-drinking, bowler-hat-wearing middle classes, today that class structure is not so easily identifiable; now we all have to share the responsibility for communicating what makes for acceptable behaviour.

It is certainly true to say that Britons are associated with a sense of fair play more than any other characteristic, but that's not to say that other nations are not associated with fair play and democracy!

Trevor Phillips, former Chair of the Commission for Racial Equality – 167 words.

E If Britishness means anything, it is essentially about Britons defending human rights. What is Britishness? It's about free speech and fair trials. It's not about whether you know the recipe for fairy cakes or which cricket teams you support. It's about hard-edged values.

Shami Chakrabarti, Director of Liberty, a human rights group – 43 words.

From "Britishness – comments and analysis", *Catalyst*, online magazine, March 23, 2006.

Text D: 60 to promote to support · **62 fluid** not fixed · **65 to appreciate s.th.** to welcome s.th. · **66 to derive from** [dɪ'raɪv frəm] to come from · **66 to reinforce** to make an idea stronger · **67 bowler-hat** [ˌbəʊlə'hæt] *(GB)* refers to a hard, black hat, traditionally worn by businessmen · **69 to make for** to make s.th. possible; **Text E: 75 recipe** ['resɪpɪ] a set of baking instructions · **75 fairy cake** a small cake baked in a paper case like a muffin · **76 hard-edged** strong, realistic · **Shami Chakrabarti** [ˌʃɑ:mɪ ˌtʃækrə'bɑ:tɪ]

Before you read: "Debating race …" on page 126.

1 Find out which nationalities are represented in your class or which ethnic backgrounds your classmates come from.

2 Describe your own ethnic background, e.g. German, Turkish, Russian, Croatian, and the characteristics you think are typical of your nationality or nationalities.

Understanding the text

3 Outline the difficulties in defining 'Britishness' that are mentioned in text A on page 126.

4 Explain what John Denham means when he says that Britain is "confident in its imperial history" ‹L 22›.

5 In text B David Goodhart talks about the "several dimensions" of Britishness ‹L 25›. Describe these dimensions.

6 Explain the definition which Yasmin Alibhai-Brown gives for "British identity" in text C.

7 Outline Trevor Phillips' understanding of traditional British behaviour in text D. What is different nowadays?

8 In text E Shami Chakrabati talks about "free speech and fair trials" ‹L 74›. Think of reasons why these two aspects might be important for new British citizens.

Language and grammar

9 Define the following terms.

a) patriot	d) multiculturalism	g) separatist
b) race	e) identity	h) ethnicity
c) nationality	f) integration	i) citizenship

10 Make a table with the nouns in exercise 9. Add the corresponding adjectives as well as other nouns from each word family.

11 Rewrite text D on page 127 in reported speech. You can use the connectives and verbs in the box below. Check the *Online-Link* for help with reported speech.

801005-0011

Example: Trevor Phillips explained that Britishness was not a static, backward-looking set of symbols. He said that it was about …

then • furthermore • in addition • finally • explain • add • say • continue • tell

Hotspot

a) Design a questionnaire to find out people's opinions on, "Who should be allowed to become a German citizen?" What questions would you ask to find out whether someone qualifies for permanent citzenship, or not?

b) Check the web and compare your questionnaire with the official one of your state. Discuss the similarities and differences you find in class.

→ **Questionnaires and surveys**
See *skills file* on page 168.

Intercultural competence (1)

We have been looking at the term 'Britishness' and what is often expected of immigrants on entering Britain. When we go to Britain, e.g. for a short visit, it is also important to behave correctly in public and in social situations. In the text on page 130 the writer examines one particular case of unacceptable behaviour in Britain and people's reactions to it.

Before you read: "The hidden rules …" on page 130.

1 What would happen if you used your mobile phone in class? Discuss.
2 Can you think of situations in which you shouldn't use your mobile phone? Give examples.

Understanding the text

3 How are British people characterized in the text?
4 Describe some people's behaviour when they are on the mobile phone.
5 Describe how other passengers react to the "noisy mobile-phone ostriches" ‹L 24›.
6 In which way(s) is the problem dealt with? Give examples.

A step further: Cartoon and text

7 Relate the cartoon on the right to the text on page 130. Say whether the writer and the cartoonist have similar or different ideas about people's reactions to loud mobile-phone users. Find examples in the text to support your answer.
8 Would people in Germany react differently in a similar situation, or not? Give reasons for your opinion.

→ **Cartoons**
See *skills file* on page 155.

Mediation

9 Imagine that your dad is going to England on business. As he uses his mobile phone a lot, and often very loudly, warn him politely about the British dislike of loud mobile-phone users by summarizing the main points of the text.

→ **Mediation**
See *skills file* on page 158.

Further activities: Comment and role play

10 Modern mobile phones are multitasking devices and young people often use them to listen to music, which can annoy the people around them when the music is very loud.
Do you consider such behaviour to be rude and selfish, or not? Write a comment of about 150 words in complete sentences.
11 a) You have a summer job in a modern media store and you have to know all about the newest mobile phone models. List all of the features of a modern mobile phone, and the advantages and disadvantages of these features.
b) Work in pairs and act out a situation with a customer who wants to buy a new mobile.

→ **Comments**
See *skills file* on page 155.

The hidden rules of English behaviour

2|52

I mentioned earlier that there are two aspects to the denial rule: pretending that other people do not exist, and also, much of the time, pretending that we do not exist either. On public transport, it is considered unseemly to draw attention to oneself. There are people who violate this rule, talking and laughing loudly with each other instead of hiding quietly behind their newspapers in the approved manner, but they have always been a much-frowned-upon minority.

Until the advent of the mobile phone, which brings out the ostrich in us: just as the dimwit ostrich with its head in the sand believes that it is invisible, the dimwit English passenger on a mobile phone imagines that he or she is inaudible. People on mobiles often seem to go about in a little personal bubble, oblivious to the crowds around them, connected only to the person at the other end of the phone. They will happily discuss the details of their domestic or business affairs, matters that would normally be considered private or confidential, in tones loud enough for half a train carriage to hear. Tremendously useful for eavesdropping nosey researchers – I get a lot of data from mobile-phone ostriches – but irritating for all the other passengers. Not that they would actually *do* anything about it, of course, except tut and sigh and roll their eyes and shake their heads.

We are not all ostriches. Many English passengers – the majority, even – are smart enough to realize that other people can in fact hear what you are saying on your mobile, and we do our best to keep our voices down. The oblivious loudmouths are still a minority, but they are a highly noticeable and annoying minority. Part of the problem is that the English will not complain – not directly, to the person making the noise, only quietly to each other, or to colleagues when they get to work, or to their spouse when they get home, or in letters to the newspapers. Our television and radio comedy programmes are full of amusing sketches about the infuriating stupidity of noisy mobile-phone ostriches, and the banality or utter pointlessness of their 'I'm on the train!' conversations. Newspaper columnists are equally witty on the subject.

In typically English fashion, we channel our anger, into endless clever jokes and ritual moans, reams of print and hours of airtime, but fail to address the real source of the problem. Not one of us is brave or blunt enough to go up to a mobile-phone ostrich and simply ask him or her to keep it down. The train companies are aware of the issue, and some have designated certain sections of their trains as 'quiet' carriages, where the use of mobile phones is prohibited. Most people observe this rule, but when an occasional rogue ostrich ignores the signs, nobody dares to confront the offender. Even in a designated 'quiet' carriage, the worst an ostrich can expect is a lot of glares and pointed looks.

From *Watching the English. The Hidden Rules of English Behaviour*, by Kate Fox, Hodder, pp. 145–146 – 504 words.

1 **denial** saying that s.th. does not exist · 3 **unseemly** *(formal)* not correct · 4 **to violate** to break (a rule) · 5 **much-frowned-upon** [ˌmʌtʃˈfraʊndəˌpɒn] regarded as being unacceptable · 7 **advent** [ˈadvent] arrival · 7 **ostrich** [ˈɒstrɪtʃ] *Strauß; (informal, figurative)* person who ignores problems instead of dealing with them · 8 **dimwit** stupid · 9 **inaudible** not loud enough to be heard · 10 **oblivious** unaware of · 12 **confidential** private, secret · 13 **tremendously** extremely · 13 **eavesdropping** listening secretly to other people's conversations · 13 **nosey/nosy** *(negative)* interested in other people's affairs · 15 **to tut** to make a sound of disapproval · 22 **spouse** [spaʊs] husband or wife · 23 **infuriating** [ɪnˈfjʊərieɪtɪŋ] making s.o. very angry · 24 **utter pointlessness** having absolutely no purpose · 25 **witty** amusing · 26 **to channel one's anger** *here:* to show anger in one certain way · 26 **moan** a long, low sound expressing unhappiness · 27 **reams of print** large quantities of writing · 27 **airtime** discussion on radio and TV · 28 **blunt** very direct · 29 **to designate s.th.** to mark s.th. for a certain purpose · 31 **rogue** [rəʊg] *here:* unusually loud · 33 **glare** a long, angry look · 33 **a pointed look** looking at a person in a critical way

Intercultural competence (2)

The text on page 130 describes how not to behave on public transport in Britain. If you were planning to study abroad, you would have to find out how to behave correctly in the host country (i.e. about intercultural competence). The quiz below looks at intercultural competence worldwide.

Over to you

1 Read the examples of behaviour around the world and guess where people would behave in such a way.

Quiz

Behaviour around the world

a) You go into a restaurant and wait for the waiter to show you to your table.
b) You take a taxi to someone's house and you do not tip the taxi driver.
c) You stroll around the city and you are careful not to drop anything at all on the street, not even an old cinema ticket.
d) You are invited to someone's house and you avoid admiring any of your host's belongings too openly as he might give them to you.
e) You are talking to some people you do not know very well. They tend to stand close to you during the conversation so you move away. They follow you.
f) A group of students asks you out one evening. You go to a café, have one or two drinks and talk a lot.
g) You are invited to someone's house and you take off your shoes in the hall.
h) At a business meeting, some business people you meet for the first time immediately ask you to call them by their first names.
i) You buy a small packet of sweets from the tobacconist and forget your receipt on the counter. The tobacconist insists that you take it with you.
j) You avoid touching anyone with your left hand – even accidentally – as you know they would be highly offended.

Ideas according to Terri Morrison/Wayne A. Conaway, *Kiss, bow, or shake hands, The bestselling guide to doing business in more than 60 countries*, Avon Business, 2nd edition, 2006 – 234 words.

i) **receipt** [rɪ'si:t] paper that proves goods or services have been paid for
j) **offended** upset by s.o.'s behaviour

Language: if-clauses

2 Analyse the situations in a) – j) and use if-clauses to say what you think would happen if someone did not behave appropriately.
Example: "If I went into a restaurant and sat down at the first free table, then the waiter would probably..."

Further activity

3 What behaviour would you personally consider to be very polite or very rude? In pairs, discuss what you think are good and bad manners.

→ **Discussions**
See *skills file* on page 177.

The legacy of Empire

Before you read

1 All of the countries below used to be part of the British Empire. What do you know about them and what problems do you associate with them? Consider ethnic, religious, cultural, economic, linguistic and geographical/territorial issues.

a) Pakistan and India
b) Israel and Palestine
c) Afghanistan
d) Iraq
e) Northern Ireland
f) Gibraltar
g) Sri Lanka
h) Zimbabwe

Check the web
Get more information about the British Empire at:
www.britishempire.co.uk

In the following statements top commentators say what difference they think the imperial past made to the role that Britain plays in the world today. The statement in A caused much controversy in Britain at the time.

Consequences of a colonial past

A A lot of the problems we are having to deal with now are a consequence of our colonial past.

Jack Straw, British Foreign Secretary (2001–2006)

B There is a direct link between failed states and contemporary Islamic terrorism. States like Afghanistan and Pakistan have had huge difficulties in fulfilling the aspirations of their citizens and developing genuine legitimacy because they were hamstrung by borders that made no ethnic, cultural, linguistic or even geographic sense imposed by imperial powers. Discontent at illegitimate regimes led to protest, protest has been crushed and its root causes have not been dealt with. Result: violent terroristic activism. Iraq is inherently unstable. So is the Sudan.

Jason Burke, Chief Reporter, *The Observer*

C Because of the British Empire and the incredible sprawl that it achieved, Britain has interests and responsibilities on a global scale. Where Jack Straw is wrong is to assume that so many global problems were caused by the Empire. The problems were always there – but the Empire allowed two centuries of respite from the bloodshed that had been there before and which was likely to come again.

Andrew Roberts, historian

D Britain's withdrawal from the Empire often left a great deal of unfinished business. In the case of partition (e.g. Ireland, the British Raj, and the Palestinian Mandate), the creation of new states was based primarily on religious affiliation making it harder for post-colonial states to build multi-cultural societies. In other parts of the world, borders were left unresolved (e.g. Belize-Guatemala; Guyana-Venezuela), giving rise to dangerous tensions. In Africa, the 'Westminster model' proved difficult to sustain and even more difficult to replace once it had been discredited. Britain's colonial past is not glorious and the first step is to recognize this, but it does provide an opportunity to contribute to a resolution of these problems.

Victor Bulmer-Thoma, Director,
Royal Institute of International Affairs

283 words in total.

Text B: 6 **to fulfil aspirations** to do everything s.o. wants you to do · 8 **hamstrung** prevented from working properly · 10 **to impose s.th.** to force s.th. on s.o. · 12 **to crush** to use violent methods to defeat s.th. · 14 **inherently** *here:* permanently; Text C: 17 **sprawl** a very large size · 22 **respite** a break (from a conflict); Text D: 27 **partition** division of a country into two or more parts · 29 **religious affiliation** *here:* religious belief · 32 **unresolved** not properly defined · 35 **Westminster model** parliamentary system based on the democratic parliamentary system in the UK · 36 **to sustain** to support · 37 **to discredit s.th.** to make people stop respecting s.th.

Understanding the text on page 132.

2 Find reasons in the statements on page 132 to support the view that the British Empire was responsible for current global problems. Classify your findings according to political, economic, ethnic, geographical or other problems.

Presentation

3 a) What relations do Germany, Holland and France have with their former colonies? Choose one of these countries and compare with Britain's relationship with its former colonies.
b) Make a poster with your findings and present your results in class.

→ **Presentations**
See *skills file* on page 160.

The Commonwealth (1)

Presentation

1 Read the "Xtra-File" on this page and on page 134 and choose a key event in Britain's history that is linked to the Commonwealth. Examine its causes and effects, and present your results in class.

→ **Presentations**
See *skills file* on page 160.

Xtra-File: The Commonwealth of Nations

The Commonwealth of Nations, formerly the British Commonwealth of Nations, is an association of 53 independent nations, plus several British dependencies such as Bermuda, the Falkland Islands and Gibraltar. Most members used to be part of the British Empire. Any nation wishing to join the Commonwealth must be independent, and its application must be acceptable to existing members. The symbolic head of the Commonwealth is the British monarch.

Members of the Commonwealth have special links with the United Kingdom and with each other. All members are equal and agree to work together towards world peace, the encouragement of trade, the defence of democracy and improvements in human rights, health and education. During World War II, Commonwealth forces played an important role in the war effort. Critics say that the Commonwealth is pointless or little more than an exclusive club. However, Commonwealth nations united to oppose apartheid in South Africa, and they also encourage joint cultural activities and sports events, particularly the Commonwealth Games, which are held every four years.

Australian athlete, Cathy Freeman holds the baton for the Queen's Baton Relay. Similar to the Olympic torch, the baton is brought from Buckingham Palace, London to the city hosting the Commonwealth Games.

Xtra-File: The Commonwealth and Europe

1931 The British Commonwealth of Nations is founded.

1947 India, known as the "Jewel in the Crown" of the Empire, becomes independent. Other colonies follow. This period of de-colonization is generally peaceful, and most of the newly independent states join the Commonwealth.

1961 South Africa is suspended from the Commonwealth because of its apartheid regime.
Britain applies to join the Common Market (European Community). France vetoes the application, arguing that Britain's links with the USA and the Commonwealth are too strong.

1972 Britain joins the Common Market.

1982 Argentina invades the Falkland Islands and Britain recaptures them in the Falklands War.

1991 Britain signs the Single European Act at Maastricht, the Treaty on the European Union.

1994 South Africa rejoins the Commonwealth after the abolition of apartheid and the election of Nelson Mandela as president.
The Channel Tunnel linking Britain and France is opened. (cf. photo above right)

1995 Nigeria is suspended from the Commonwealth because its regime is considered to be undemocratic. Nigeria was reinstated in 2000.
Cameroon and Mozambique (the latter an ex-Portuguese colony) join the Commonwealth.

The Channel Tunnel is opened by Queen Elizabeth II and French President François Mitterrand (1994).

1997 Hong Kong is handed back to China.

2002 The British government considers handing Gibraltar back to Spain.

2003 Zimbabwe is indefinitely suspended from the Commonwealth because it is considered that people in Zimbabwe do not have adequate democratic rights, e.g. the right to vote in free democratic elections.

2004 Pakistan's suspension from Commonwealth councils is lifted.

2006 Fiji's membership is suspended after a military coup.

2010 Commonwealth Games will take place in Delhi, India.

32 **indefinitely** lasting for an unlimited period of time

The Commonwealth (2)

On March 22, 2007, the Commonwealth Secretary General, Don McKinnon, spoke about the challenges facing the Commonwealth of Nations at the Indian Council of World Affairs, in New Delhi, India.

1|24 **India** The beginning of the speech covers India's key role in the Commonwealth and its growing economic power.

Understanding the text "21st century ..." on page 135.

1 Outline the challenges which Don McKinnon talks about in his speech.
2 Why is democracy sometimes seen in a bad light?
3 How does Don McKinnon see the African attitude to democracy?
4 How does he describe the advantages of democracy?
5 Outline the ways in which the Commonwealth can promote democracy.
6 What powers does the Commonwealth have to make its members stick to the rules of democracy?
7 In the end, what issue is often more important to Commonwealth states than democracy, and why?

2|54

21st century challenges

[…] I have chosen to speak to you this evening on '21st century challenges'. […]

On the one hand, our challenges include upholding constitutional government, or fundamental human rights, or the rule of law, or combating the scourge of terrorism and other international crimes, or creating more harmonious societies.

On the other hand they involve alleviating poverty, eradicating illiteracy and disease, helping to create an equitable multilateral trade regime, bridging the digital divide, or protecting our precious environment.

Let me just touch on some of these, however lightly. I shall perhaps raise more questions than I answer. So let us talk later. I view the Question & Answer session as every bit as important as this lecture.

For now, let me start by raising the challenge of early 21st Century democracy – and how we in the Commonwealth are trying to address it.

There are those who contend that democracy is something of a dirty word. Certainly, it's seen as the stuff of rhetoric, not reality. Nightly television scenes of the way that the much vaunted democracy is playing out in Iraq and Afghanistan do nothing for its share price. Nor do bad headlines anywhere raise its stock – be it 'cash for honours' in the UK, or even legislators hurling microphones and furniture at each other in one of your own state assemblies in India! Each morning, I receive press clippings from around the 53-nation Commonwealth and, every now and then, read headlines like these in each and every Commonwealth country. […]

I was in Lesotho recently, meeting political parties before the February elections. I found it inspiring to see political opponents sitting around a table and committing one-and-all to nurturing their country's democracy. This is the secret of Commonwealth Africa's democracy, for all its flaws: Africa owns it; cares for it; and wants it to mature.

So where does all this good news meet the bad, and what is the challenge of 21st Century democracy?

I have two answers. First, let's keep the faith. Democracy isn't easy but it's the best way we know to give individuals freedom, control over their lives, and opportunities to do better. It is 'work-in-progress' wherever it is – always evolving, often making mistakes, always adapting to circumstances.

Don McKinnon

3 to uphold s.th. to support s.th. that you think is right · **5 to combat** to fight against · **5 scourge of s.th.** ['skɜːdʒ əv ˌsʌmθɪŋ] trouble caused by s.th. · **7 to alleviate poverty** to help poor people · **7 to eradicate illiteracy** to teach people to read · **8 equitable** treating everyone the same · **8 multilateral** involving many countries · **9 trade regime** system of buying and selling goods · **18 to contend** to say that s.th. is true · **20 much vaunted** [ˌmʌtʃ'vɔːntɪd] praised greatly · **22 share price** *(figurative)* value · **22 to raise its stock** to raise its value · **23 to hurl** to throw · **31 to commit to** to give time and effort · **33 flaw** mistake

Second, let's try and nurture democracy at three levels, [...]

We have to support the forms of democracy, like free and fair elections. We have to support the institutions of democracy, like a parliament, a judiciary and an executive which are apart but work together; responsible armed forces and police; an independent and responsible media; a lively civil society. And finally we have to support a real culture of democracy ... of citizens having a say in how they are governed.

Of all these things, perhaps the culture is the greatest. Democracy is often fragile, because it is precious. If we are committed to it, we are always chiseling away to make it better and stronger.

The Commonwealth helps countries do that. In high profile cases, it will suspend members who flout its shared principles: such was the case for Fiji after a democratically elected government was overthrown by a military coup in December. But in general we keep a lower profile – working alongside governments as trusted partners on those three areas: the forms, the institutions, the culture.

These then are some of the challenges of democracy itself. And their links to the challenges of development were most forcibly brought home to me by an African leader who said to me: 'yes Don, but you can't eat democracy'.

Because it is food on the table – and all the other fruits of development, like jobs, investment, education, health – which must be the dividends of democracy. [...]

Extracts from a speech by Don McKinnon, March 22, 2007, www.thecommonwealth.org – 615 words.

42 **to nurture s.th.** to help s.th. to develop and be successful · 52 **to chisel away** *(figurative)* to work at s.th. constantly · 54 **to flout** to show no respect

Language and style

8 Find examples of rhetorical devices used in the speech.

→ **Style analysis**
See *skills file* on page 162.

Listening comprehension

1|27

Respecting difference, promoting understanding

Listen to Queen Elizabeth's message for Commonwealth Day on March 22, 2007.

Hotspot

Find out more about India's role as a modern member of the Commonwealth of Nations and write your own five-minute speech on this topic. You could refer to the rhetorical devices that you found in task 8 for ideas to make your speech more interesting.

→ **Presentations**
See *skills file* on page 160.

Britain and Europe

Before you read

1 Write the word "EUROPE" in a column in your notebook and match each letter with a term that represents the European ideal for you.
2 Do you personally see yourself as a European, or not? Give reasons.

Britain's future tied to Europe

By Hugh Cortazzi

[…] Douglas Hurd, a former conservative British foreign secretary, has said that Britain often "punches above its weight" in world affairs. It can only do so when it works with its friends and not against them. The British have recognized, at least ever since the Suez debacle of 1956, that they cannot exercise force in the world in opposition to policy adopted by the United States, the only superpower. They know that Britain must remain on good terms with the U.S., although that does not and should not mean that we become a tool of the Americans.

Most Britons also recognize that Britain is a part of Europe and that Britain cannot flourish without the closest cooperation with other states in Europe. Britain on its own cannot exercise the sort of authority in international affairs that could accrue to a united Europe in competition with such growing powers as China and India.

Unfortunately, a number of people in Britain still believe the European Union undermines British independence and sovereignty, and see the European Commission in Brussels as a meddling bureaucracy that threatens British national interests. The tendency to blame Brussels for every irritating regulation sadly reflects an ingrained British suspicion of anything foreign, but the problem lies much deeper in British psyche. Some British people have yet to fully adjust to the inevitable decline in their economic and political power in the world since World War II. Some politicians suffer from nostalgia for past glories and have not yet come to terms with the realities of the modern world.

Flags in front of the European Parliament in Brussels, Belgium

Britain generally managed to escape from its colonial commitments without too much loss of good will or bloodshed. The British Commonwealth, which former British possessions overseas tended to join after gaining independence, depended on shared democratic values and cultural connections. It was neither an alliance nor a free trade area. It was more highly regarded in London than in most of the overseas "dominions."

Heading: **tied to s.th.** connected closely to s.th.; **Text: 6 Suez debacle** refers to a military attack on Egypt by the UK, France and Israel, when Egypt closed the Suez Canal to Israeli ships · **14 to flourish** to be successful · **18 to accrue to** *here:* to reach the same level as s.th. else · **21 to undermine s.th.** to make s.th. weaker · **23 meddling** *(negative)* trying to decide things for others · **26 ingrained** fixed · **28 psyche** ['saɪki:] mind · **30 inevitable** unavoidable · **30 decline** loss · **32 nostalgia** [nɒs'tældʒə] feeling of sadness mixed with pleasure when you think of happier times · **44 dominion** *(old)* country of the Commonwealth that had its own government

Unfortunately, too much sentimental value was attached to the Commonwealth for too long by many British politicians. By some it was seen as a substitute for joining the EU. […]

For too long, Britain has accepted overseas commitments for which it has inadequate resources. British armed forces are overstretched, and equipment and manpower have not been increased to match the demands made on them by politicians. Britain cannot go on trying to do so much in places like Iraq and Afghanistan without an increase in defense expenditures. Since this cannot be achieved without cuts in other public services such as health, education and police, it would not be acceptable to the electorate.

The British believe that they can remain as the bridge between the U.S. and Europe, but it is far from clear that either the Americans or the Europeans see Britain as such a bridge. The Americans are glad to have a dependable ally in Europe willing to commit their armed forces to support American-led campaigns, but the inability of Blair to persuade the Americans to give more than passing support to the causes to which he attached importance, such as trying to find a solution to the problems of Palestine, suggests that the foundations at the American end of the bridge are shaky.

The European end also looks rather brittle. German Chancellor Angela Merkel and French President Nicolas Sarkozy do not share their predecessors' attitude toward the U.S. and want to improve relations. They would also like to bind Britain more closely to Europe, but they do not see Britain as their bridge to America. […]

By Hugh Cortazzi, *The Japan Times*, June 30, 2007 – 595 words.

50 commitment involvement · **65 ally** ['ælaɪ] helper, supporter · **68 Blair** Tony Blair, former British Prime Minister (1997–2007) · **74 brittle** easily broken

Understanding the text

3 Why does the writer think that Britain should cooperate with the EU?

4 Describe the attitude of some Britons towards the EU.

5 Summarize the positive and negative aspects of EU membership for Britain in a table.

6 How does the writer describe Britain's role in Europe, as well as its attitude towards the Commonwealth and the United States?

7 Outline other EU members' attitudes to Britain and its role in Europe. What does the term "bridge" refer to in this discussion?

Language

8 Explain the following expressions from the text in your own words.
a) "exercise force" ‹L7›
b) "remain on good terms" ‹L9–10›
c) "suffer from nostalgia" ‹L32›

9 Look at the following examples of figurative language from the text and rewrite them in your own words.
a) "punches above its weight" ‹L3›
b) "become a tool of" ‹L11›
c) "the foundations … of the bridge are shaky" ‹L72–73›

→ **Figurative language**
See *glossary* on page 202.

Translation

10 Translate from, "For too long, Britain has accepted…" ‹L49› to "… the bridge are shaky." ‹L73›.

→ **Translation**
See *skills file* on page 165.

A step further: Cartoon

11 Describe the cartoon and explain the figure's attitude towards foreign influences on Britain. To what extent does he contradict himself?
12 Compare the attitude in the cartoon with the attitudes expressed in the text on pages 137–138.

Cartoons
See *skills file* on page 155.

1|28

Listening comprehension

Britain's role in Europe

Listen to Ben Bradshaw talking about Britain's role in Europe.

Hotspots

a) **1** Find out about the functions of the European Commission.
2 What other EU institutions do you know? What are their powers?
3 Organize your information in a mind map.

b) You work as a journalist for a newspaper called *The European News* which is sold throughout Europe and deals with topics of European interest. Working in groups, design the front page of tomorrow's issue using, e.g. photos, articles, a short comment, European news. Think of issues that might be vital for EU member states and should be placed on the front page, such as the advantages or disadvantages of the Euro, working conditions, global concerns, science projects, etc.

c) **1** Check your local newspaper for one week and collect articles, comments, news items and photos that are linked to European topics.
2 Design a poster using your findings and present it in class.

Check the web:
Key word: "European Commission"

Mind maps
See *skills file* on page 186.

Unit 10 Globalization

801005-0010

Getting started

1 Work in small groups. Look at the pictures above and come up with a heading for each one.

2 Draw a mind map about 'globalization' starting with the aspects presented in the photos. Add more ideas and present the mind map to your class.

3 Think of examples of the effects of globalization visible in your hometown. Present and discuss your findings in class.

Mind maps
See *skills file* on page 186.

Global business

Globalisation shakes the world

Globalisation is a word that is on everyone's lips these days, from politicians to businessmen. [...]

Few places in the world have seen the dramatic effects of globalisation more than Bangalore, the Silicon Valley of India, which is experiencing an unprecedented IT boom that is transforming the prospects of the Indian economy.

For Santosh, a tour guide in Bangalore, life is good. As a result of the IT boom, he has launched his own web-based travel firm, getoffurass.com, and is doing a booming business selling weekend getaway holidays to stressed-out IT workers.

For Dean Braid, a skilled car engineer in Flint, Michigan, life is not so good. He – and 28,000 other workers – were laid off from Buick City when GM closed the complex in 1999, and hasn't worked since. Globalisation is blamed for many of the ills of the modern world, but it is also praised for bringing unprecedented prosperity.

But what is globalisation, and what are the forces that are shaping it?

The accelerating pace of globalisation is having a profound effect on life in rich and poor countries alike, transforming regions such as Detroit or Bangalore from boom to bust – or vice versa – in a generation.

Many economists believe globalisation may be the explanation for key trends in the world economy such as:

- Lower wages for workers, and higher profits, in Western economies
- The flood of migrants to cities in poor countries
- Low inflation and low interest rates despite strong growth.

Queue at an employment office

And globalisation has played a key role in the unprecedented increase in prosperity in the last 50 years, which is now spreading from the United States and Europe to include many formerly poor countries in Asia, including China and India.

Defining globalisation

In economic terms, globalisation refers to the growing economic integration of the world, as trade, investment and money increasingly cross international borders (which may or may not have political or cultural implications).

Globalisation is not new, but is a product of the industrial revolution. Britain grew rich in the 19th century as the first global economic superpower, because of its superior manufacturing technology and improved

7 unprecedented never seen before · **10 tour guide** person who shows tourists famous places · **16 skilled** trained for a special job · **18 to lay s.o. off** to make s.o. redundant · **18 Buick City** [ˌbjuːɪkˈsɪtɪ] car production complex in Flint (1904–1999) · **21 ills** evil · **26 accelerating pace** increasing speed · **27 profound** *here:* major · **30 bust** *(informal)* bankruptcy · **38 interest rate** *Zinssatz* · **51 implication** consequence · **56 manufacturing** production global communications such as steamships and railroads.

But the pace, scope and scale of globalisation have accelerated dramatically since World War II, and especially in the last 25 years. The rapid spread of information technology (IT) and the internet is changing the way companies organise production, and increasingly allowing services as well as manufacturing to be globalised.

Globalisation is also being driven by the decision by India and China to open their economies to the world, thus doubling the global labour force overnight.

The role of trade

Trade has been the engine of globalisation, with world trade in manufactured goods increasing more than 100 times (from $95 bn to $12 trillion) in the 50 years since 1955, much faster than the overall growth of the world economy.

Since 1960, increased trade has been made easier by international agreements to lower tariff and non-tariff barriers on the export of manufactured goods, especially to rich countries.

Those countries which have managed to increase their role in the world trading system by targeting exports to rich countries – such as Japan, Korea and now China – have seen dramatic increases in their standard of living.

In the post-war years more and more of the global production has been carried out by big multinational companies who operate across borders.

Multinationals have become increasingly global, locating manufacturing plants overseas in order to capitalise on cheaper labour costs or to be closer to their markets.

And globalisation is even harder to track now that one-third of all trade is within companies, for example, Toyota shipping car parts from Japan to the US for final assembly.

More recently, some multinationals like Apple have become "virtual firms" outsourcing most of their production to other companies, mainly in Asia. [...]

By Steve Schifferes, *BBC News*, Bangalore, January 21, 2007, news.bbc.co.uk – 633 words.

59 scope range · **59 scale** extent · **69 thus** in this way · **76 overall** general · **80 tariff barrier** *Zollschranke* · **85 to target s.th.** to concentrate particularly on s.th. · **96 to track** to trace · **99 final assembly** last stage in production · **101 outsourcing** to have work done by another company

Understanding the text

1 Describe Santosh's and Dean Braid's experiences of globalization.
2 According to the text, what problems does globalization cause?
3 List the stages in the emergence of globalization.

Further activities

4 In what ways is Silicon Valley similar to Bangalore? Give examples.
5 What do you know about Britain in the 19th century? Write ten sentences.
6 The writer mentions that India is "experiencing an … IT boom" ‹L7›. Give other examples of Indian industries which have been successful worldwide.

Essay/Composition

7 a) Find pros and cons of globalization in the text and list them in a table.
b) Add your own arguments.
c) Write an essay using the points you found. Think of a suitable heading.

→ **Essays/Compositions**
See *skills file* on page 157.

Translation

8 Translate the first part of the text into German, starting with the heading "Globalization shakes the world" up to ‹L25›, "… shaping it".

→ **Translation**
See *skills file* on page 165.

Food from around the globe

Before you read: Cartoon and text

1 Describe the cartoon below and point out its message.

→ **Cartoons**
See *skills file* on page 155.

Talking about the cartoon and text

2 Read the text and relate the message in the cartoon to it.

Carrier of culture

"Food is the oldest global carrier of culture. In fact, food has always been a driving force for globalization, especially during earlier phases of European trade and colonial expansion. The hot red pepper was introduced to the Spanish court by Christopher Columbus in 1493. It spread rapidly throughout the colonial world, transforming cuisines and farming practices in Africa, Asia, and the Middle East."

From *Britannica online*, www.britannica.com – 63 words.

4 hot red pepper *scharfer, roter Pfeffer, Chilipfeffer* ·
7 farming practice way of growing food

"I wish you were more adventurous sometimes, Gerald!"

Essay/Composition

3 Exotic dishes are fashionable in the industrialized world while some Third World countries have difficulties feeding their populations. Do you think that a change in eating habits in industrialized countries could improve the situation in developing countries, or not? Discuss.

→ **Essays/Compositions**
See *skills file* on page 157.

Hotspot: Show and tell

a) Choose a country and present its food specialities. Check the web for information about eating habits, typical foods, recipes, cooking methods, etc. in that country. Collect interesting pictures or even objects to present in class. You could even prepare some food for your classmates to try!

b) Present the country's specialities in class. Write down key words which you can use in a free speech. You should speak for at least five minutes.

→ **Presentations**
See *skills file* on page 160.

Better chances for Third World farmers

Before you read: Translation

1 Translate the statement below into German.

"We believe in a total transformation of the coffee industry, so that all coffee sold in this country should be Fair Trade Certified, or if produced on a plantation, that workers' rights should be guaranteed and independently monitored. Our view includes social justice and environmental sustainability: all coffee should be certified organic and shade grown where applicable."

From *Global Exchange*, www.globalexchange.org – 57 words.

4 **to monitor** to observe over a time · 4 **environmental sustainability** not causing damage to nature · 5 **shade grown** grown in a place that is sheltered from the sun · 6 **applicable** relevant

2 Do you agree with the values mentioned in the text, or not? Give reasons.
3 What other points could be more important for producers and consumers?

Summary

4 Work with a partner. Read the flier on pages 144–145 and summarise the situation of small farmers.

Fairtrade, established in 1997, is an umbrella organization that unites 20 labelling initiatives in 21 countries and producer networks representing organizations in Central and South America, Africa and Asia. The texts on pages 144–145 are taken from a Fairtrade flier.

2|57

TRADING UP

THE **FAIRTRADE MARK** GUARANTEES SMALL FARMERS A STRONGER POSITION IN WORLD MARKETS

In the Windward Islands, in the Caribbean, thousands of families make their living growing bananas on small, hilly farms. During the 1990s, many of them were forced out of business by large-scale Latin American banana plantations where labour is cheaper and costs are lower.

"When prices dropped, the economy went down to zero because bananas are the heartbeat of the country," explains Amos Wiltshire, National Fairtrade Co-ordinator for Dominica, one of the Windward Islands.

Amos joined forces with other farmers who saw Fairtrade as the only way to survive in a cut-throat market. Through Fairtrade, producers learn how best to sell their products and what the international market and consumers want. Today, nearly 100% of Dominica's banana farmers are members of Fairtrade groups.

"FAIRTRADE HAS BEEN THE SAVIOUR OF THE FARMERS IN DOMINICA – OF AGRICULTURE AND THE WHOLE ECONOMY. WITH FAIRTRADE, SMALL FARMERS HAVE BEEN TRANSFORMED FROM MARGINALISED FARMERS INTO BUSINESSMEN.
AMOS WILTSHIRE, BANANA FARMER, DOMINICA"

4 **large-scale** big · 10 **to join forces** to unite · 11 **cut-throat** aggressive · Statement, Amos Wiltshire: 17 **saviour** s.th. that helps s.o. to survive · 24 **marginalised** pushed aside

Role play

5 Imagine you are the owner of a coffee plantation. What arguments can you find to justify how you run your business?

6 With a partner improvise a discussion between a small farmer and a large-scale farmer. Use the arguments from tasks 4 and 5.

Mediation

7 You work for an import firm which wants to include fair trade products in their range. Use the information in the flier and in the box on Global Exchange on page 144 and create a German information sheet for your customers which convinces them to buy the new products.

Mediation
See *skills file* on page 158.

1|32

Listening comprehension

The situation of women in Chile

Listen to Rosa Palleres as she talks about the situation of female agricultural workers in Chile.

2|58

A BETTER DEAL

THE **FAIRTRADE MARK** GUARANTEES A CLOSER LINK BETWEEN SHOPPERS AND PRODUCERS

More and more of us want to know where our shopping comes from and that the people who produce it have received a fair deal. Fairtrade encourages more direct trading relationships so that producers get a bigger share of the export price.

Sweet rewards

In Ghana, liberalisation of the internal cocoa market created big challenges for small farmers; they responded by forming Kuapa Kokoo, a farmer-owned business. Their decision proved wise: 10 years on, Kuapa Kokoo owns a one-third share in a UK-based company selling Fairtrade chocolate. As well as supplying the cocoa, they have a direct share in the company's success.

"I WANT TO BE SURE THAT FARMERS GET A FAIR PRICE AND BENEFIT DIRECTLY FROM MY PURCHASE. AS THE DAUGHTER OF A GHANAIAN FATHER, I KNOW HOW IMPORTANT FAIRTRADE IS TO SMALL PRODUCERS. WITH MORE SHOPS STOCKING MORE GREAT QUALITY PRODUCTS CARRYING THE FAIRTRADE MARK, IT'S A WIN-WIN SITUATION. WE CAN EAT AND DRINK IN GOOD HEALTH AND GOOD CONSCIENCE."
ADJOA ANDOH, ACTRESS (PICTURED TOP RIGHT)

FAIRTRADE

Guarantees a **better deal** for Third World Producers

33 **liberalisation** removal of restrictions · 34 **to respond** to react · 34 **Kuapa Kokoo** [ˌkwɑːpæ'kɒkəʊ] · 37 **to supply** *liefern* · 40 **purchase** s.th. you buy · 40 **Ghanaian** [ɡɑː'neɪən] · 41 **to stock** *here:* to offer to customers · 42 **win-win situation** situation in which there are no losers · 43 **conscience** ['kɒnʃəns] sense of what is right and wrong · 44 **Adjoa Andoh** [əˌdʒəʊə 'ændəʊ]

Global understanding

Before you read

1 What do you think are the most important languages in Europe? Which language is the most important in the world? Give reasons.
2 What dialects or types of English can you think of? Make a list with a partner and try to give examples for each type.
3 Explain the terms 'lingua franca', 'creoles' and 'pidgins'. Check the web or other sources of information for ideas.

→ **Map**
See map on page 208.

English as lingua franca

English is a global language. It is the language most often studied in the European Union, and also in China, Japan, South Korea and Taiwan. India now has more people who speak or understand English than any other country in the world. It is the language of the United Nations and of most international sports bodies (including the International Olympic Committee), and 95 per cent of all science articles are written in English.

English is not, however, regulated, and so there are hundreds – if not thousands – of dialects, creoles and pidgins, from "Euro-English" to "Singlish" (Chinese English spoken in Singapore). It is precisely this adaptability, the lack of regulation that has helped the English language to achieve its current status. As it spreads, it reflects local cultural practices. And when people adopt English they immediately adapt it, maintaining cultural variation and linguistic diversity in new ways.

"But Dr Johnson ov wat yuse wil this dicshunary of yors be?"

From *"By Hook or by Crook: a journey in search of English*, by David Crystal" by Nick Groom, *The Independent*, May 18, 2007 – 148 words.

11 **international sports body** worldwide sports organization · 17 **to regulate a language** to establish rules for a language · 23 **adaptability** ability to change · 29 **to adopt** *here:* to begin to use · 30 **to adapt** to change · 30 **to maintain** to support

Understanding the text

4 According to the text, why has the English language become so popular?
5 Find a definition for the term "global language" ‹L1›.

A step further: Cartoon and text

6 Describe the cartoon on the right. What point does it make?
7 Does the cartoon agree or disagree with the ideas mentioned in the text? Give examples.

→ **Cartoons**
See *skills file* on page 155.

Talk

8 a) What do you think of the regulation of languages, e.g. the reform of the German language? Write down key ideas and give a talk in class using the ideas as prompts.
b) Note down questions while listening to your classmates' talks. Discuss the different opinions in class.

The language of tomorrow

Before you read

1 Which languages may become increasingly important in the future? Give reasons for your opinion.

Schools import China's teachers for lessons in 'language of tomorrow'

All the country's 250 specialist language schools have been told by a government adviser that they should put Mandarin on the curriculum as "the language of tomorrow".

Sir Cyril Taylor, chairman of the Specialist Schools and Academies Trust, said it should be seen as the key language for future generations to learn – replacing European languages.

The trust, which represents 90 per cent of England's 2,950 state secondary schools, has clinched a deal with the Chinese government, which will send 200 teachers a year over to the UK to teach Mandarin in schools. Pupil exchanges are also being arranged, Sir Cyril revealed at a meeting of the Commons Select Committee on Education yesterday.

If Sir Cyril Taylor has his way, these students may have the option of studying GCSE Chinese.

He told MPs: "I want all language colleges to be teaching Mandarin. It is a strategic world language. The difficulty in the past has been getting Chinese teachers. However, exchanges between our schools and Chinese schools will help to change that. We learn from them and they learn from us."

Around 4,000 pupils in the UK are studying GCSE Chinese. However, most of them are of Chinese origin and Sir Cyril wants to extend its take-up.

Richard Cairns, headmaster of Brighton College – the independent school which became the first school in the country to make the language compulsory for all pupils and introduced it to youngsters from the age of three – said he believed it would replace German in the "pecking order" of languages.

Sir Cyril added: "The state of modern language teaching in this country means we need to do a lot more to promote it. I'd like to see all language colleges having Mandarin on the curriculum as soon as possible and I'd like to extend it to a number of other schools as well." In his government inquiry into language teaching, Lord Dearing successfully argued that ministers should drop the requirement for all schools to teach a European language from the ages of 11 and 14. Instead, they should be allowed to include Mandarin, Arabic and Urdu on the list of languages that could be taught.

By Richard Garner, *The Independent*, May 24, 2007 – 351 words.

2 adviser s.o. who gives s.o. else advice · **5 Cyril** ['sɪrəl] · **5 chairman** president · **6 key language** most important language · **12 to clinch a deal** to reach an official agreement · **18 to reveal** *here:* to inform the public · **30 take-up** acceptance · **31 Cairns** [keənz] · **32 independent school** *(GB)* a private school · **33 compulsory** obligatory · **37 pecking order** hierarchy · **48 inquiry** investigation

Understanding the text

2 Describe the agreement which has been reached by Britain and China.

3 Sum up Sir Cyril Taylor's arguments in favour of teaching Mandarin in British schools.

Language

4 Find nouns which correspond to the following verbs from the text.

a) to see ‹L6›
b) to represent ‹L9›
c) to arrange ‹L17›
d) to reveal ‹L18›
e) to extend ‹L30›
f) to introduce ‹L34›
g) to believe ‹L35›
h) to replace ‹L36›
i) to add ‹L38›
j) to promote ‹L41›
k) to allow ‹L52›

5 Find the adverbs which correspond to the following adjectives from the text.
a) strategic ‹L 23›
b) origin ‹L 29›
c) independent ‹L 32›
d) first ‹L 32›
e) compulsory ‹L 33›
f) possible ‹L 45›

6 Find suitable English definitions for the following words from the text.
a) curriculum ‹L 3›
b) pupil exchanges ‹L 16›

Language barriers

Before you read: The English Language

1 Globalization has led to greater mobility on the job market. In what ways can good language skills be an important factor for integration in a foreign culture?

The English Language

2|59

When I arrived in England I thought I knew English. After I'd been here an hour I realised that I did not understand one word. In the first week I picked up a tolerable working knowledge of the language and the next seven years convinced me gradually but thoroughly that I would never know it really well, let alone perfectly. This is sad. My only consolation being that nobody speaks English perfectly.

Remember that those five hundred words an average Englishman uses are far from being the whole vocabulary of the language. You may learn another five hundred and yet another five thousand and yet another fifty thousand and still you may come across a further fifty thousand you have never heard before, and nobody else either.

If you live here long enough you will find out to your great amazement that the adjective nice is not the only adjective that the language possesses, in spite of the fact that in the first three years you do not need to learn any other adjectives. You can say the weather is nice, a restaurant is nice, Mr. Soandso is nice, Mrs. Soandso's clothes are nice, you had a nice time, and all this will be very nice.

Then you have to decide on your accent. [...]

I have known quite a number of foreigners who tried hard to acquire an Oxford accent. The advantage of this is that you give the impression of being permanently in the company of Oxford dons and lecturers on mediaeval numismatics; the disadvantage is that the permanent singing is rather a strain on your throat and that it is a type of affectation that even many English people find hard to keep up incessantly. You may fall out of it, speak naturally, and then where are you?

The Mayfair accent can be highly recommended, too. The advantages of Mayfair English are that it unites the affected air of the Oxford accent with the uncultured flavour of a half-educated professional hotel-dancer.

3 to convince s.o. to make s.o. believe s.th. · **4 let alone** to say nothing of · **4 consolation** comfort · **10 amazement** great surprise · **18 don** *(BE)* teacher at university · **18 mediaeval numismatic** [ˌmedɪ'i:vl ˌnju:mɪz'mætɪk] *Sachverständige(r); Text für mittelalterliche Münzen* · **19 strain** effort · **19 affectation** unnatural behaviour · **20 incessantly** continually

George Mikes (1912–1987)
was born in Hungary and studied law in Budapest before going to England to live and work as a journalist in the 1930s. His book *How to be an Alien* describes his impressions of Britain in a humorous way as well as considering how language can be a means of integration.

Info-box: **Mikes** [maɪks]

The most successful attempts, however, to put on a highly cultured air have been made on the polysyllabic lines. Many foreigners who have learnt Latin and Greek in school discover with amazement and satisfaction that the English language has absorbed a huge amount of ancient Latin and Greek expressions, and they realise that (a) it is much easier to learn these expressions than the much simpler English words; (b) that these words as a rule are interminably long and make a simply superb impression when talking to the greengrocer, the porter and the insurance agent.

Imagine, for instance, that the porter of the block of flats where you live remarks sharply that you must not put your dustbin out in front of your door before 7:30 a.m. Should you answer "please don't bully me," a loud and tiresome argument may follow, and certainly the porter will be proved right, because you are sure to find a clause in your contract (small print, bottom of last page) that the porter is always right and you owe absolute allegiance and unconditional obedience to him. Should you answer, however, with these words: "I repudiate your petulant expostulations," the argument will be closed at once, the porter will be proud of having such a highly cultured man in the block, and from that day onwards you may, if you please, get up at four o'clock in the morning and hang your dustbin out of the window. […]

When you know all the long words it is advisable to start learning some of the short ones, too.

You should be careful when using these endless words. An acquaintance of mine once was fortunate enough to discover the most impressive word *notalgia* for backache. Mistakenly, however, he declared in a large company:

"I have such a nostalgia."

"Oh, you want to go home to Nizhne-Novgorod?" asked his most sympathetic hostess.

"Not at all," he answered. "I just cannot sit down."

Finally, there are two important points to remember:

1. Do not forget that it is much easier to write in English than to speak in English, because you can write without a foreign accent.

2. In a bus and in other public places it is more advisable to speak softly in good German than to shout in abominable English.

Anyway, this whole language business is not at all easy. After spending eight years in this country, the other day I was told by a very kind lady: "But why do you complain? You really speak a most excellent accent without the slightest English."

From "How to be a Brit" by George Mikes, *Penguin Humour*, 1977, pages 37–43 – 762 words.

25 on the polysyllabic lines [ɒn ðə ˌpɒlɪsɪˈlæbɪk ˌlaɪnz] by using words of more than one syllable (= *Silbe*) · **29 interminably** endlessly · **33 dustbin** *(BE)* container for waste · **36 allegiance** loyalty · **37 I repudiate…** I do not accept your annoying criticism · **42 an acquaintance of mine** a person I know · **44 to declare** to state · **44 company** crowd at a party · **45 nostalgia** [nɒsˈtældʒə] homesickness · **46 Nizhne-Novgorod** [ˌnɪʒnɪˈnɒvgərɒt] · **51 advisable** wise · **52 abominable** terrible · **54 to complain** to say one is not satisfied with a situation · **55 slight** *here:* a little

Understanding the text: "The English Language" on pp. 148–149.

2 Describe the writer's first experiences with the English language.
3 Outline his attitude to English vocabulary.
4 In what way does he describe English pronunciation and accent?
5 Explain why the writer thinks that words borrowed from other languages are useful.

Analysing style

6 Analyse the writer's use of language. Which stylistic devices create humour in the text? Give examples.

→ **Style analysis**
See *skills file* on page 162.

Discussion

7 Do you agree with the writer's attitude that words borrowed from other languages can make a good impression, or not? Give reasons.
8 Think of particular situations in which you might have to use formal language.

→ **Discussions**
See *skills file* on page 177.

Check the web: artificial languages

9 Artificial languages such as Esperanto, Volapük, Ido and Interlingua were created to allow people with different mother tongues to communicate. Check the web to find out:
a) when and why they were created;
b) how important they are/why they couldn't be established.
10 Think of some examples of artificial languages created for movies or literature. Why were these languages used? Check the web for information.

Mediation/Intercultural competence

11 Based on the text, write a short set of instructions in German for someone planning to stay in England for a period of time. Give advice on how to use the English language.

→ **Mediation**
See *skills file* on page 158.

Global politics

Understanding the text: "Xtra-File" on page 151.

1 Describe the origins of the G8.
2 What have been the most fundamental changes since the G8's early years?
3 Outline the main issues dealt with at G8 summits.
4 In what way are the G8 meetings criticized?

Role play

5 a) Form groups of eight people. Each person represents a G8 country. Decide on topics which you consider to be important. Consider how the G8 countries and developing countries might be affected by these issues.
b) Write a role play in which you discuss these issues and act it out in class.

Xtra-File: Profile of the G8

The photo shows a meeting between representatives from African states and the G8 leaders during the G8 summit held in Heiligendamm, Germany from June 6–8, 2007.

The origin of the first G8 meetings lies in the oil crisis and the worldwide economic recession at the beginning of the 1970s. In 1973 the so-called Library Group was formed from senior financial officials from Europe, Japan and the USA, who met informally. In 1975 governments leaders were also included. Members came from the UK, France, Italy, Germany, the USA and Japan. Initially called the G6, the group was renamed the G7, and later the G8, as Canada and Russia both joined.

Originally, the G8 concentrated on economic and trading issues but by the late 1970s politics had become more important. Nowadays, G8 summits deal with the problems of developing countries as well as global warming, global security, peace in the Middle East and other current issues. Although its agreements are not binding for member states, decisions made by the G8 can affect other countries because of their enormous economic and political power.

Each summit requires months of preparation. Only the second day is free for members to meet informally without the presence of the media.

The EU does not take part in or influence G8 political discussions, although the president of the European Commission and the leader of the country holding the EU presidency are both present at the summit. Neither China nor India – both fast-growing economies with large proportions of the world population – are allowed to vote. African and Latin American countries are also not incuded in decision making.

The leadership of the G8 rotates between the member states on an annual basis. The G8's main aims are to encourage cooperation in trading and financial issues, to develop the global economy, to strengthen democracy and peace, and to prevent international conflicts and try to find solutions.

In recent years G8 summits have been criticized for only representing the elitist interests of the industrialized world. The summits have also seen protests by anti-globalization groups. Riots and demonstrations, such as the violent protests in Italy in 2001, make headlines before and during summits. This has resulted in greater security and given the summit an increasingly closed-door image. In recent years the G8 has made attempts to fight diseases such as Aids and has created development programmes for the Third World. The environment has also been an important issue.

2 **recession** [rɪ'seʃn] a serious slowdown in economic activity · 4 **library** *here:* room(s) where books are stored · 5 **official** civil servant · 15 **summit** conference of national leaders · 35 **to rotate** *here:* to go from one country to the next · 36 **on an annual basis** every year · 45 **riot** fight between demonstrators and the police

Intercultural competence

Before you read

1 a) Which nationalities are represented in your neigbourhood?
b) Do people get on well there or are there any problems?

Test yourself

2 Flexibility and open-mindedness are key qualities if you want to find a job in the global world. Test yourself and find out whether you have these qualities, or not. Choose the most suitable answer to each question.

Quiz

A Can you imagine moving to a foreign country and working there?

1 Definitely not. I want to stay in my hometown with my friends and family.
2 Perhaps I would like that. But I would like to stay in Europe.
3 That would be great. I would like to live in different places all over the world.

B How good are you at languages?

1 I am not good at languages, so I just do what is required at school.
2 My English is okay but I don't have any other languages.
3 I am trying to improve my English. I am also quite fluent in a second language.

C Do you like food from different countries?

1 No, I prefer food which is typical of my culture.
2 I like pizzas, burgers and sometimes I try something new, but nothing too exotic.
3 Yes, of course. I'm interested in new tastes, spices and foods.

D What nationalities are your friends?

1 Mostly the same as I am.
2 I like the foreign students in my class but I have no close friends from other countries.
3 I have a lot of friends of different nationalities and we get on very well.

E Do you buy Fairtrade products?

1 No, they are too expensive.
2 Yes, I do, but only now and then. It depends on what is available.
3 I try to buy them as often as possible because I think that it is good to support fair trade.

F What do you do to protect the environment?

1 Not much. Nothing I can do will have an effect on the environment anyway.
2 I recycle waste, and I sometimes walk to school or use public transport.
3 I try to think of our environment and other people and countries. So I avoid wasting raw materials and try not to buy things that harm the environment.

G Where would you like to spend your holidays?

1 I would like to stay in my own country.
2 I am keen on travel but only in Western cultures like Europe and the US.
3 That's difficult to say. The world is full of interesting places.

3 Check whether you had mostly 1's, 2's or 3's and read the interpretation of your result below.

Key
Mostly 1's: You like to stick to the things you know well. That's not always a good idea. Try to be more flexible. It can make life more interesting if you try new things now and then.
Mostly 2's: You are on your way to having a global attitude. In some areas you still prefer people and things you know, in others you can be quite adventurous. Try to keep a balance without losing your interest in new things.
Mostly 3's: You seem to be an open-minded person who is eager to learn and to try out something new. That can be a very useful attitude at work or when making friends. Just don't forget that traditions are important, too.

Your opinion

4 Think of some things in your own life which are a product of globalization. Give examples.

Debating

5 Should countries keep up their traditions or try to grow together and adopt each other's cultural values? Discuss.

→ **Discussions**
See *skills file* on page 177.

Hotspot: Mind map

Work in small groups. Go back to the mind map about 'globalization' that you started at the beginning of the unit. Add new aspects to it based on what you have discussed in this unit. Complete the mind map and display it in your classroom.
Example:

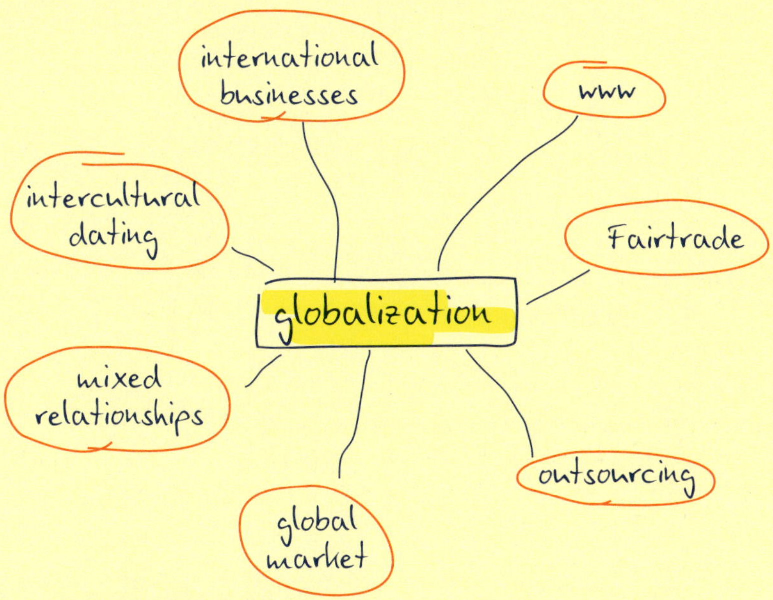

→ **Mind maps**
See *skills file* on page 186.

Skills files

Exam skills
Cartoons *155*
Comments *155*
Essays/Compositions *157*
Illustrations and photos *158*
Mediation *158*
Presentations *160*
Statistics *161*
Style analysis *162*
Summaries *164*
Translation *165*

Projects
Projects and group work *167*
Questionnaires and surveys *168*

Business communication
Agendas *169*
Formal and business letters *170*
Letters of application and CVs *173*
Interviews *174*
Mails *175*

Speaking
Discussions *177*
Phone calls *178*
Small talk *180*

Writing
Personal letters *181*
Reports *182*

Analysing visual materials
Adverts *183*
Film analysis *184*

Vocabulary
Collecting words *184*
Mind maps *186*
Surviving without a dictionary *187*
Using an English-English dictionary *187*
Dictionary page *188*

The following exam skills concentrate on the main points you should consider in an exam situation. An interactive description of the necessary skills, which also gives you extra practice, is given in *Exam Training: Englisch Abitur, Berufliche Gymnasien/Oberschulen mit bundeslandtypischen Abiturprüfungen* (ISBN: 978-3-12-801007-6).

Cartoons

Cartoons are funny but often critical. When looking at a cartoon the most important thing is to work out what point the cartoonist is making. Generally, the point is made by a combination of the illustration and the text. Thus, you should analyze and understand both parts.
The illustration often shows caricatures of well-known people or particular stereotypes, so you need to define the person or group of people illustrated.
The text can be in one or all of the following forms:
- A caption (a statement in quotation marks under the illustration). You need to work out who is speaking, as in the cartoon on page 28.
- A speech bubble or speech bubbles, as in the cartoon strip on page 60.
- Text that is integrated in the cartoon, e.g. on a sign or poster, as in cartoon a) and c) on page 22.

Useful phrases

» Describing the cartoon

The cartoon consists of an illustration of …
The illustration shows …
There is a caption under the cartoon, which says "…".
In the (first) speech bubble it says "…".
The text in the speech bubble is spoken by …
The figure is a stereotype/caricature of …
The drawing is detailed/clear/sketchy/abstract.

» Talking about the point

The cartoonist is making fun of …
The cartoonist is satirizing …
The cartoon is funny because of the misunderstanding between …

» Giving your opinion

I think/I don't think the cartoon is (very) funny because …
I get the joke/point. /I don't get the joke/point.
I think/I don't think the cartoon is easy to understand because …
I agree/I don't agree with the point the cartoonist is making because …

Comments

In a comment you are expected to give your opinion about a topic. Make sure you give your own opinion as well as including counter-arguments. In an exam situation in particular, you should prepare your comment carefully before you begin to write. Try to remember the following piece of advice:
"Tell 'em what you're gonna tell 'em; then tell 'em; then tell 'em what you've told 'em."

Preparing your comment

- Plan the time you have available for writing the comment: use approximately a quarter of your time for preparation, half of the time to write the comment, and the final quarter of your time to check it.
- Have a close look at the topic of your comment so that you really know what you are going to write about.
- Write down your initial opinion in one sentence.
- Collect as many facts and arguments (pros and cons!) as possible.
- Decide on the main arguments you want to include (3–5 points). Then try to think of one or two supporting arguments for each main argument.
- Put your facts or arguments into a logical order. For example, you could:
  - start with general ideas and then go on to talk about details;
  - put things into chronological order;
  - start with the arguments in favour and then give the counter-arguments;
  - follow each argument in favour with a counter-argument.
- Once you have written down your arguments check whether your opinion has changed and adjust your comment.

Writing your comment

In the **introductory paragraph** you should introduce your topic and catch the reader's interest. You could also state what your comment is going to be about in one or two sentences and/or ask a question which you will answer in your comment.

In the **main paragraphs** you should:
- start a new paragraph for each new idea;
- begin each paragraph with a main idea or argument and then follow it up with your supporting or counter-arguments;
- write simple sentences;
- arrange your sentences in a logical order;
- join your sentences using suitable connectives;
- use adjectives and adverbs to emphasize points;
- use examples where possible;
- make sure that the arguments supporting your opinion are more convincing than the counter-arguments.

> → **Connectives**
> See list on the back inside cover (IV).

In the **final paragraph**, the conclusion, you should:
- summarize what you have said in your comment;
- make a brief concluding statement expressing your opinion;
- include a quotation or anecdote, if you can;
- answer any questions you asked in the introduction.
- not introduce any new ideas!

Checking your comment

- Read your comment again after a break of one or two minutes. If possible, leave the room or think of something completely different.
- Make sure your comment really deals with the topic of the exercise, **and** it contains your opinion and reasons for it.
- Check that all of your sentences are complete and that they make sense.
- Check for grammar and spelling mistakes.

Essays/Compositions

An essay or composition is a clearly structured piece of writing which presents important points on a topic. An essay is generally written in the present tense.
In an expository essay you explain an idea or set of related facts.
In an argumentative essay you express your opinion and give arguments for and/or against a given topic.

Preparation

- Define the topic clearly.
- Brainstorm ideas and collect them in a mind map, diagram or table.
- Formulate your opinion on the topic.

→ **Mind maps**
See *skills file* on page 186.

Arranging your material

- Decide on the most important points (maximum 5 items).
- For each main argument try to think of two supporting arguments.
- Put your points in a logical order. E.g.
  - general ideas followed by details.
  - chronological order.
  - all of the arguments in favour first followed by all of the counter-arguments.
  - each argument in favour followed by a counter-argument.

Writing your essay

The introductory paragraph

- Introduce your topic and catch the reader's interest, e.g. with a relevant quotation, a provocative statement or a relevant (humorous) personal experience.
- Say what your essay is going to be about in one or two sentences.
- Ask a question or questions which you will answer in your essay.
- Outline the problem/topic now and in the past.

The main paragraphs

- Start a new paragraph for each new idea.
- Begin each paragraph with a main idea or argument. Follow it up with your supporting or counter-arguments.
- Write simple sentences and arrange them in a logical order.
- Join sentences using suitable connectives.
- Use adverbs to emphasize points.
- Use examples where possible.

→ **Connectives**
See list on the back inside cover (IV).

The conclusion

- Do not introduce new ideas!
- Make a brief concluding statement summarizing what you have said in your essay.
- Include a quotation or anecdote if you can.

Checking your essay

- Check that all your sentences are complete and that they make sense.
- Check your essay for grammar, spelling and punctuation mistakes.
- Write out the final version of your essay.

Illustrations and photos

Visual materials can usually be divided up into the following categories: photo, print, transparency, slide, painting, drawing, sketch, illustration, image, collage, electronic image, snapshot, skyline, panorama, close-up, action photo or still (from a film).
When describing a photo or illustration you should describe the type of picture and its content before interpreting it. The aspects you could mention are given in **bold print** below.

Useful phrases

» Saying what a picture is of
This is a photo/an illustration of ...
This photo was taken in ...
The illustration shows ...
In this illustration/photo you can see (that) ...

» Saying where things are in a picture
on the right-hand/left-hand side of the picture • in the centre • in the foreground • in the background • at the top • at the bottom • in the upper right-hand corner • in the lower left-hand corner

» Adjectives of style & colour
colour • black & white • bright/dull • hand-painted/hand-drawn/drawn by hand • clear/in focus • blurred/not in focus/out of focus • lifelike • to scale/not to scale • posed/staged

» Describing the impression a picture makes
The person in the picture looks ... (+ adjective, e.g. confused)
The photo/illustration supports the point made in the text that ...
The photo/illustration gives you the impression that ...
The impression I get from this photo is that ...
The illustration makes me feel ... (+ adjective, e.g. worried).
The colours the artist has chosen make me feel ... (+ adjective, e.g. happy, sad, worried)
In my opinion the illustration would be better, if ... (+ simple past, e.g. if it was more life-like)

Mediation

FAQs is an acronym for 'Frequently Asked Questions'. These may arise when a topic is rather new, which is certainly true of mediation. If you have not frequently asked yourself the following questions, you may already be an expert!

FAQs about mediation

Q: What does 'mediation' mean?
A: It normally means communicating the main points of a text, written in one language, in another language. For example, the text may be in English and you have to formulate the main points in German, or the text may be in German and the text you produce should be in English.
Q: What is mediation not?
A: It is definitely not a word-for-word translation. Instead, it is about getting a message across in a different language.
Q: What is the difference between 'mediation' and 'translation'?
A: The example at the top of page 159 should make this clear.

Example (English-German mediation):

Original text	Translation	Mediation text
An analysis of census data in the US has overturned long-held assumptions that women were still lagging behind men in wages. (*The Independent*, August 4, 2007)	Eine Analyse statistischer Daten in den USA hat die langjährigen Vermutungen, dass die Löhne von Frauen immer noch hinter denen der Männer zurückbleiben, widerlegt.	In den USA verdienen Frauen doch nicht weniger als Männer.

As you can see, the complex structures in the original text have been reduced to the key message in the mediation text.

Q: How do I know what the main points of the text are?

A: The task description will tell you who the mediation is for and what the person wants to know. These two points are the basis for your decision about how to write the mediation text and which points of the original text to include in your version. Look at the following examples:
Example – English original and German mediation text:
Imagine your brother, who is not good at English, asks you what the text XYZ is about.
Note: You should isolate the main ideas in the text and express them in German.
Example – German original and English mediation text:
Imagine you are an intern in a German company. Your boss asks you to write down the main ideas of a German text in English which he needs for a presentation abroad.
Note: Isolate the main ideas in the text and express them in English.
In your exam, you will not just have to refer to all of the main ideas in the text in general, instead you will have to select the ideas indicated in the task description.

Q: How do I know how many points I have to come up with in my mediation?

A: Again, you have to decide this based on the task description. However, you should practice separating the relevant points from the irrelevant ones.

Q: Do I have to translate the heading of the original text?

A: No, you don't. It is fine to mention the topic in the introduction to your mediation text and start without a heading.

Q: Is there a word limit for the mediation text?

A: No, there isn't. But it will be much shorter than the original.

Q: Am I allowed to use a bilingual dictionary?

A: No, you aren't, sorry about that.

Q: How can I use a monolingual dictionary for a mediation exercise?

A: English-German mediation: The dictionary is useful to find out the meaning of words you do not know or remember.
German-English mediation: The dictionary contains sample sentences which can help you to express yourself correctly.
Note: A dictionary is more than just a collection of words. It usually includes illustrations and tables, CVs, sample letters and many more things which can be very useful. Get to know your dictionary!

Q: Can I present my mediation text in a table or just give the key words?

A: As a rule, no, you can't. The task description will tell you what type of text is expected. Use complete sentences.

Q: How do I proceed to do a mediation exercise?

A: – Read the task description carefully to understand what you are supposed to do.
- Read the text and underline the words you need to look up in the dictionary.
- Read the text again and mark the most important points based on the task description. You can also write key words in the margin. Pay attention to words such as 'but', 'however', and other signals which indicate a new point. You do not normally need to include examples in your mediation text as these usually only illustrate the main points in the original text.
- Plan the structure of your mediation text: Think of a good introduction to your text. Which points will you start with? Do you want to have a conclusion? Note: Your mediation does not need to have the same structure as the original text.

Q: How can I practice mediation?

A: Any text will do, although in your exam the mediation text will have something to do with the 'world of work'.

Presentations

Preparation

- Brainstorm to find ideas on the topic and make a mind map.
- Find information from relevant sources (library, school books, the internet, newspapers, etc.)
- Choose which main points you want to talk about.
- Make a set of prompt cards in English, to help you during your talk (cf. card 2 below).
- Arrange your prompt cards in a logical order. You could:
  - start with the most important point and move to the least important (or vice versa).
  - present points chronologically.
  - present points in favour and then all those against.
- Make prompt cards for your introduction (see card 1) and for your conclusion (see card 6).

Mind maps
See *skills file* on page 186.

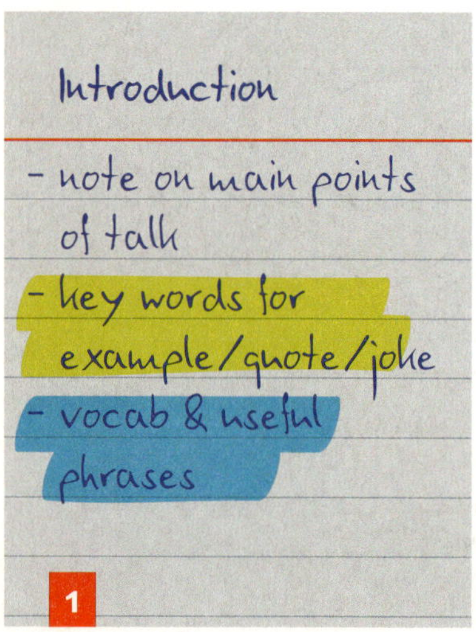

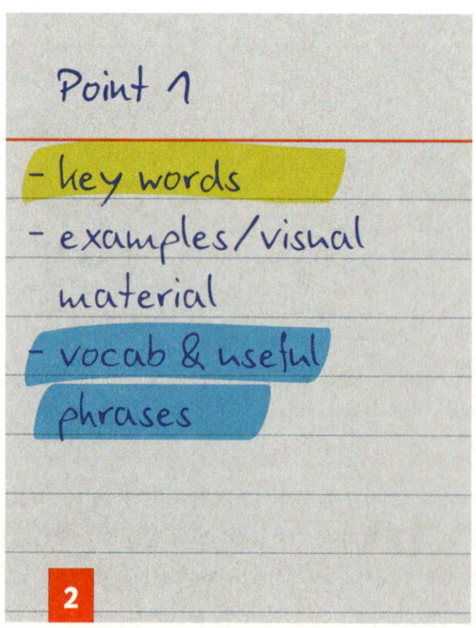

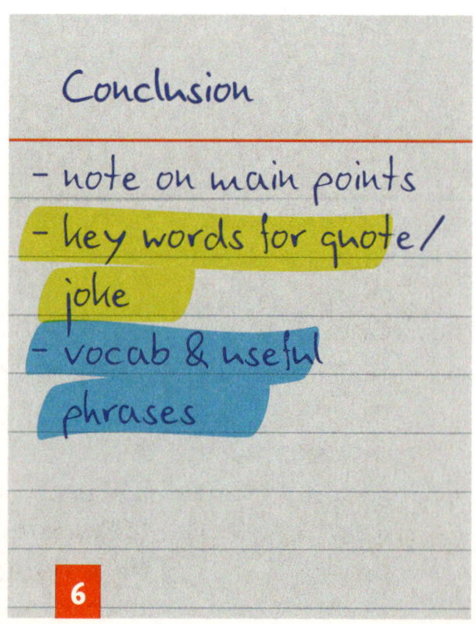

Giving a talk or presentation

- Speak slowly and clearly and use short, clear sentences.
- Vary your voice so that you don't sound boring. For example, emphasize important points by speaking a little more loudly.
- Look at your audience. Don't look at your prompt cards all the time.
- Try not to make distracting movements such as waving your hands.
- Smile! (But don't laugh nervously!)
- Start by introducing yourself (if necessary) and your topic. Finish by thanking your audience for listening. Ask if anyone has any questions.

Useful phrases

» Starting your talk

Good morning/afternoon, my name is …
Today I'm going to talk about …
The subject of my talk today is …
Can everyone hear me alright?
Can everyone see the board/screen/etc.?

» Structuring your talk

I'd like to begin by (-ing form of the verb)
Let me start by saying a few words about …
Let me give you an example.
As you can see on the chart/graph/cartoon/etc. …

» Finishing your talk

I'd like to finish/conclude by (-ing form of the verb)
Let me finish by (-ing form of the verb)
Finally …
Thank you very much for your attention.
I hope you've all enjoyed my talk.
I'd be happy to answer any questions.

Statistics

Statistics give us detailed information in the form of figures. So, instead of describing current trends (using the present progressive) in words, e.g. "Unemployment is rising again", we could say: "The unemployment rate was 10% and now it stands at 12%."
Statistics may be integrated in a text or presented in the form of graphs or tables. Here are some ideas how to describe figures, statistics and trends.

Describing figures

- Decimals: In English decimals come after the 'point' (not 'comma').
  Example:
  - 2.5 = two point five
  - 3.06 = three point oh six
  - 0.53 = (nought) point five three or (zero) point five three
- Money: £5.20 = five pounds twenty (pence)
  - €98.99 = ninety-eight euros ninety-nine (cents)
  - $23,454 = twenty-three thousand, four hundred and fifty-four dollars

Useful phrases

» Describing statistics

the figures for the last year/the last month • the latest figures • the total number of … • a significant/insignificant number of … • a high/small percentage of … • the statistics • a majority/minority of …

Useful phrases (continued)

» Increases

to rise • to increase by • growth • an increase (in the number of ...)

» Decreases

to decrease • to drop • to decline • a decrease • a decline • a drop (in the number of ...)

» Adjectives and adverbs

sharp(ly) • slow(ly) • steady/steadily • continuing/continual(ly) • gradual(ly) • significant(ly) • insignificant(ly) • negligible/negligibly • large • high • small • dramatic(ally)

Examples: Sales figures have risen sharply over the last two years.
There has been a steady decline in the sales of mobile phones.
Growth is expected to be negligible.

» Qualifiers

a total of • over • under • nearly • more/less than • between • the same number as • the same amount of • from over/under ... to just over/under • half • a third • two thirds • a quarter • (25) per cent • twice/three times as many • on average • roughly • exactly • precisely

Types of graphs

A graph

A pie chart

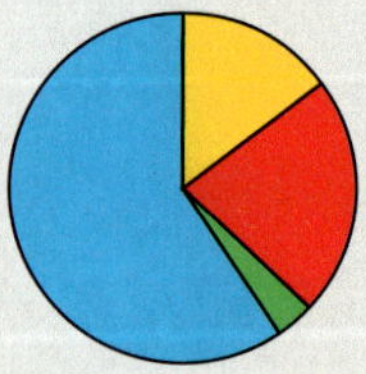

A bar chart

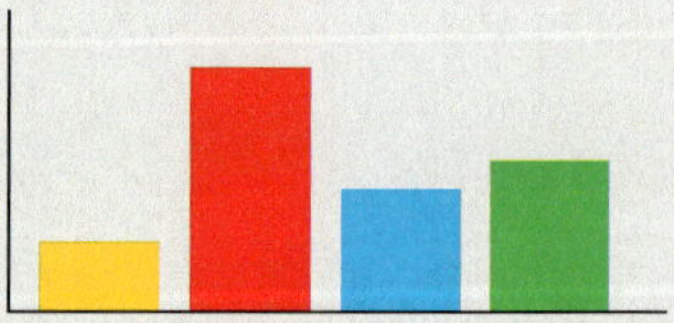

Useful phrases

» Describing graphs and tables

The figures in the table show that ...
As you can see from the graph ...
The dotted line on the graph represents...
The pie chart compares ...
The figures prove that...
The statistics suggest that ...
This table gives information about ...
The diagram makes it clear that ...

Style analysis

The way a writer uses words, phrases, structure and rhetorical devices defines the style of a text. Consider the points below and on p. 163 when you analyse style. Always support your points with quotes, examples, etc. from the text. You will find the *italicized words* in the glossary on pp. 201–203.

Text form

Mention the *text form* involved, e.g. *poem*, *short story*, *play*, *novel*, a factual article, letter, *essay* or speech.

→ **Essays/Compositions**
See *skills file* on page 157.

Text type

Describe the *text type*. Identify the writer's intention in writing the text: is it argumentative, instructive, narrative, descriptive or expository? One type is usually dominant in a text although more than one type may be present.

Text structure

Describe the structure of the text.
- Novels: the structure is usually determined by the sequence of the chapters.
- *Dramas* (plays) are composed of acts and scenes.
- Poems are made up of *stanzas*.
- Essays, *comments* and articles are composed of a series of paragraphs (sometimes divided by subheadings).

Describe the presentation and development of the *theme*, events, issues and ideas, etc. Most texts contain a progression of ideas that help the reader to understand the point(s) the writer wants to make.
- Novels, short stories, dramas: The progression of ideas is determined by the *plot*.
- Essays, factual articles, speeches: The main point is usually presented in the first (or sometimes the last) paragraph, and the other paragraphs support and develop this point with various techniques.
- Poems contain descriptions, and *figurative language* which portray ideas, tell stories and/or create emotions.

Say whether you think the text structure has been successful.
- Are important ideas presented clearly and effectively? Why, or why not?
- What structural changes would you suggest?

Register

Register refers to a writer's language choice in a situation. It indicates the type of audience he or she wants to reach, and the relationship that he or she intends to establish with them.
- *Formal language* and complex sentence structure keep this relationship more academic and distant.
- *Informal language* and simpler sentence structures often establish a closer relationship.

When analysing register, consider the vocabulary, the sentence structure and the tone.
- **Vocabulary**
  - Is the writer's vocabulary formal or informal?
  - Is the vocabulary descriptive and concrete, or abstract and theoretical?
  - Are a lot of the terms specific to a certain field?
  - Does the vocabulary create a certain *atmosphere*?
  - Is the choice of vocabulary appropriate, or not?
- **Sentence structure**
  - Are most of the sentences simple and short, as with most dialogues, or are they mainly complex?
  - What grammatical elements do you notice, e.g. participles, gerunds, infinitives? Why do you think the writer uses these elements?
- **Tone**
  - Describe the tone, or the writer's attitude toward the subject, the characters and the readers of the text.
  - How does the tone affect your understanding of the text and your own attitude toward it?

Rhetorical devices

Rhetorical devices (often referred to as 'literary devices' or 'stylistic devices') involve the use of language in a non-literal sense or in an unusual way. You should explain the function of the rhetorical devices in the text and say what effect they have on you.
Examples: *alliteration, assonance, hyperbole, irony, simile, metaphor, personification, rhetorical questions, understatement.*
These devices can organize, emphasize, explain and vary the expression of ideas within a text. Other examples, that are commonly used in talks and in written texts, are shown below with their functions.

Rhetorical devices	Functions
repetition of key words and ideas	emphasize
quotations and proverbs	support a statement
rhetorical questions	structure the text, keep listeners'/ readers' attention
personal pronouns (we/our/you)	make the audience feel personally involved

Summaries

A summary is a short text in which you restate the main points of another text in your own words. A summary is almost always written in the present tense.

Summarize a non-fictional text

- Read the original text at least twice.
- In your own words, make a note of the main arguments or points, e.g. list the key words or write one sentence to go with each paragraph.
- Rewrite some or all of your sentences to say what the writer's intention was.
- Link sentences with connectives.

→ **Connectives**
See list on the back inside cover (IV).

Useful phrases

» Summarize a non-fictional text

The author/writer points out that … • emphasizes … • suggests that … • describes (how) … • concludes by saying that …

Summarize a fictional text

- Briefly describe the characters and the setting.
- Briefly describe what happens and how the events are connected.
- Link your sentences with connectives.
- Do not…
  - copy any phrases or sentences from the text.
  - use statistics, numbers, figures, details or quotations from the text.
  - give your personal opinion.
  - produce a summary that is more than a third of the length of the original.

→ **Connectives**
See list on the back inside cover (IV).

Useful phrases

» Summarize a fictional text

The scene/story/extract takes place in (the present/past/future ...)
The scene/story/extract ... is set in ...
The main character is ...
There are two/three/etc. main characters.

Translation

Preparation

- Always read the whole text at least twice.
- Make a note of the main points in German.

First version

- Don't translate word for word, but do keep as close to the original as possible.
- Write words and phrases you can't translate in English.
- In an exam you may not have time to write a second or third version, so make sure your first version is legible and easy to correct.

Second version

- Read through your first version and try to translate any remaining English words from the context. If you can't, look them up in a dictionary. As time is limited in an exam, you shouldn't look up more than ten words.
- Check your translation word for word against the English text and make sure you haven't left anything out. Make corrections as necessary.

Final version

- Reread your text and decide if it sounds German. If it doesn't, you haven't translated properly. Think about what you are trying to say and how you would say it in German. Make corrections.

Tips and tricks

- Don't improve texts when you translate. For example, if one verb is used repeatedly in the text use one verb in your translation, even if you think another would sound better.
- When translating long sentences, define the main clause and translate this first, then translate the other clauses in their order of importance.
- Try to keep to the same number of sentences in the text and in your translation. (Don't split sentences up or join them in your translation, unless it is really necessary.)
- Be prepared for your German text to be longer than the English original: English sentences are often shorter than German ones.
- Be careful with false friends (= words in English that look like German words but they have a different meaning). Here are some examples.

False friends	Incorrect translation	Correct translation
actual	≠ aktuell	eigentlich
after all	≠ nach allem	doch, zum guten Schluss
brave	≠ brav	mutig

→

False friends	Incorrect translation	Correct translation
briefcase	≠ Brieftasche	Aktentasche
critic	≠ Kritik	Kritiker
gift	≠ Gift	Geschenk
gymnasium	≠ Gymnasium	Turnhalle
however	≠ wie auch immer	jedoch
to overhear	≠ überhören	zufällig mitbekommen
physician	≠ Physiker	Arzt
rent	≠ Rente	Miete
rubber hose	≠ Gummihose	Gartenschlauch
sensible	≠ sensibel	vernünftig

Certain structures in English are difficult to translate. Here are some useful tips for when you meet these structures in a text.

Translation problems	Solutions
Present perfect sentences with 'since'/'for' Example: I have had my car for 2 years now.	Use the present tense in German. Example: Ich habe mein Auto jetzt seit zwei Jahren.
Constructions using past participles and -ing forms Example 1: I thanked them for the lovely weekend spent with them. Example 2: A group of American students visiting our town were at college today.	Try using a relative clause. Example 1: Ich dankte ihnen für das schöne Wochenende, das ich mit ihnen verbracht hatte. Example 2: Eine Gruppe amerikanischer Studentinnen, die unsere Stadt besuchen, waren heute in der Schule.
'It' when it does not mean 'es'. Example: I couldn't get a seat on the train: it was totally crowded.	Check what 'it' refers to. Example: Ich konnte im Zug keinen Platz kriegen: er war total überfüllt.
'You' and 'they' Example: In Britain you often see double decker buses.	Try using the German 'man'. Example: In Großbritannien sieht man oft Doppeldeckerbusse.
'Do' or 'did' in positive sentences when used to emphasize the verb Example: I *did* do my homework!	You usually use an adverb. Example: Ich habe sehr wohl meine Hausaufgaben gemacht!
'There is/are' and 'there was/were' Example 1: There's so much to do and see in New York! Example 2: There was nothing to eat.	Use 'es gibt' or 'es gab'. Example 1: Es gibt so viel zu tun und zu sehen in New York! Example 2: Es gab nichts zu essen.
an adjective + noun combination Example: congressional elections (adjective + noun)	Use one noun in German. Example: Kongresswahlen (compound noun)

→

Translation problems	Solutions
'with + -ing form' Example 1: Roads are becoming busier and busier with more and more people driving cars. Example 2: With winter approaching, they decided to leave.	Use a separate clause and begin with a conjunction (weil, da, wo, wenn, wobei, etc.). Example 1: Die Straßen werden immer voller, weil immer mehr Leute Auto fahren. Example 2: Jetzt, wo der Winter sich näherte, beschlossen sie zu gehen.
Passive sentences Example: The stolen money was found in a phone box.	Try using 'man'. Example: Man hat das gestohlene Geld in einer Telefonzelle gefunden.
Proper names Examples: Henry VIII • Cologne • Prince Charles	Only translate when there is a real German equivalent. Examples: Heinrich der VIII. • Köln • Prince Charles
Miles, pounds, etc. Example: She runs 5 miles every day.	Do not convert them. Example: Sie läuft jeden Tag 5 Meilen.

Projects and group work

The type of project you may do can vary from a "hotspot" where you prepare and carry out a survey (cf. page 19) or design the front page of a newspaper cf. page 139, task b), to a group role play of a radio programme (cf. page 11, task 13). How you go about doing a project will depend on the assignment. These tips are very general.

Finding information

The first place you will probably look for information is the internet. Some good sources are the website addresses of search engines, schools and colleges, youth organizations, political parties, newspapers, magazines, and government agencies in America and the UK.
However, you could also try the following information sources:
- your local library.
- the nearest university or college library.
- your twin-town association (if your area has one).
- travel agencies and tourist information bureaus which can give you brochures and leaflets.

Doing a project

- Read the information you are given about the assignment carefully.
- In your groups, brainstorm to find ideas about:
  - what you already know about the topic.
  - which aspects you want to concentrate on.
  - where you can find information.
- If necessary, decide which points are more important (concentrate on these) and which are less important (and can possibly be left out).
- Decide which tasks each member of the group is going to do.
- If not specified in the assignment, decide how you want to present your material. You can produce: a talk using visual aids, a video, a CD, a leaflet, a brochure, a file of written information, a poster or wall chart, a written report or a website.
- Keep a record of where you found material, statistics, extracts, etc.

→ **Presentations**
See *skills file* on page 160.
Reports
See *skills file* on page 182.

Questionnaires and surveys

Questionnaires and surveys are a good way of getting an overview of how people, e.g. in your class or college, feel about a particular topic. They are a very useful basis for a discussion in class. It is important to have a clear idea of the kind of information you hope to get from your survey before you start.

Preparation

- Write one or two sentences describing your topic and explaining why you are doing the survey. You can include these sentences at the start of your questionnaire so that the interviewees (= participants or people you ask) have a clear idea of what the survey is about.
- Briefly state what you expect the results of your survey to be – or give alternatives (see below).

Useful phrases

» Outlining expectations

I think the survey will show/prove that ...
The survey might prove that ...
On the other hand, it might show that ...

- Decide how many people you want to interview and which social groups they should belong to. For example, is the age of participants important? Should they be male or female? Should they have a certain job or hobby?

Making the questionnaire

The success of a survey depends largely on how good your questions are. If possible, ask an independent person to answer your questions before you carry out the survey to make sure your questions are clear.

- Decide what type of questions you want to ask. Your questions need not all be of the same type, but it is best not to include too many different types. The most common types are described below.

Multiple choice questions: The interviewee chooses from given answers. Example: Which of the following do you own? ☐ a) a TV ☐ c) an mp3 player ☐ b) a DVD player ☐ d) a CD player	**Graded questions:** The interviewee chooses to what extent they agree/disagree with, like/don't like, etc. something. Example: How often do you eat fruit or vegetables on average per day? ☐ a) never ☐ b) less than three times ☐ c) more than three times
Yes/No questions: Questions that can be answered 'Yes' or 'No'. Example: Do you exercise more than three times a week? ☐ yes ☐ no	**Open-ended questions:** Interviewees must give their own answer. The questions usually begin with a question word: who, what, when, where, why or how. Example: How could the recycling system in your area be improved?

- Keep the aim of your survey in mind when you are formulating questions.
- Word your questions clearly and concisely. Use formal language.
- Don't ask too many questions (between 10 and 15 is usually enough).
- Put your questions in a logical order.
  - Group questions relating to particular aspects together.
  - Start with simpler, more general questions and then go on to more detailed questions.
  - Your last question can be an open-ended question (see page 168).

Carrying out the survey

- Don't try to make people take part in the survey or answer certain questions if they don't want to.
- Explain why you are doing the survey, who you will be presenting the results to and in what form.
- It is usually best to conduct anonymous surveys: that is, without keeping a record of the names of the people you interview. However, in order to evaluate the results it can be important to make a note of details, such as age and sex. If you need this information, explain why to the interviewee.
- Explain exactly what interviewees are expected to do. Be prepared to give more details or explain what certain questions mean.
- If you want to make an audio or visual recording of the interview, ask participants for their permission.
- Smile and always be polite!

Agendas

An agenda is a list of points to be discussed in a meeting. The agenda is usually sent out in advance so that participants have time to prepare.

Preparation

Start with the title, date, time and venue (place) of the meeting, followed by a list of the points to be discussed.
- The first points are often: apologies for absence and matters arising from the last meeting.
- The last points are often: A.O.B. (any other business), i.e. any other topics not included in the agenda and the date of the next meeting.

Example:

Management Meeting

Date: 28 August 20... **Time:** 2.00 pm – 3.00 pm
Venue: Conference Room, Block B

AGENDA
1 Matters arising from last meeting
2 Spring collection
3 Price review
4 Customer complaints
5 Problems with supplier
6 A.O.B.

Formal and business letters

A formal letter can be a letter of application, a reservation, a request for information, etc. Business letters are basically formal letters written in a business context, i.e. from one company to another. However, mails are increasingly taking over from business letters.
There are different ways of layouting formal and business letters. The example below is in 'block form', which is probably the best to use because it is accepted everywhere.

→ **Letters of application**
See *skills file* on page 173.
Mails
See *skills file* on page 175.

Example:

Letterhead	**GiLa's Diners** 321 Venture Blvd. Cleveland, 123 Ohio Tel. +44(0)189 9879 (Fax. 9889) www.gilasdiner.com
Date	14 September 20…
Reference initials	Our ref. AR/PR
Address of recipient	Astra Inc. Human Resources Department 1000 Third Avenue Cleveland, 123 Ohio
Attention line	Attention: Dr Dick Branson, Human Resources Manager
Salutation (cf. p.171)	Dear Mr Branson,
Subject line	**Invitation to launch of GiLa's Executive Catering Service**
1st paragraph: Introduction	Are your employees fit for work? Or do they just grab a quick snack in their lunch break? We know you care about the health of your staff, and we have the perfect solution.
2nd paragraph: The message	We are proud to announce the launch of GiLa's Executive Catering Service, a 24-hour delivery service with a selection of tasty meals and snacks at fair prices.
3rd and 4th paragraph: Future action	To celebrate our launch we would like to invite you to a reception at our headquarters in Cleveland on Friday, October 20th. at 4pm. You will have the opportunity to try some delicious meals from our exciting menu. If you wish to attend the launch, please send me an acceptance mail at a.roberts@gilasdiner.us. Details about GiLa's Executive Catering Service together with our menu and price list are also enclosed.
Last paragraph: Friendly reference to future contact	We hope to see you at our launch and would be pleased to serve you and your staff in the future.
Complimentary close (cf. page 171)	Sincerely yours
Signature	Ashley Roberts
Name and position of sender	Ashley Roberts (Ms) Public Relations Director
Enc. = Enclosures (items sent with a letter)	Enc.

Salutations and complimentary closes

The salutation you use to address the person you are writing to depends on whether you know their name, sex, etc.
The complimentary close you use before signing off usually depends on the salutation, but variations are possible. Follow the guidelines below.
Note: Nowadays the use of 'Yours faithfully' and 'Yours sincerely' is not always divided up as strictly as given below.
Americans usually close formal letters with: 'Sincerely yours' or 'Yours truly'.

Salutation	Complimentary close	When used
Dear Sir or Madam, Dear Sirs	Yours faithfully/sincerely (faithfully is seldom used nowadays)	*(UK)* to a company and when you don't know a person's name or sex
Dear Mr Brown,	Yours sincerely	*(UK)* to a man, whose name you know
Dear Ms Brown,	Yours sincerely	*(UK)* to a woman, whose name you know but whose marital status is not known
Dear Jenny	Best wishes/Yours	to a person you know well
(Ladies and) Gentlemen:	Sincerely/Sincerely yours	*(US)* to a company and when you don't know a person's name or sex
Dear Mr Brown:	Yours truly/Sincerely yours	*(US)* to a man whose name you know
Dear Arnold:	Regards	*(US)* to a person you know well

Useful phrases

» Explaining the purpose of the letter

We are writing/I am writing
… in connection with …
… with reference/regard to …
… to advise you of …
… to confirm …
… to let you know …
… to tell you that …
… to ask/enquire (whether) …

» Stating a reference

Thank you for your mail of July 1st.
Many thanks for your letter dated 26th July.
We refer to your order for 2000 ABC Widgets.
I have received your enquiry regarding our new widgets.
Further to our telephone conversation today, …
With reference to your mail of June 5th, …
With regard to your enquiry of June 5th about …

» Giving good news

I am delighted to tell you that …
You will be pleased to hear that …

» Giving bad news

We regret to inform you that …
I am afraid that …
We are sorry to have to tell you that …

» Making a request

Please …
Please could you … ?
Could you possibly…?
We would be grateful if you could/would …
We would be much obliged if you could …
I would appreciate it if you could …

» Offering help

If you wish, we would be happy to …
Would you like us to … ?

→

Useful phrases

» Giving information

We wish to advise you that …
We are pleased to inform you that …

» Enclosing documents

I am enclosing …
Please find enclosed …
Please find attached … (= mail attachment/papers fixed to the letter with a paper clip/etc.)

» Thanking

Thank you for sending me …
Many thanks for …
I am grateful to you for …
I am much obliged to you for sending me … *(formal)*

» Apologizing

I am sorry about the delay in replying.
We were (very/extremely/most) sorry to hear about the problem.
We regret that this problem has happened.
We apologize for any inconvenience caused.

» Setting deadlines/Insisting/ Threatening

Please ensure that the goods reach us by (+ deadline).
We must insist on payment of the sum by (+ deadline) at the latest.
If the goods do not reach us by (+ deadline), we will … (+ threat).

» Assuring

Please rest assured that we will do our utmost to help you.
We assure you that we will do our best to put the matter right.
We promise to look into the matter immediately.
You can count on us to ensure smooth delivery in future.

» Making concessions

We agree to reduce the price by (percentage/sum of money).
We are happy to grant you a discount of 3% on the goods.
We will let you have the goods at a reduced price of …

» Closing remarks

If you have any questions, please do not hesitate to call me/us on (tel. no.).
Should you have any questions, feel free to contact me/us.
If you require further information, please do get in touch/ask.
Should you require further details, please contact us again.
If we can help in any way we would be happy to be of assistance.

» Referring to future contact

I look forward to hearing from you soon/meeting you next week/ seeing you on the 29th.
I am looking forward to receiving your proposal/order.
I hope to receive your comments in due course.

Letters of application and CVs

A letter of application is a specific type of formal letter and should follow the guidelines for this type of letter. The letter should be accompanied by your CV and its main aims are to demonstrate your interest in a vacancy and to present you, your qualifications and skills in the best possible light to potential employers.

Formal and business letters
See *skills file* on page 170.

Example:

Writer's address	Stefan Wollinger Vinckestr. 1 70183 Stuttgart Germany Tel/Fax: 0711 768232 Mail: s.wollinger@mail.com
Addressee	Ms Jane Taylor Human Resource Manager 11270 White Blvd. Los Angeles CA 91430 USA
Date	January 11, 20…
Salutation (cf. page 171)	Dear Ms Taylor
Subject line	**Your advertisement on www.jobs4U.com**
	With reference to your advertisement on www.jobs4U.com, I would like to apply for the position of bilingual buying assistant.
Main part of letter: State your reasons for writing	I am particularly interested in this job as I would very much like to gain work experience abroad. As well as speaking fluent English and Spanish, I have a working knowledge of French. My mother tongue is of course German. I can supply references from former employers if you wish. I enclose my curriculum vitae. Please do not hesitate to contact me if you should require further information.
Complimentary close	Yours sincerely
Signature	Stefan Wollinger Stefan Wollinger
Enc. = Enclosures (items sent with a letter)	Enc.

CV is short for 'Curriculum Vitae'. There are no rules about how to write a CV in English. Use the following 'Do's and Don'ts' and the model CV as a guide.

Do's and Don'ts

- Do include skills and interests which are relevant to the job, if possible.
- Do give the English equivalents of German terms, where possible.
- Don't write more than one page.
- Don't include a photo, unless asked to.
- Don't use handwriting for your CV.
- Don't sign your name at the end.

Example:

Curriculum Vitae

Name:	Ute Braun
Address:	Vinckestr. 1, 70183 Stuttgart, Germany
Telephone:	0711/234567
Mail:	u.braun@e-mail.de
Date of birth:	6. 5. 1988
Nationality:	German
Schools attended:	2004–2006: Language college, Stuttgart 1997–2004: Pfeiffer Realschule (Comprehensive)
Qualifications:	Diploma course as a bilingual secretary (English, Spanish)
Work experience:	July 2005 – September 2005: kitchen work at McDougall's July 2004 – September 2004: office assistant in the export department of Bosch
Skills, Interests and Experience:	fluent English and Spanish, a working knowledge of French; good computer skills (Word, Excel); a clean driving license; tennis and member of the local repertory company (latest role: the Nurse in *Romeo and Juliet*)

Interviews

If a company finds your letter of application and CV interesting, their human resource department may invite you for an interview. For the interviewee, the interview process starts beforehand with good preparation.

Preparation

- Find out about the business or institution where you will have your interview.
- Think of questions that you might be asked, and come up with suitable answers.
- Have a friend ask you the questions (plus some surprise ones) and give you a critique of how you have answered them.
- Think of questions to ask the interviewer about the business or institution. You want to show that you already know something about them.
- Dress nicely and arrive early so that you can collect your thoughts before the interview.

During the interview

- Smile and maintain eye contact with your interviewer (although it isn't a good idea to stare).
- The interviewer knows that you are nervous, so he or she might try to lighten the atmosphere with small talk. Be prepared to chat with him or her.
- Speak clearly and not too quickly! It is perfectly alright to pause for a moment and think about what you want to say.
- If necessary, ask the interviewer to repeat or explain a question. This also gives you more time to think!
- Do not answer questions with a *yes, no, or I don't know.* However, keep answers clear and concise. This is your chance to convince the interviewer that you are the right person for the job!
- If possible, ask the question(s) about the business or institution that you thought of.
- Thank your interviewer at the end.

→ **Small talk**
See *skills file* on page 180.

After the interview

- After a short time, send a short, follow-up mail thanking your interviewer and expressing interest in the position again. If you haven't been told when the decision will be made, ask politely when you can expect a reply.
- If you don't get the job, don't worry! Think of what you can do better next time, and work on these points. As with any other skill, the more interviews you do, the better you will get!

→ **Mails**
See *skills file* on page 175.

Mails

Mails have largely replaced traditional letters, both in business and in private correspondence, as they enable us to communicate in real time. However, whether you write a mail or a letter you should remember to follow the rules for these types of communication.

→ **Formal and business letters**
See *skills file* on page 170.
Personal letters
See *skills file* on page 181.

FAQs about mails

Q: How do I spell 'e-mail/email' correctly?

A: According to current dictionary entries, 'email' is now the most common form for both the verb and the noun. In spoken English, 'to mail' and a 'mail' have become common.

Q: What should I consider when creating my email address?

A: The mail address you use to communicate with your friends can be creative and funny, but you should also have a serious address. Why? Imagine you apply online for an internship or a job. What will a human resource manager think when he/she gets a mail from wieobercool@...? These mails also risk being treated as spam.

Q: Do I have to use capital letters in mails?

A: Yes, absolutely. The rules for punctuation, spelling and style are valid for all written communication. Not applying these rules is a sign of carelessness, ignorance and laziness – all of which are inappropriate in business communication.
Structure your mail by using short paragraphs and remember to fill in the subject line. All of these things make your mails clearer and easier to read.

Q: How do I read out my mail address?

A: There are some symbols that you should know.
m.com = m/dot/com
m_m = m/underscore/m
@ = at
m-m = m/hyphen/m (Don't say 'minus'!)
Note: *(German) Kein Leerzeichen* = *(English)* 'no space'

Q: May I use abbreviations?

A: There are many useful and widely accepted abbreviations you may use:
Example: FYI = for your information; as an introduction to the subject line
e.g. = for example
i.e. = that is
In business communication you should avoid the abbreviations that are acceptable in text messages.
Example: asap = as soon as possible
BTW = by the way
got ur msg = got your message.
Do not use emoticons e.g. ;-) in formal business communication.

Q: What is the difference between business letters and business mails?

A: Mails, of course, are usually shorter, but there are no big differences. In business communication, mails are as formal as business letters when dealing with people you do not know.
Start and close your business mail as you would a business letter, e.g. "Dear Mr/Mrs/Ms" … "Yours sincerely". In less formal mails you may use "Hello" to start. "Best regards" (alternatively: "Best wishes" or "Regards") is a less formal way of closing business letters and mails alike.
With regard to language and style, make sure you learn the "Useful phrases" for business correspondence on pp. 171–172 to be on the safe side. You will also find useful lists on the internet.

Q: Do I have to use commas after the salutation and the complimentary close?

A: There is no need to do so. Commas are often used in American correspondence. If you do use commas, make sure to do so after both the salutation and complimentary close.
Note: The first letter of the body of a letter or a mail is always capitalized, whether you use a comma after the salutation, or not.

Q: How can I make my mail sound polite?

A: Using the standard letter phrases and the words "please" and "thank you (for)" are the best way to sound polite. You should also keep sentences short and clear. If you want to request a price list, you should say so briefly but politely, e.g. "Please send me your current price list." Do not write: "Would it be possible to send me your current price list? I would be very happy about this."

Q: What is the last thing I should do before clicking the "send" icon?

A: You should check your mail for mistakes. (see Q: above on capital letters) And if you want to send an attachment, remember to attach it to your mail.

Discussions

Whether you are involved in a discussion in class or at work it is important to listen carefully to what other people are saying and keep to the point when you speak. Always be polite! The phrases below and on page 178 should help you to express your ideas.

Useful phrases

» Make a suggestion

Let's consider …
I suggest/propose that you/we …
I suggest/propose + (verb in -ing form)
What do you think about …?
If I were you, I would …

» Respond to a suggestion

That's a good idea!/Fine!
OK/Yes, why not?
OK, if you want, I don't really mind.
I think it would be a better idea to consider …
Couldn't we look at this/do this another way?
What about …?
I'm not sure. How about …?

» Ask for an opinion

What do you think/feel about …?
What is your view/opinion on/about …?
What would you say?

» Give an opinion

As far as I'm concerned …
I think/feel/believe/am of the opinion that …
To my mind …
In my opinion …/In my view …

» Agree

You are (quite/absolutely) right.
That's a very good point!
Absolutely!/Exactly!
I agree (with you/Susie/etc.).
You have a point.
You might/could be right.
I think you're right to a certain extent/up to a point.

» Disagree

I disagree (entirely).
I'm sorry, but I completely disagree.
Stop exaggerating!
I think you're oversimplifying things.
That's an interesting point, but …
That's not the point.
You've missed the point (entirely).

» Interrupt someone

Sorry to interrupt, but (could you please explain/repeat the point you just made).
Excuse me for interrupting, but (I don't understand what you just said).
Sorry for interrupting but …

» Deal with being interrupted

Can I just finish what I was saying, please?
Just a second. I haven't quite finished.
Would you let me finish?
Would you allow me to make my point, please.
You could at least let me finish my sentence!

» Change the subject

There is something else that I'd like to say …
Have you ever thought of/considered …?
On the other hand …
Try looking at things another way/from a different angle.
I'd like to bring up another point.

» Return to the original subject

Let's get back to what we were saying/discussing.
Let's get back to the point.
As I was saying before, …
Getting back to what we/you/… said earlier …

» Ask for a further explanation

Did I get that right?
Do you really mean that …?
Did I understand correctly that you think …?
Could you explain what you just said/the point you just made again, please?
Could you give me/us a concrete example, please?

» Say that a point has been misunderstood

That's not what I meant to say (at all)!
You've got me (completely) wrong.
You've (completely) misunderstood me.
That's not what I was trying to say!
I didn't make myself clear. I'll try and explain again.

A discussion leader has a particular role to play in a discussion (see ideas in **bold print** in the table below). He/she makes sure the discussion is held in an orderly way and that participants are always polite to each other. He/she always remains neutral.

Useful phrases

» Introduce the discussion and the participants
(As you know,) our discussion today is about …
On my right/left I have … (name of person or group), who is/are in favour of/against …

» Choose whose turn it is to speak
Who would like to open the discussion?
… , would you like to open the discussion?
The next person to speak is … , followed by … and then …

» Make sure everyone has an equal chance to speak, including people who are shy
Is there anything you would like to say, …?

» Do not allow one person to monopolize the discussion
I'm sorry to interrupt you, but I'm afraid you'll have to stop there.
Sorry, but I must give the others a chance to put forward their arguments now.

» Make sure that only one person is speaking at a time
Please wait your turn, you'll have a chance to speak in a minute!
If you'd just let … finish, please.

» Note down the most important points and summarize the discussion at the end
Time is running out, so I'd like to sum up what we've been discussing.
We heard from … that …

» Thank everybody for taking part at the end
Thank you for taking part in the discussion.

Phone calls

In a job situation it is not unusual to have to ring someone whose first or second language is English, which is your only way of communicating with them. You can make the experience easier for yourself if you prepare well beforehand.

Preparation

- Make notes in English or write out a rough draft of the main things you want to say. Also, think of things the contact person is likely to ask or say and work out your responses.
- If possible, find out the name and number of a contact person in advance.
- Be prepared to spell words, especially people's names, the names of places and mail addresses.

Making phone calls

- Speak clearly and slowly. State your requests clearly and to the point.
- Don't worry about making mistakes.
- Be polite! Say 'please' when you ask for information and 'thank you' when you receive help.
  Note: please = *bitte*
  you're welcome/not at all = *bitte schön; gern geschehen*
- When making a formal/business call give your first name and surname, and address people using 'Mr', 'Mrs' or 'Ms' [mz] + surname.

- State telephone numbers as single digits. When the same number occurs twice consecutively, you can say 'double' (e.g. 33: double 3). 0 = Oh (*BE* & *AE*) or zero (*AE*)
  Example: 07145 14406: Oh/zero – seven – one – four – five – one – double four – oh/zero – six
- Ask the caller to spell names, etc. for you to avoid confusion (cf. "Checking spelling" below).
- Repeat important information to be sure that you have understood everything correctly (cf. "Checking information" below).
- You could put the following useful telphone phrases onto a card which you could refer to.

Useful phrases

1 = Your name **2** = Name of person you want to speak to **3** = State telephone number

» Greeting
Hello/Good morning./Good afternoon.
(This is) **1** speaking.
Can I help you?
What can I do for you?

» Asking to speak to someone
Can I speak to **2** , please?
Can you put me through to **2** , please?
I'd like to speak to someone in your … department.

» Holding the line and putting calls through
Please hold (the line).
One moment, please.
I'll connect you with **2** /with the … department.
I'll put you through (to **2** /to the … department).

» When someone isn't available …
I'm sorry, **2** isn't here/available at the moment/today/etc.

» Getting the right extension, etc.
Can you give me **2**'s extension number, please?
I'd like to receive more information about …
I'm calling about …
I can give you his/her extension number/voice mail number/fax number/mail address. It's **3**.

» Giving and taking messages
Would you like to leave a message?
Can I take a message?
Would you like me to pass on a message?
Could you pass on a message, please?

» Ringing back
Shall I ask him/her to call you back?
Could you call back later/in half an hour/etc., please?
Could you ask him/her to call me back, please? My number is **3**.
Can I call back later?
I'll call back later/in half an hour/etc. if that's OK.
When would be the best time to call back?

» Checking spelling
Would you like me to spell …/that for you? It's spelt …
I'll just spell that for you. It's …
Could you spell …/that for me, please?
Would you mind spelling …/that for me, please?

» Checking information
Let me just check that I've understood all the information you've given me/asked for correctly.
I'll just repeat that back to you to make sure I've got everything down correctly.
Let me just check that I've spelt your name correctly.

» Ending a call
Thanks for your call!/Thanks for calling!
Thank you very much for your help!
Sorry I can't be of any more help.
Have a nice day!
Goodbye!

Don't expect to understand every single word that is said during the phone call. If you don't understand something ask the person to repeat what they have just said, explain it in a different way or speak more slowly.
If you think you've got the wrong number, check and apologize. Don't just hang up. If the caller has got the wrong number, explain politely.

Useful phrases

» Solving telephone problems

I'm sorry. I'm afraid I don't understand what you mean. Could you explain that again, please?
Could you speak a little more slowly/loudly, please?
I'm sorry, (it's a very bad line,) I didn't quite catch that! Could you speak up a bit, please?
Could you repeat that, please?
Is that (+ number you want)?
I'm sorry, I think I've dialled the wrong number,
I'm sorry, but I think you've got the wrong number. This is (+ your number/name/company name).
I'm sorry, there's no-one here with that name. This is (+ your number/name/company name).

Small talk

Small talk is light (casual) conversation. It is a way of showing interest in others, communicating in a friendly way and avoiding conflict! At a social event, like a party, you might spend the whole time in casual conversation. At a business meeting, on the phone, at an interview, etc. you can start (and end) with a few minutes of small talk. Here are some topics and useful phrases that you can use.

Topics for small talk

- The weather (especially popular in Britain!)
- A journey (to or from the place where you are)
- Where you live/Where your conversation partner lives
- Your family and/or your conversation partner's family (if you know them)
- A recent/well-known TV programme or film
- Tips about what to see and do in a certain town or city (i.e. cultural events, attractions, restaurants, local specialities, etc.)
- Sport (e.g. a current sports event)
- A holiday
- Where you/your conversation partner went to school or university
- What you do for a living/what your conversation partner does for a living
- Hobbies and interests
- An experience/event that you and your conversation partner are both currently involved in or have been involved in
- A non-controversial item in the news

Topics to avoid in small talk

- Controversial political issues
- Religious beliefs
- Illnesses

Useful phrases

» Starting a conversation
Hi!/Hallo!
Do you mind if I join you?
Nice to see you (again).
How are you doing?

» Finding a topic
Did you see … on TV last night?
Have you seen the new (James Bond) film yet?
Did you read about … in the newspaper this morning?
How was your journey?
How did you get here?

» Using question tags
You know,… don't you?
He's … isn't he?

» Responding
That's the funniest/strangest/most interesting thing I've heard in ages!
I couldn't agree more.
That's funny! Exactly the same thing happened to me the other day.
I've never thought of it like that before.

» Finishing a conversation
It was nice talking to you!
Oh no, is that the time?
Excuse me, I've got to go now.
Hope to see you again soon.
Take care.
Give my regards to…

Personal letters

A personal letter is written to someone you know well, e.g. a friend or relative. A few basic rules are given below next to the model letter.
You can use informal language in a personal letter, as if you were speaking to the person.
Example:

Dinkelstr. 1
70183 Stuttgart
Germany

Your address goes in the top right hand corner.

May 3, 20…

Write the date under the address.

Start the letter: Dear + name

Use a capital letter for the first word.

Dear Frank,
Just a few lines to let you know I'm still alive! Sorry for not having written for so long, but I've been very busy at college with exams.

How are things with you? What are you doing for the summer? Unfortunately my applications for jobs in the States have all been turned down so far. Oh well, I'll keep trying…

Please drop me a line when you have a minute. We really must keep in touch. Give my regards to your family.

Group your news, etc. in paragraphs.

All the best,
Thomas

Finish the letter with one of these phrases:
All the best,
Best wishes,
Bye for now,
Love,
Lots of love,

P.S. If I do get to the States, I'll let you know my address. Maybe we'll be able to meet up!

Reports

A report usually gives information and (sometimes) recommendations based on research findings. Before starting it is important to read the task description carefully so that you know what exactly the reader wants to know.
As a rule, reports should be kept simple and the language should be concrete. The date can be written at the top or under the signature at the end. The report should include the following items:

Contents

- Title or title page
- Table of contents
- Introduction/Summary/Terms of reference/Procedures stating the purpose and scope of the report.
- Findings (= main part of the report) giving the results of investigations. Key facts should be clearly identified by numbering or the use of bullet points (•).
- Conclusion(s) giving an analysis of the facts or findings.
- Recommendations i.e. action recommended by the writer on the strength of the findings and conclusions
- Appendices (graphs, diagrams, statistics, etc. referred to in the report)
- Bibliography and/or references (titles of books, magazines, websites, etc. used in finding information or related to the subject of the report)

Example:

GiLa's Diners

Proposal to Launch Executive Catering Service

Terms of reference
Ginny Largo, President, has asked for a report about the market potential of catering service to executives.

Procedures
The Marketing Department has conducted extensive research and analysed the findings.

Findings
1 87% of executives interviewed eat regularly at GiLa's Diners.
2 GiLa's Diners is generally perceived as an up-market and socially responsible classic family diner providing quality and convenience.
3 Most respondents were critical of their company's cafeteria. 45% never use it. Common reasons were "slow service", "poor quality", "no vegetarian meals", "tasteless food" and "downright unhealthy".
4 Competition is limited to down-market, fast-food takeaways.
5 Executives are prepared to pay for healthy food, especially the 18–45 age group.

Conclusions
There is a clear gap in the market for an executive catering service. Executives value speed and quality over price. GiLa's Diners already has high brand recognition among an increasingly health-conscious target group. However, GiLa's Diners is still seen primarily as a traditional family diner.

Recommendations
I recommend that an executive catering service be introduced, tailored to the target group. The existing brand image of wholesome family dining must be adapted to project a more professional image.

Dolores Gregory
Marketing Manager

February 17th 20…

Adverts

Advertising is all around us. On the one hand, it can be entertaining, but on the other, we should be aware that advertisers are trying to influence the way we see a product so that we will buy it. To know how an advert works we should first look at the AIDA formula: Advertisers often use this formula to plan advertising campaigns.
The acronym, AIDA, stands for:

Attention How can we catch the consumer's attention?
Interest How can we arouse the consumer's interest in the product?
Desire What arguments can we use to make the product desirable?
Action What arguments would make the consumer go out and buy the product?

Analysing an advert

Here are some more questions to help you analyse an advert and see how the formula works.

- **Attention**
  - How big is the advert? Is it a full-page ad or a half-page ad?
  - Where in the publication is the advert located?
  - How creative are the colours, the illustrations and the slogan?
  - How do the illustrations, the text and the product relate to one another?
- **Interest**
  - What rhetorical devices does the slogan use?
  - What does the publication, in which the advert appears, tell you about the potential target group?
- **Desire**
  - What does the slogan promise the customer?
  - Can you identify a particular need which the product fulfils?
  - What benefits of the product does the advert mention?
  - How will the product give the consumer satisfaction?
  - What image does the advert convey both of the product and of the person who buys it?
- **Action**
  - In your opinion, how effective is the advert in making people actually buy the product?
  - Does the advert show that the product is value for money?

In order to answer these questions, you should first collect suitable adjectives in a mind map like the one below. The mind map is only a starting point and you can add other key words as you need them.

Example:

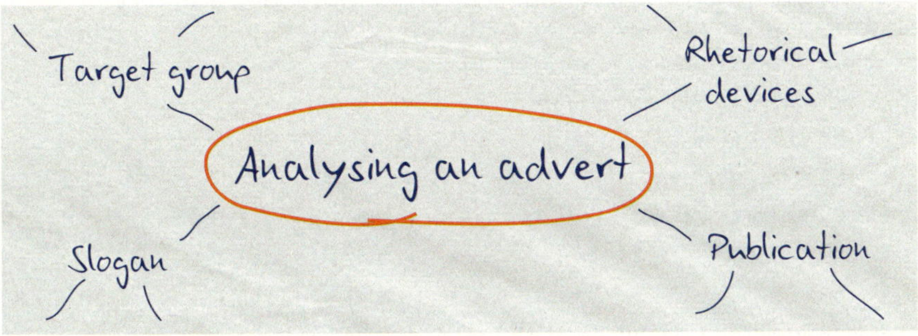

→ **Rhetorical devices**
See *skills file* on page 164.

Film analysis

In films, the atmosphere in a scene or the impression you get of a character is not only conveyed by the actors themselves and the dialogues, but also by the varied use of lighting, camera movements, sound effects and music.
- **Lighting:** Bright light is used to make the atmosphere in a scene friendly and happy. If the lighting is reduced the scene can suddenly become gloomy and tense.
- **Camera positions:** Depending on the position of the camera, the viewer may observe a scene from a distance, e.g. from far away or from a height, or he/she may become part of the scene and observe the action from a character's perspective. In a close-up shot the camera zooms in to show the details of a scene or a character's face. If the camera is placed below the actor in a low-angle shot, he/she can be made to seem bigger or more dominant than if he/she was presented in a full shot at eye-level.
- **Music and sound effects:** These elements also help to create a certain atmosphere. Try pressing the mute button before watching a scene. Then look at the scene again with sound and you will notice a big difference!

Analysing a film scene

In order to analyse a film sequence, you have to watch it several times. If you answer the following questions and interpret your answers, you should be able to analyse a scene quite well.
- How is light used in a particular scene, e.g. is it very bright or dark? Is there a spotlight on one particular person or thing? Does the spotlight move during the scene?
- From which point(s) of view are the characters presented? Where are they positioned or how do they move during the scene?
- How do the music and sound effects contribute to the atmosphere in the scene?
- Is there a cut between the different scenes or does one scene end slowly (fade out) before being followed by the next?
- In general, what means are used to grab the viewers' attention and to keep their interest, i.e. what makes the scene funny, sad, dramatic, serious, violent, tense, etc.?

Collecting words

Everyone learns new vocabulary differently. It is worthwhile organizing vocabulary so that you can learn it more easily. Then when you study for your exam you will immediately have the most relevant vocabulary at your fingertips. Below you will find some ideas as to how you could organise vocabulary.
Note: When you meet new English words don't just write a German translation. Always write an explanation or give a synonym or opposite in English! See the format of *Challenge 21 Band 2 Vocabulary Notebook* (978-3-12-801009-0) for ideas.

Where to write new words

- On cards with the English word on the front and the English definition (and the German translation) on the back.
- In a vocabulary book.
- On the computer.

Ways of collecting and organizing words

- Alphabetically (A–Z): You can find words easily, but you have to know what the word is in the first place. It is a good method to use in addition to the other methods listed below.
- By writing synonyms and opposites: Group together words with similar meanings, e.g. pretty, nice, lovely, or with their opposites, e.g. pretty ≠ ugly.
- In word families: When you note a new word, include the other words which can be formed from it, e.g. the verb, adjective, adverb, etc. Also make a note of the word with its prefix or suffix (see below).
- In collocations: Make a note of words which are often written together (verb + preposition, verb + noun, etc.). Always try to learn words with their collocations, e.g. to make allowances.
- In semantic fields: Group words according to topics. Include nouns, adjectives, verbs, idioms, phrases, etc.,
  Example: School: to attend, to be absent from, classroom, hall, staff room.
- In mind maps by topic: Start with the topic heading and add words in a logical way.

Mind maps
See *skills file* on page 186.

You can increase the number of words you know if you add prefixes or suffixes to verbs, nouns, adjectives, etc.

Prefixes

A prefix is added to the beginning of a word to change its meaning.

– You can give a word a negative or opposite (≠) meaning.		– You can show an increase (+) or decrease (–)	
Prefix	**Example**	**Prefix**	**Example**
in-	inactive	over- (+)	overheat
im-	impossible	out- (+)	to outgrow
il-	illiterate	super- (++)	supernatural
ir-	irrelevant	under- (–)	to underpay
un-	unhappy	sub- (–)	substandard
dis-	to dislike		
de-	to destabilise		

Suffixes

A suffix is usually added to the end of a word to give it a different meaning, usually to make a verb or adjective into a noun.

– You can form nouns from verbs and adjectives.					
Suffix	**Verb**	**Noun**	**Suffix**	**Adjective**	**Noun**
-ence	to differ	difference	-ness	happy	happiness
-ment	to improve	improvement	-(i)ty	difficult	difficulty
-ion/-ation/-ision	to nationalize	nationalization	-th	true	truth
-er	to teach	teacher			
-or	to act	actor			
-ing	to begin	beginning			

Mind maps

Mind maps are useful for collecting and organizing information about a topic. You can make a mind map for yourself or as a group. The basic structure of a mind map is always the same.

How to make a mind map

Use a pencil so that you can easily delete things or change their position, if necessary.

- Write your main topic in the middle of a page and draw a circle around the word or phrase. (Fig. 1)
- Think of important things directly related to the main topic. Write each idea (subtopic) in a circle around the outside of your first circle. Draw lines connecting the subtopics to the main topic. (Fig. 2)
- Now add more circles with related ideas around the subtopics. (Fig. 3).
- You can also use lines with 'branches' for subtopics. (Fig. 4)

Fig. 1

Fig. 2

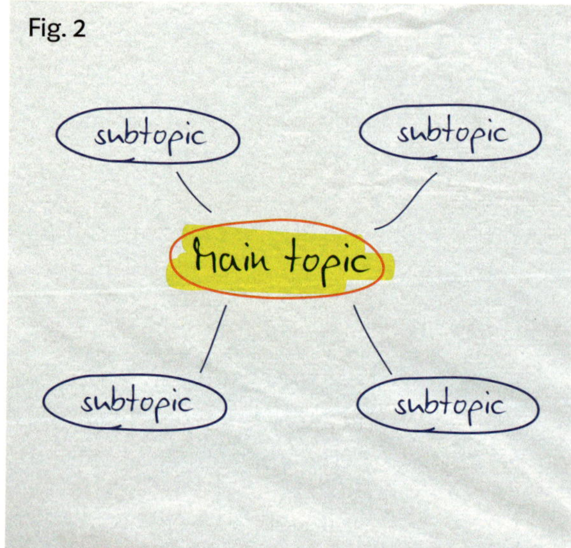

Fig. 3

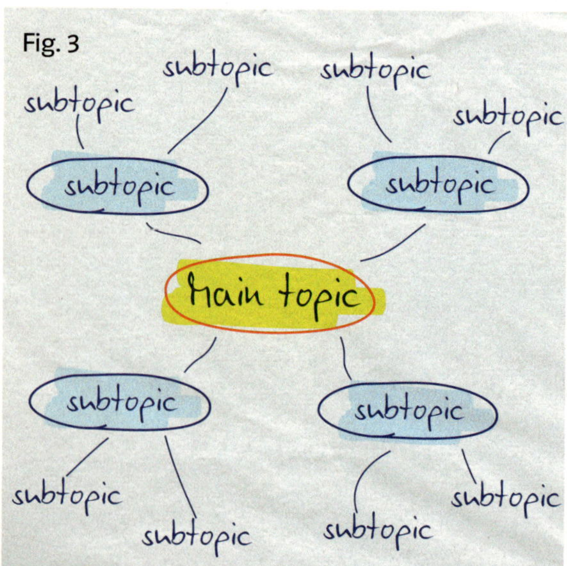

Fig. 4

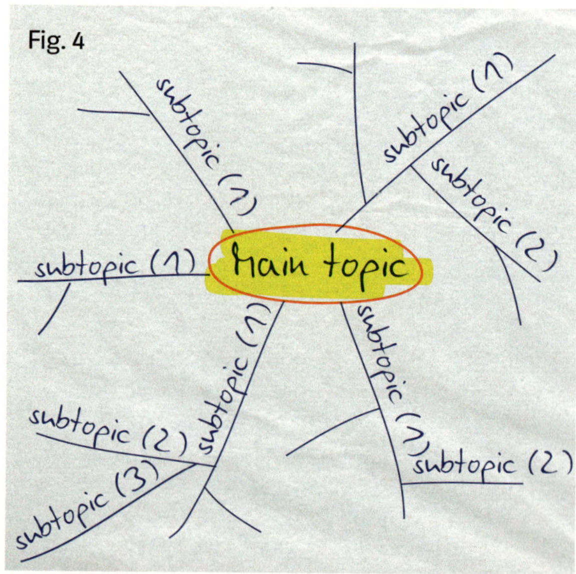

Ways of using mind maps

- To brainstorm ideas on a given topic: Write the topic heading in the centre circle and add all new and related aspects.
- To organize information from a text or other source: Start with the most important point in the text, add the main subtopics, then add relevant detailed information or quotations from the text.
- To develop word fields: Start with the generic term and add all related words.
- To organize arguments: Start with the topic of discussion. Add a branch or circle: 'for' and another one 'against'. Continue by adding further branches/circles with arguments 'for' and 'against'.

Surviving without a dictionary

The following techniques will help you to 'survive' without a dictionary, when you come across words you don't know.

- Always read a text once through without looking up any words. Try to understand the gist, i.e. the basic meaning of a text. You don't need to understand all the details at first.
- See whether the words and sentences before and after an unknown word (the context) help you to understand it! Can you guess its meaning from the context? Or can you understand the sentence without that word?
- Try to identify the word family. Part of the word may be related to a known English word. Look out for prefixes, suffixes and compounds, e.g. disapproval = approve + prefix & suffix.
- Many English words are of French or German origin, so think about whether there is a similar word in your own language or other foreign languages you know, e.g. discipline – *Disziplin*.
- Does the sound of the word help? Say it out loud, e.g. "Ping!".

→ **Collecting words**
See *skills file* (prefixes and suffixes) on page 185.

Using an English-English dictionary

A good English-English (monolingual) dictionary provides you with:

- the different forms of a word.
- the class of the word (noun, verb, adverb, etc.).
- the pronunciation (phonetics).
- the stress
- the different meanings.
- grammatical information.
- examples showing how the word is used in context.
- the prepositions, etc. commonly used with the word.
- idioms, etc. in which the word is commonly used.

Tips for using an English-English dictionary

- Before looking up a word identify whether it is a verb, noun, adjective, etc.
- When you have found the entry for the word make sure you look at the meaning for the correct class of word.
- Read any additional information which the dictionary gives you about the word.
- Take your time to read the entry carefully.
- Make sure you find the entry which matches the use of the word in the given context.

Dictionary page

This dictionary entry was taken from *Cambridge Learner's Dictionary*, 978-0521682022.

Bb

B, b /biː/ the second letter of the alphabet

BA /biːˈeɪ/ *noun* [C] *abbreviation for* Bachelor of Arts: a university or college qualification in an arts (= not science) subject which usually takes 3 or 4 years of study

baa /bɑː/ *noun* [C] the sound that a sheep makes

babble /ˈbæbl/ *verb* [I] to talk quickly in a way which is confused, silly, or has no meaning • **babble** *noun* [U] *the babble of voices*

babe /beɪb/ *noun* [C] **1** *very informal* a young, attractive woman **2** *literary* a baby

WORD PARTNERS FOR *baby*

have/be expecting/give birth to a baby • a baby **is born** • a **new/newborn** baby

⊶**baby** /ˈbeɪbi/ *noun* [C] **1** a very young child *a baby girl/boy* ○ *baby clothes* ○ *Liz has **had a baby**.* ○ *Maria's **expecting a baby*** (= she is pregnant). **2** a very young animal *a baby bird*

ˈbaby ˌboom *noun* [C] a time when a lot of babies are born in a particular area *the postwar baby boom*

ˈbaby ˌcarriage *noun* [C] *US* a small vehicle with four wheels for carrying a baby

babyish /ˈbeɪbiɪʃ/ *adjective* Babyish behaviour is silly, like the behaviour of a young child.

babysit /ˈbeɪbɪsɪt/ *verb* [I, T] **babysitting**, *past* **babysat** to look after children while their parents are not at home • **babysitter** *noun* [C] *We'd like to come, but we can't get a babysitter.* • **babysitting** *noun* [U]

bachelor /ˈbætʃələr/ *noun* [C] **1** a man who is not married **2 Bachelor of Arts/Science/Education, etc** a university or college qualification which usually takes 3 or 4 years of study, or a person who has this qualification

⊶**back** /bæk/ *adverb* **1** [RETURNING] where someone or something was before *When do you go back to college?* ○ *I put it back in the cupboard.* **2** [BEHIND] in a direction behind you *Anna stepped back.* ○ *Flint leaned back in his chair.* **3** [REPLY] as a reply or reaction to something *UK to ring back/ US to call back* ○ *I signalled to her and she waved back.* **4** [STATE] to the state something or someone was in before *Hopefully things will **get back to normal** again now.* ○ *I'm sure we can **put** it **back together** again* (= repair it). ○ *Try to go back to sleep.* **5** [EARLIER] at or to an earlier time *We first met **back in** 1973.* ○ *Looking back, I think we did the right thing.* **6** [AWAY FROM] in a direction away from something *He pulled back the curtain.* **7 back and forth** (*also UK* **backwards and forwards**) in one direction, then the opposite way, then in the original direction again many times *He has to travel back and forth between London and Paris every week.*

COMMON LEARNER ERROR

back to

Remember to use the preposition **to** when you are talking about returning to a place.

I haven't seen her since she went back to Korea.

~~*I haven't seen her since she went back Korea.*~~

⊶**back²** /bæk/ *noun* [C] **1** [NOT FRONT] the part of something that is furthest from the front or in the opposite direction to the front *He wrote his number down on the back of an envelope.* ○ *I always keep a blanket in the back of the car.* **2** [BODY] the part of your body from your shoulders to your bottom *back injuries/pain* ○ *He was lying on his back.* ➲See colour picture **The Body** on page Centre 13. **3** [SEAT] the part of a seat that you lean against when you are sitting *the back of a chair* **4 back to front** *UK* with the back part of something where the front should be *You've got your trousers on back to front.* **5 in back of** *US* behind *They sat in back of us on the plane.* **6 at/in the back of your mind** If you have a thought or idea at the back of your mind, you are always thinking about it. **7 behind sb's back** If you do something behind someone's back, you do it without them knowing, often in an unfair way. *Have they been saying things about me behind my back?* **8 be glad/happy, etc to see the back of sb/sth** *UK* to be pleased when someone leaves or something ends because you did not like them **9 be on sb's back** to remind someone again and again to do something, or to criticize someone in an annoying way **10 turn your back on sb/sth** to decide to stop having contact with someone or something, or to refuse to help someone *She turned her back on Hollywood and went to live in Florida.* ➲See also: a **pat²** on the back, be (like) **water¹** off a duck's back.

back³ /bæk/ *verb* **1** [T] to give support or help to a person, plan, or idea *He backed Mr Clark in the recent election.* **2** [T] to risk money by saying that you think a horse, team, etc will win a race, game, or competition in order to win more money if they do *Many people are backing Holyfield to win the fight.* **3 back (sth) away/into/out, etc** to move backwards or drive backwards *She saw he had a gun and backed away.*

back away to show that you do not support a plan or idea any more and do not want to be involved with it *The government has backed away from plans to increase taxes.*

back down to admit that you were wrong, or agree not to do something *The council **backed down over** rent increases.*

back off 1 to move away from someone, usually because you are afraid *I saw the knife and backed off.* **2** *mainly US* to stop supporting a plan *The president has **backed off from** a threat to expel U.N. soldiers.*

back out to decide not to do something you had planned or agreed to do *Nigel backed out at the last minute, so we had a spare ticket.*

back sb up 1 to support or help someone *My family backed me up in my fight for compensation.* **2** to say that someone is telling the

| j **yes** | k **cat** | ŋ **ring** | ʃ **she** | θ **thin** | ð **this** | ʒ **decision** | dʒ **jar** | tʃ **chip** | æ **cat** | e **bed** | ə **ago** | ɪ **sit** | i **cosy** | ɒ **hot** | ʌ **run** | ʊ **put** |

Vocabulary

The words explained in the annotations in this book are listed here in alphabetical order with their German meanings. The German meaning is given for the use of the English word in the given context. Some words appear in the book more than once. The page numbers refer to the first occurrence of the word.

A

abominable [ə'bɒmɪnəbl] schrecklich *149*
absently ['æbsəntlɪ] (geistes-) abwesend *102*
abuse [ə'bju:s] Missbrauch *68*
to accelerate [ək'seləreɪt] beschleunigen *91*
accelerating pace [əkˌseləreɪtɪŋ 'peɪs] zunehmende Geschwindigkeit *141*
acceleration [əkˌselə'reɪʃn] Beschleunigung *20*
to access ['ækses] erreichen *29*
accidental [ˌæksɪ'dentl] zufällig *39*
accolade ['ækəleɪd] Auszeichnung *91*
to accomplish [ə'kʌmplɪʃ] erfüllen *85*
to account for [ə'kaʊnt fɔ:] ausmachen, entfallen auf *27, 41, 49*; in die Überlegungen einbeziehen *95*
to accrue to [ə'kru: tu:] zu einem bestimmten Ziel führen *137*
acid ['æsɪd] LSD *101*
an acquaintance of mine [ənə'kweɪntənsəvˌmaɪn] ein Bekannte(r) von mir *149*
to acquire [ə'kwaɪə] erwerben *23*; **acquisition** [ˌækwɪ'zɪʃn] Erwerb *23*
to act pissed off [akt ˌpɪst'ɒf] zeigen, dass man verärgert ist *117*
adamant ['ædəmənt] unnachgiebig *51*
to adapt [ə'dæpt] anpassen *146*; **adaptability** [əˌdæptə'bɪlətɪ] Anpassungsfähigkeit *146*
to address s.o. [ə'dres‿ˌsʌmwʌn] jemanden ansprechen *32*
adept [ə'dept] erfahren, sehr geschickt *93*
Adjoa Andoh [əˌdʒəʊə 'ændəʊ] *145*
adjustment [ə'dʒʌstmənt] Anpassung *126*
to adopt [ə'dɒpt] annehmen *146*
adorned [ə'dɔ:nd] verziert *16*
advances [əd'vɑ:nsɪz] Fortschritte *93*
advent ['ædvent] Aufkommen *130*
advisable [əd'vaɪzəbl] ratsam *149*; **to advise** [əd'vaɪz] raten *120*; **adviser** [əd'vaɪzə] Ratgeber(in) *147*
advocacy group ['ædvəkəsɪˌgru:p] Interessengruppe *39*
to advocate ['ædvəkeɪt] unterstützen *119*
to affect [ə'fekt] Einfluss nehmen auf *39*
affectation [ˌæfek'teɪʃn] Affektiertheit *148*
to affirm [ə'fɜ:m] bestätigen *101*
affluence ['æflʊəns] Wohlstand *12*
aficionado [əˌfɪʃɪən'ɑ:dəʊ] Anhänger(in) *16*
Agent Provocateur [ˌæʒɒŋprəˌvɒkə'tɜ:] Markenname für Luxusunterwäsche *44*
to air [eə] senden *39*
Air Res Traffic ['eəˌrezˌtræfɪk] *101*
airtime ['eəˌtaɪm] Sendezeit *130*
to alert [ə'lɜ:t] warnen *79*
alien ['eɪlɪən] Ausländer(in) *51*; **alienated** ['eɪlɪəneɪtɪd] entfremdet *58*
allegiance [ə'li:dʒəns] Gehorsam *149*
to alleviate poverty [əˌli:vɪeɪt 'pɒvətɪ] die Armut erleichtern *135*
allogeneic donor [ˌæləʊdʒəneɪk'dəʊnə] Spender(in) mit nahezu identischen Genen *87*
alloy ['ælɔɪ] Legierung, Mischung *113*
ally ['ælaɪ] Verbündete(r) *138*
aloft [ə'lɒft] empor, hoch oben *93*
along with [ə'lɒŋwɪð] zusammen mit *36*
amazement [ə'meɪzmənt] Erstaunen *148*
amenable [ə'mi:nəbl] zugänglich *126*
annihilation [əˌnaɪɪ'leɪʃn] Vernichtung *91*
to announce [ə'naʊns] ankündigen *16*
anomaly [ə'nɒməlɪ] Anomalie *97*
anticipation [ænˌtɪsɪ'peɪʃn] Vorfreude *45*
antidote ['æntɪdəʊt] Gegengift *45*
anti-gerasone [ˌæntɪ'dʒerəsəʊn] erfundenes Lebenselixier *98*
anvil ['ænvɪl] Amboss *87*
anxiety [æŋ'zaɪətɪ] Angst *56*
apparent [ə'pærənt] offenbar, offensichtlich *45, 93*
appealing [ə'pi:lɪŋ] attraktiv *24*
applicable [ə'plɪkəbl] zutreffend *144*; **application** [ˌæplɪ'keɪʃn] Anwendung *78*
to appreciate s.th. [ə'pri:ʃɪeɪt ˌsʌmθɪŋ] etwas schätzen *127*
approach [ə'prəʊtʃ] Ansatz *29*
appropriate [ə'prəʊprɪət] angemessen *93*
aptitude ['æptɪtju:d] Fähigkeit *24*
aquifer ['ækwɪfə] Grundwasserleiter *97*
arid ['ærɪd] dürr *63*
to arrest s.th. [ə'rest ˌsʌmθɪŋ] die Aufmerksamkeit auf sich ziehen *35*
aside [ə'saɪd] Nebenbemerkung *26*
to assault [ə'sɔ:lt] angreifen *21*
to assess [ə'ses] beurteilen *71*
assisted braking [əˌsɪstɪd'breɪkɪŋ] Bremshilfe *79*
associated with [ə'səʊʃɪeɪtɪd wɪð] verbunden mit *126*
assumption [ə'sʌmpʃn] Annahme *126*
Astronomer Royal [əsˌtrɒnəmə'rɔɪəl] *93*
asylum [ə'saɪləm] Asyl *108*
at a go [ətə'gəʊ] in einem Rutsch *13*

at random [ət'rændəm] ohne Methode *73*
automata (singular **automaton**) [ɔ:'tɒmətə] Automaten *82*

B

backbone ['bækbəʊn] Rückgrat, Charakterstärke *12*
to backfire [ˌbæk'faɪə] schiefgehen *33*
backlash ['bæklæʃ] Gegenreaktion *113*
Bangladeshi [ˌbæŋglə'deʃɪ] *53*
bar [bɑ:] Stange *50*; Hinderungsgrund *119*;
to bar [bɑ:] verriegeln *119*
bargain ['bɑ:gɪn] Schnäppchen *44*
Barnsley ['bɑ:nzlɪ] *54*
barrister ['bærɪstə] Anwalt/Anwältin (vor Gerichten) *16*
a battery of s.th. [ə 'bætərɪ‿əv ˌsʌmθɪŋ] eine große Anzahl an *67*
to be an ass [bɪ‿ən 'æs] sich blöd verhalten *117*
to be between May and December [bɪ bɪˌtwi:n‿ˌmeɪəndɪ'sembə] kurzlebig sein *98*
to be clad [bɪ 'klæd] sich kleiden *50*
to be down to [bɪ 'daʊn tu:] zurückzuführen sein auf *44*
to be exceeded by s.th. [bɪ‿ɪk'si:dɪd‿baɪ ˌsʌmθɪŋ] von etwas übertroffen sein *78*
to be exposed to [bɪ‿ɪk'spəʊzd‿tu:] treffen auf, in Kontakt kommen mit *110*
to be out of kilter [bɪ‿ˌaʊtəv'kɪltə] aus dem Gleichgewicht geraten sein *14*
to be rooted in [bɪ 'ru:tɪd ɪn] verwurzelt sein in *23*
to be set [bɪ 'set] erwartet werden *27*
to get smeared [get 'smɪəd] überfahren werden *99*
beam [bi:m] Strahl *81*
beermat ['bɪəˌmæt] Bierdeckel *13*
to benefit ['benɪfɪt] nützen *32*
Berkshire ['bɜ:kʃə] *73*
Berwick ['berɪk] *54*
to besiege [bɪ'si:dʒ] belagern, bedrängen *103*
bête noir [ˌbet'nwɑ:] ein Gräuel *73*
betwixt and between [bɪˌtwɪkstənbɪ'twi:n] zwischen den Stühlen sitzen *12*
bewildering [bɪ'wɪldərɪŋ] verwirrend *20*
biodiversity [ˌbaɪəʊdaɪ'vɜ:sətɪ] Artenvielfalt *63*
Blair [bleə] *138*
bleakly ['bli:klɪ] trostlos, trübe *98*
blend [blend] Mischung *23*;
to blend [blend] mischen *29*
to blot out [blɒt 'aʊt] verdecken *101*
blunt [blʌnt] unverblümt *130*
boldly ['bəʊldlɪ] mutig *93*
to bolt [bəʊlt] festschrauben *50*;
to bolt up [bəʊlt 'ʌp] hochfahren *101*
bond [bɒnd] Verbindung *126*
bone marrow ['bəʊnˌmærəʊ] Knochenmark *87*
Border Patrol ['bɔ:dəpəˌtrəʊl] Grenzkontrolle, Grenzpatrouille *51*
border watch ['bɔ:dəˌwɒtʃ] Grenzbewachung *50*
borderline sane ['bɔ:dəlaɪn ˌseɪn] fast verrückt *29*
borough ['bʌrə] Bezirk, Gemeinde *54*
boundary ['baʊndrɪ] Grenze *63*
bowler-hat [ˌbəʊlə'hæt] Melone *127*
to brag [bræg] angeben *18*
branch [brɑ:ntʃ] Zweigstelle *58*
brief [bri:f] kurz *32*;
to brief s.o. ['bri:f ˌsʌmwʌn] jemanden informieren *102*
brittle ['brɪtl] brüchig *138*
Brussel sprout [ˌbrʌsl'spraʊt] Rosenkohl *21*
buggy ['bʌgɪ] Einspänner *70*
Buick City [ˌbju:ɪk'sɪtɪ] *141*
bulge [bʌldʒ] Ausbuchtung, Rundung *117*
to bump into s.o. by accident [ˌbʌmp 'ɪntʊ ˌsʌmwʌn baɪ‿'aksɪdənt] jemanden zufällig anrempeln *54*
a bundle of figures [ə ˌbʌndl əv‿'fɪgəz] eine Handvoll Zahlen *9*
bunk [bʌŋk] Etagenbett *101*
burden ['bɜ:dən] Last *26*
to bust [bɜ:st] brechen *98*;
bust [bʌst] Pleite, Bankrott *141*
to buy s.th. ['baɪ ˌsʌmθɪŋ] jemandem etwas abnehmen *68*
to buy into s.th. [ˌbaɪ‿'ɪntʊ ˌsʌmθɪŋ] an etwas teilnehmen *126*
buzzphrase ['bʌzfreɪs] Schlagwort *29*
by heaven [ˌbaɪ'hevn] Bei Gott! *68*
by way of [ˌbaɪ'weɪ‿əv] um … zu *32*
byproduct ['baɪˌprɒdʌkt] Nebenprodukt *66*

C

to cackle ['kækl] gackern, schnattern *99*
Cairns [keənz] *147*
calibrated ['kælɪbreɪtɪd] geeicht *97*
canola [kə'nəʊlə] Raps *47*
carbon dioxide [ˌkɑ:bndaɪ'ɒksaɪd] Kohlendioxyd *62*
carer ['keərə] Betreuer(in), Pfleger(in) *26*
Carlisle [kɑ:'laɪl] *54*
a case in point [əˌkeɪsɪn'pɔɪnt] ein einschlägiger Fall *71*
cast off ['kɑ:stɒf] weggeworfen *101*
cattle ['kætl] Vieh *51*
to cave to [ˌkeɪv'tu:] sich einer Sache beugen *39*
celebrity endorsement [səˌlebrətɪ‿ɪn'dɔ:smənt] Werbung mit Prominenten *41*
chairman ['tʃeəmən] Vorsitzende(r) *147*
to change beyond recognition [ˌtʃeɪndʒ bɪˌɒndrekəg'nɪʃn] bis zur Unkenntlichkeit verändern *16*
to channel one's anger [ˌtʃænl wʌnz 'æŋgə] seinem Ärger auf eine bestimmte Art und Weise Luft machen *130*
charitable ['tʃærɪtəbl] wohltätig *29*;
charity ['tʃærɪtɪ] Wohltätigkeitsverein *9*
chest [tʃest] Brust *43*
Chief of Staff [ˌtʃi:fəv'stɑ:f] Stabschef *102*
chills [tʃɪlz] Schauer, Frösteln *107*
to chisel away [ˌtʃɪzlə'weɪ] permanent daran weiterarbeiten *136*
chore [tʃɔ:] Haushaltspflicht *26*
cinnamon twist [ˌsɪnəmən'twɪst] Zimtgebäck *47*
circuit ['sɜ:kɪt] Stromkreis *89*
to cite [saɪt] zitieren *41*
civic ['sɪvɪk] bürgerlich *113*
to claim [kleɪm] behaupten *9*
clarity about purpose ['klærətɪ əˌbaʊt 'pɜ:pəs] ein klares eindeutiges Vorhaben *23*
to clinch a deal [ˌklɪntʃ ə 'di:l] ein Abkommen abschließen *147*

to cling on to s.th. [ˌklɪŋ'ɒntʊ ˌsʌmθɪŋ] an etwas hängen *73*
clock conscious ['klɒk‿ˌkɒnʃəs] zeitbewusst *32*
to cloud s.o.'s objectivity ['klaʊd ˌsʌmwʌnz ˌɒbdʒɪk'tɪvətɪ] jemands Objektivität beeinflussen *33*
Co [kəʊ] ['kaʊntɪ] Bezirk *54*
to cohabit [kəʊ'hæbɪt] (ohne Trauschein) zusammen leben *9*
to coincide [ˌkəʊɪn'saɪd] zufällig zusammentreffen *14*
collaboration [kəˌlæbə'reɪʃn] Zusammenarbeit *126*; **collaborator** [kə'læbəreɪtə] Mitarbeiter(in) *85*
to collate [kə'leɪt] zusammenstellen und vergleichen *36*
the collective voice [ðə kəˌlektɪv‿'vɔɪs] die gemeinsame Stimme *16*
to combat ['kɒmbæt] bekämpfen *135*
combustion engine [kəm'bʌstʃnˌendʒɪn] Verbrennungsmotor *70*
to come out in favour [ˌkʌmaʊtɪn'feɪvə] bevorzugen *93*
to commission s.th. [kə'mɪʃn ˌsʌmθɪŋ] etwas in Auftrag geben *27*
to commit to [kə'mɪt‿tu:] Kraft und Zeit für eine Sache investieren *135*; **commitment** [kə'mɪtmənt] Bindung, Engagement *138*
commonality [ˌkɒmə'nælətɪ] Gemeinsamkeit *113*
commonplace ['kɒmənpleɪs] alltäglich *79*
company ['kʌmpənɪ] Gesellschaft *149*
to compensate for ['kɒmpənseɪt fɔ:] ausgleichen *24*
competitor [kəm'petɪtə] Konkurrent(in) *95*
to complain [kəm'pleɪn] sich beschweren *149*
complementary [ˌkɒmplɪ'mentərɪ] sich gegenseitig ergänzend *81*
to compound [kəm'paʊnd] verschlimmern *56*
compressed natural gas [kəmˌprestˌnætʃərəl'gæs] komprimiertes Erdgas *71*
to comprise [kəm'praɪz] aus etwas bestehen, umfassen *49, 66*
compulsive [kəm'pʌlsɪv] zwanghaft *43*; **compulsory** [kəm'pʌlsərɪ] obligatorisch, vorgeschrieben, verpflichtend *24, 147*
concession [kən'seʃn] Zugeständnis *33*
to conduct [kən'dʌkt] ausführen *33*
confidential [ˌkɒnfɪ'denʃl] vertraulich *130*
to confine [kən'faɪn] beschränken, begrenzen *105*
connotation [ˌkɒnəʊ'teɪʃn] Konnotation *33*
conscience ['kɒnʃəns] Gewissen *145*
conscience salving ['kɒnʃəns‿ˌsælvɪŋ] Gewissensberuhigung *73*
consciousness ['kɒnʃəsnəs] Bewusstsein *82*
consensual agreement [kənˌsenʃʊələ'gri:mənt] Entscheidung mit gegenseitigem Einverständnis *33*
consolation [ˌkɒnsə'leɪʃn] Trost *148*
conspicuous [kən'spɪkjʊəs] deutlich sichtbar, auffallend *105*
to constrain [kən'streɪn] einschränken, behindern *70*
consultation [ˌkɒnsəl'teɪʃn] Beratung, Konsultation *82*
containment [kən'teɪnmənt] Eindämmung *121*
to contend [kən'tend] verfechten *135*
contractual [kən'træktʃʊəl] vertraglich *33*
convenience [kənˌvi:nɪəns] Bequemlichkeit *36*
to converse [kən'vɜ:s] sich unterhalten *32*
to convey [kən'veɪ] vermitteln *32*
to convince s.o. [kən'vɪns‿ˌsʌmwʌn] jemanden überzeugen *148*
core [kɔ:] Kern *113, 126*
corporate ['kɔ:pərət] vom Unternehmen *29*
corps [kɔ:] Besatzungen *94*
to counter ['kaʊntə] erwidern, dagegen sprechen *119*; **counterpart** ['kaʊntəpɑ:t] Gegenstück *58*
courtesy of ['kɜ:təsɪ‿əv] auf Kosten von *73*
to cover ['kʌvə] senden *41*
craftsman ['krɑ:ftsmən] Handwerker *23, 57*
to creep [kri:p] sich ranken; kriechen *101*
crêpe paper ['kreɪp‿ˌpeɪpə] Krepppapier *114*
crisply ['krɪsplɪ] scharf, knapp *51*
crucial ['kru:ʃəl] entscheidend *32, 51*
crucible ['kru:sɪbl] Schmelztiegel *113*
crumbling ['krʌmblɪŋ] Zerbröckeln *61*
to crush [krʌʃ] unterdrücken *132*
crutch [krʌtʃ] Krücke *115*
cub scout ['kʌbˌskaʊt] junger Pfadfinder *114*
curriculum [kə'rɪkjələm] Lehrplan *23*
cut-price [ˌkʌt‿'praɪs] stark herabgesetzt *44*
cut-throat ['kʌtθrəʊt] halsabschneiderisch *144*
to cycle ['saɪkl] kreisen *97*
Cyril ['sɪrəl] *147*

D

dandelion ['dændɪlaɪən] Löwenzahn *99*
daybed ['deɪˌbed] Ruhebett *98*
debris ['deɪbri:] Schutt, Trümmer *67*
decaf ['di:kæf] koffeinfrei *47*
to decay [dɪ'keɪ] zerfallen *66*
to declare [dɪ'kleə] angeben *54*; erklären, feststellen *149*
to decline [dɪ'klaɪn] ablehnen *39*; **decline** [dɪ'klaɪn] Niedergang *137*
to deem [di:m] halten für *29, 58*; machen *73*
deliberation [dɪˌlɪbə'reɪʃn] Überlegung *121*
delicate ['delɪkət] heikel *26*
to delight in s.th. [dɪ'laɪt ɪn ˌsʌmθɪŋ] Freude an etwas haben *126*
demeaning [dɪ'mi:nɪŋ] erniedrigend *39*
demographer [dɪ'mɒgrəfə] Bevölkerungswissenschaftler(in) *12*
denial [dɪ'naɪəl] Ablehnung *130*
dent [dent] Delle *67*
to deny [dɪ'naɪ] verleugnen *126*; **to deny s.th.** [dɪ'naɪ ˌsʌmθɪŋ] etwas vorenthalten *58*
depleted [dɪ'pli:tɪd] fast aufgebraucht *21*
depletion [dɪ'pli:ʃn] Abnahme *97*
to deploy [dɪ'plɔɪ] (Truppen) einsetzen *117*
deposit [dɪ'pɒzɪt] Anzahlung *95*

to derive from [dɪ'raɪv frəm] ableiten von *127*
descent [dɪ'sent] Abstammung, Herkunft *53*
to designate s.th. ['dezɪgneɪt ˌsʌmθɪŋ] etwas ausweisen *130*
despite [dɪ'spaɪt] trotz *113*
to detect [dɪ'tekt] feststellen, wahrnehmen *81, 97*
to deter [dɪ'tɜ:] verhindern *51*
devastating ['devəsteɪtɪŋ] verheerend *9*
device [dɪ'vaɪs] Gerät, Vorrichtung *77*
devolution [ˌdi:və'lu:ʃn] Übertragung von parlamentarischer Gewalt *126*
DFS [ˌdi:ef'es] eine Einkaufskette, die Sofas verkauft *44*
diametrically opposed [daɪəˌmetrɪklɪ‿ə'pəʊzd] völlig entgegengesetzt *44*
dictum ['dɪktəm] Spruch, Sprichwort *20*
dignitary ['dɪgnɪtərɪ] Würdenträger *115*
to dilute [daɪ'lu:t] verdünnen *98*
dimwit ['dɪmwɪt] dumm *130*
14-19 diplomas [ˌfɔ:ti:ntə'naɪnti:n dɪˌpləʊməz] Qualifizierungsnachweise *23*
dire [daɪə] schrecklich *21*
disability [ˌdɪsə'bɪlətɪ] Behinderung *27*; **disabled** [dɪ'seɪbld] behindert *29*
discarded [dɪs'kɑ:dɪd] ausrangiert, weggeworfen *101*
to discredit s.th. [dɪ'skredɪt ˌsʌmwʌn] in Verruf bringen *132*
to disinherit [ˌdɪsɪn'herɪt] enterben *98*
to dismiss [dɪ'smɪs] nicht beachten *61*
dispensable [dɪ'spensəbl] entbehrlich *93*
to disperse [dɪ'spɜ:s] verstreuen *56*
to display [dɪ'spleɪ] zeigen *56*
to dispose of s.th. [dɪ'spəʊz əv ˌsʌmθɪŋ] etwas beseitigen *66*
disproportionately [ˌdɪsprə'pɔ:ʃənətlɪ] unverhältnismäßig viel bzw. stark *113*
distinction [dɪ'stɪŋkʃn] Unterscheidung *86*
distraught [dɪ'strɔ:t] verzweifelt *39*
to ditch [dɪtʃ] aufgeben *27*
diversion [daɪ'vɜ:ʃn] Umleitung *97*
dominion [də'mɪnjən] (Herrschafts-)Gebiet *138*
don [dɒn] Dozent *148*
dose [dəʊs] Überdosis *45*
to draft [drɑ:ft] entwerfen *52*
to drag [dræg] sich schleppen *97*
to drain the household budget [ˌdreɪn ðə ˌhaʊshəʊld‿'bʌdʒɪt] das Haushaltsgeld verprassen *9*
to draw fire [ˌdrɔ: 'faɪə] ins Kreuzfeuer der Kritik geraten *39*
drawback ['drɔ:bæk] Nachteil *51*
drawn to ['drɔ:n tu:] angezogen von *43*
to drive [draɪv] (an)treiben *113*
drought [draʊt] Dürre *63*
drum majorette [ˌdrʌm‿meɪdʒər'et] Tambourmajorin *114*
durian ['djʊərɪən] Durian *20*
dustbin ['dʌstbɪn] Mülleimer *149*

E

eager ['i:gə] eifrig *23*
to ease s.th. ['i:z‿ˌsʌmθɪŋ] etwas erleichtern *26*
easily obtainable [ˌi:zɪlɪ‿ɒb'teɪnəbl] leicht erhältlich *17*
eavesdropping ['i:vzdrɒpɪŋ] heimlich lauschend *130*
economic deprivation [ˌi:kənɒmɪkˌdeprɪ'veɪʃn] wirtschaftliche Entbehrung *56*
to embolden [ɪm'bəʊldən] ermutigen *39*
to embrace [ɪm'breɪs] begrüßen *20*
to emerge [ɪ'mɜ:dʒ] auftauchen *43, 119*
émigré ['emɪgreɪ] politischer Auswanderer *94*
to emit [ɪ'mɪt] ausstoßen *62*
emulsifier [ɪ'mʌlsɪfaɪə] Emulgator *47*
enclave ['enkleɪv] Enklave *21*
to endear oneself [ɪn'dɪə wʌnˌself] sich beliebt machen *32*
endeavor [ɪn'devə] Unterfangen *39*
to endure [ɪn'djʊə] Bestand haben *105*
to engulf [ɪn'gʌlf] verschlingen *101*
to enhance [ɪn'hɑ:ns] verbessern *43*; **enhancement** [ɪn'hɑ:nsmənt] Verbesserung *78*
to enlist s.o. [ɪn'lɪst ˌsʌmwʌn] jemanden anwerben *77*; jemanden aufnehmen *85*
enormous [ɪ'nɔ:məs] riesig *101*
entangling alliance [ɪnˌtæŋglɪŋə'laɪəns] verpflichtendes Bündnis zwischen Staaten *120*
entire [ɪn'taɪə] ganz *51, 81, 110*
entrenched [ɪn'trentʃt] festgefahren *26*
entrepreneur [ˌɒntrəprə'nɜ:] Unternehmer(in) *94*
environmental sustainability [ɪnˌvaɪərənmentlsəˌsteɪnə'bɪlətɪ] umweltschutztechnische Nachhaltigkeit *144*
to envisage [ɪn'vɪzɪdʒ] sich etwas vorstellen *29*
to epitomize [ɪ'pɪtəmaɪz] verkörpern, darstellen *113*
equitable ['ekwɪtəbl] gleichberechtigt *135*
to eradicate [ɪ'rædɪkeɪt] vollständig löschen *39*
to eradicate illiteracy [ɪˌrædɪkeɪt ɪ'lɪtərəsɪ] Analphabetentum besiegen *135*
erratic [ɪ'rætɪk] launenhaft, unberechenbar *119*
estate magnate [ɪ'steɪtˌmægneɪt] Grundstückseigentümer, Baulandbesitzer *94*
esteemed [ɪ'sti:md] sehr geschätzt *91*
to estimate ['estɪmeɪt] schätzen *51*; **estimate** ['estɪmət] Schätzung *62*; **estimated** ['estɪmeɪtɪd] geschätzt *16*
estranged [ɪ'streɪndʒd] getrennt lebend *39*
euphoria [ju:'fɔ:rɪə] Euphorie *43*
to evaluate [ɪ'væljʊeɪt] be-, auswerten *93*
ever-upward [ˌevər'ʌpwəd] stetig zunehmend *9*
to evolve [ɪ'vɒlv] entstehen, sich entwickeln *53, 126*
to exacerbate [ɪg'zæsəbeɪt] verschärfen, verschlimmern *56*
to exact a greater toll [ɪgˌzækt ə ˌgreɪtə 'təʊl] einen höheren Tribut fordern *14*
to exchange a glance [ɪksˌtʃeɪndʒ ə 'glɑ:ns] einen Blick austauschen *102*
exchequer [ɪks'tʃekə] Finanzministerium *23*
to execute ['eksɪkju:t] ausführen *97*
exempt [ɪg'zempt] ausgenommen, befreit *56*

to expel [ɪk'spel] ausweisen, abschieben *53*
to expend [ɪk'spend] verwenden *123*
to expose s.th. [ɪk'spəʊz‿ˌsʌmθɪŋ] etwas darlegen *23*
extended family [ɪkˌstendɪd'fæməlɪ] Großfamilie *45*
extension [ɪk'stenʃn] Verlängerung *78*
extent [ɪk'stent] Ausmaß *62*
to extol the virtues [ɪkˌstəʊl ðə 'vɜ:tju:z] die Vorteile rühmen *45*
to extract [ɪk'strækt] gewinnen *84*; **extraction** [ɪk'strækʃn] Gewinnung *71*

F

fabric ['fæbrɪk] Gesellschaft *107*
facilities [fə'sɪlətɪz] Möglichkeiten *24*
faculty ['fækəltɪ] Fakultät *84*
fad [fæd] Modeerscheinung *12*
to fade [feɪd] verschwinden, verblassen *9, 66, 126*
fairy cake ['feərɪˌkeɪk] kleiner muffinähnlicher Kuchen *127*
faith [feɪθ] Glaube *57*
to fall short of expectation [fɔ:l ˌʃɔ:təvekspek'teɪʃn] weit hinter einer Erwartung zurückbleiben *45*
fallout ['fɔ:laʊt] radioaktiver Niederschlag *103*
falsehood ['fɔ:lshʊd] Lüge *35*
Famiglietti [ˌfæmɪl'jetɪ] *97*
farming practice ['fɑ:mɪŋˌpræktɪs] Anbaumethode *143*
far-ranging [ˌfɑ:'reɪndʒɪŋ] weit reichend *82*
FE college [ˌef'i:ˌkɒlɪdʒ] Aus- und Weiterbildungseinrichtung *24*
feasibility ['fi:zə'bɪlətɪ] Machbarkeit *81*
feat [fi:t] Leistung *81*
to feel like just up and ... [ˌfi:l‿laɪkdʒʌstˌʌpən '...] drauf und dran sein, etwas zu tun *98*
to fend for oneself [ˌfend‿fə wʌn'self] für sich (selbst) sorgen *68*
feverishly ['fi:vərɪʃlɪ] fieberhaft *102*
to file for divorce [ˌfaɪl fə dɪ'vɔ:s] die Scheidung einreichen *86*
final assembly [ˌfaɪnlə'semblɪ] Endmontage *142*
financial wherewithal [faɪˌnænʃl 'weəwɪðɔ:l] das nötige Kleingeld *12*
finite ['faɪnaɪt] begrenzt *56*
to fit the bill [ˌfɪtðə'bɪl] auf eine Beschreibung passen *29*
flamboyant [flæm'bɔɪənt] schillernd *95*
flask [flɑ:sk] Castor *67*
flattering ['flætərɪŋ] schmeichelhaft *86*
Flaubert ['fləʊbeə] *43*
flaw [flɔ:] Makel, Fehler *51, 135*
floodplain ['flʌdˌpleɪn] Flussaue, Polter *97*
to flourish ['flʌrɪʃ] gedeihen *137*
to flout [flaʊt] verspotten *136*; **to flout rules** [ˌflaʊt 'ru:lz] Regeln brechen *17*
fluctuating ['flʌktʃʊeɪtɪŋ] schwankend *101*
fluid [flu:ɪd] fließend *127*
to fool around [ˌfu:l ə'raʊnd] sinnlos herumspielen *68*
to forge [fɔ:dʒ] schmieden *113, 126*
forged [fɔ:dʒd] geschmiedet *67*
fossil fuel [ˌfɒsl'fjʊəl] fossiler Brennstoff *62*
foundation degree [faʊn'deɪʃndɪˌgri:] dualer Universitätsabschluss *24*
fourfold ['fɔ:fəʊld] vierfach *14*
to frazzle ['fræzl] versengen, verbrennen *105*
free-range birds [ˌfri:reɪndʒ 'bɜ:dz] freilaufendes Geflügel *21*
to freeze one's tail off [ˌfri:z wʌnz 'teɪlˌɒf] sich einen abfrieren *68*
frequently ['fri:kwəntlɪ] häufig *12*
fringe [frɪndʒ] Rand *52*
fudge [fʌdʒ] Karamell-Konfekt *47*
fuel cell ['fʊəlˌsel] Brennstoffzelle *70*
to fulfill [fʊl'fɪl] erfüllen *94*; **to fulfil aspirations** [fʊlˌfɪl ˌæspɪ'reɪʃnz] Verlangen nach etwas erfüllen *132*
to function ['fʌŋkʃn] arbeiten *58*
to fund [fʌnd] finanzieren *27*; **funding** ['fʌndɪŋ] finanzielle Unterstützung *59*

G

to gabble ['gæbl] gackern, schnattern *99*
gain [geɪn] Gewinn *27*
gas-guzzling ['gæsˌgʌzlɪŋ] mit einem hohen Benzinverbrauch *73*
Generation X [dʒenəˌreɪʃn 'eks] Generation, die zwischen 1964 und 1979 geboren ist *12*
generational hiccup [dʒenəˌreɪʃənl 'hɪkʌp] Problem, das nur eine Generation betrifft *12*
genuine ['dʒenjʊɪn] echt *23*
to get away with s.th. [getə'weɪwɪð ˌsʌmθɪŋ] ohne Strafe davonkommen *117*
to get by [get‿'baɪ] vorbeikommen *51*
to get off scot-free ['getɒfˌskɒt'fri:] ungeschoren davonkommen *119*
to get on with it [get'ɒnwɪð ˌɪt] trotz Schwierigkeiten weitermachen *117*
to get s.th. over to s.o. ['get ˌsʌmθɪŋ 'əʊvətʊ ˌsʌmwʌn] (eine Idee) verständlich machen, etwas rüberbringen *69*
Ghanaian [gɑ:'neɪən] *145*
to give rise to [ˌgɪv 'raɪz tu:] verursachen *16*
to give s.o. a pause [ˌgɪv sʌmwʌn ə 'pɔ:z] jemanden nachdenklich stimmen *81*
to give s.o. s.th. on a silver platter ['gɪv ˌsʌmwʌn ˌsʌmθɪŋ ɒnəˌsɪlvə'plætə] jemandem etwas auf einem Silbertablett servieren *68*
to give s.o. the benefit of the doubt ['gɪv ˌsʌmwʌn ðəˌbenəfɪtəvðə'daʊt] jemandem etwas nicht übel nehmen *117*
glacier ['glæsɪə] ['gleɪʃə] Gletscher *62*
glare [gleə] Blick, der töten könnte *130*
glaring ['gleərɪŋ] auffallend, eklatant *105*
glass ceiling [ˌglɑ:s‿'si:lɪŋ] Karrierehindernis *26*
gloomily ['glu:mɪlɪ] düster, trübselig *99*
GMB [ˌdʒi:em'bi:] eine britische Gewerkschaft *16*
to go broke [ˌgəʊ 'brəʊk] pleite gehen *60*
goal [gəʊl] Ziel *71*
to gobble ['gɒbl] verschlingen *13*
golly ['gɒlɪ] Ausruf: Donnerwetter! *98*
goosebumps ['gu:sbʌmps] Gänsehaut *107*
gosh [gɒʃ] Ausruf: Donnerwetter! *98*
to grab s.o. ['græb ˌsʌmwʌn] jemanden packen *68*

grainy ['greɪnɪ] unscharf, körnig *102*
grand marshal ['grænd‿ma:ʃel] Oberkommandierender einer Parade *114*
to grant s.th. ['gra:nt ˌsʌmθɪŋ] etwas gewähren *91*
granulocyte ['grænjələsaɪt] Granulozyt *87*
graph [gra:f] Diagramm *9*
grasp [gra:sp] Verständnis *56*
to grate on one's nerves [ˌgreɪt ɒn wʌnz 'nɜ:vz] auf die Nerven gehen *45*; **grated** ['greɪtɪd] gerieben *47*
to grip [grɪp] ergreifen *9*
guarantee of refuge [ˌgærən'ti:‿əv 'refju:dʒ] das Recht auf Asyl *57*
guzzling ['gʌzlɪŋ] schluckend *68*
gym bag ['dʒɪmˌbæg] Sporttasche *107*

H

habit ['hæbɪt] Gewohnheit *36*
habitable ['hæbɪtəbl] ermöglicht das menschliche Überleben *105*
habitat ['hæbɪtæt] Lebensraum *63*
hamstrung ['hæmstrʌŋ] gelähmt *132*
handout ['hændaʊt] Zuwendung, Almosen *68*
handy ['hændɪ] praktisch, gelegen *52, 73*
harbour ['ha:bə] Hafen *120*
hard hat ['ha:dˌhæt] Schutzhelm *50*
hard-edged [ˌha:d'edʒd] stark, realistisch *127*
to harness ['ha:nɪs] verbinden *23*
Hartlepool ['ha:tlɪpu:l] *54*
hassle ['hæsl] Ärger *73*
to have faith in s.o. [hæv‿'feɪθ ɪn ˌsʌmwʌn] jemandem vertrauen *69*
to have s.th. brought home to one ['hæv ˌsʌmθɪŋ ˌbrɔ:t 'həʊm tʊ‿ˌwʌn] sich etwas bewusst werden *47*
hazardous ['hæzədəs] gefährlich *66*
heavy losses [ˌhevɪ 'lɒsɪz] schwere Verluste *102*
hedge fund manager ['hedʒfʌndˌmænɪdʒə] Hedge-Fonds Manager(in) *94*
heroine ['herəʊɪn] Heldin *43*
to hibernate ['haɪbəneɪt] Winterschlaf halten *87*
high-flying [ˌhaɪ'flaɪɪŋ] erfolgreich *27*
to highlight ['haɪlaɪt] betonen *14*
highly publicised [ˌhaɪlɪ'pʌblɪsaɪzd] überall bekannt *50*
hindsight ['haɪndsaɪt] Rückblick *122*
to hoard [hɔ:d] horten *13*
to hold down [ˌhəʊld‿'daʊn] behalten *26*
Home Office ['həʊmˌɒfɪs] Innenministerium *56*
hon [hʌn] Liebling *99*
honeymoon ['hʌnɪmu:n] Flitterwochen *94*
to hook up [hʊk 'ʌp] zusammenpacken *86*
hospitable [hɒs'pɪtəbl] ermöglicht das menschliche Überleben *91*
host [həʊst] Gastgeber *32*
hostage ['hɒstɪdʒ] Geisel *122*
hostile ['hɒstaɪl] feindselig *56, 122*; **hostility** [hɒs'tɪlətɪ] Feindschaft *56*
hot red pepper [ˌhɒtˌred‿'pepə] scharfer roter Pfeffer, Chilipfeffer *143*
to hover ['hɒvə] herumstehen, herumhängen *101*
human-induced [ˌhju:mənɪn'dju:st] von Menschen verursacht *62*
humiliation [hju:ˌmɪlɪ'eɪʃn] Demütigung *122*
hurdle ['hɜ:dl] Hindernis, Hürde *56*
to hurl [hɜ:l] schleudern *95, 135*
to hurtle ['hɜ:tl] rasen *105*
hyphenated ['haɪfəneɪtɪd] in zwei Kulturen verwurzelt (mexikanisch-amerikanisch) *52*

I

I dunno ['aɪdəˌnəʊ] [ədə'nəʊ] Ich weiß nicht *99*
I got more than I bargained for. [aɪgɒtˌmɔ:ðənaɪ'ba:gɪndfɔ:] Ich habe mehr erfahren als ich wissen wollte. *86*
I hung up my car keys [aɪˌhʌŋʌpmaɪ'ka:ˌki:s] Ich habe meine Autoschlüssel für eine Weile weggelegt *73*
I repudiate your petulant expostulations. [aɪrɪ'pju:dɪeɪtjɔ: ˌpetjələntɪkˌspɒstʃə'leɪʃnz] Ich lehne Ihre lästige Kritik ab. *149*
to ignite [ɪg'naɪt] zünden *95*; **ignition** [ɪg'nɪʃn] Zündung *89*
ill-advised [ˌɪləd'vaɪzd] schlecht beraten *122*
illiterate [ɪ'lɪtərət] nicht lesen und schreiben können *24*
ills [ɪlz] Übel *141*
to imitate ['ɪmɪteɪt] nachahmen *78*
to impact [ɪm'pækt] beeinflussen *33*; **impact** ['ɪmpækt] Auswirkung *51, 71*
to impair [ɪm'peə] beeinträchtigen *102*
implication [ˌɪmplɪ'keɪʃn] Auswirkung *141*
to impose s.th. on s.o. [ɪm'pəʊz ˌsʌmθɪŋ ɒn ˌsʌmwʌn] jemandem etwas aufzwingen, auferlegen *33, 56, 132*
in demand [ˌɪndɪ'ma:nd] gesucht *27*
in due course [ɪnˌdju:'kɔ:s] rechtzeitig *44*
in effect [ɪnɪ'fekt] in Wirklichkeit *81*
in my mind's eye [ɪn‿maɪˌmaɪndz'aɪ] innerlich *47*
in this regard [ɪnˌðɪsrɪ'ga:d] diesbezüglich *41*
inaction [ɪn'ækʃn] Untätigkeit *50*
inappropriate [ˌɪnə'prəʊprɪət] unpassend, unangemessen *41*
inaudible [ɪn'ɔ:dɪbl] nicht hörbar *130*
incessant [ɪn'sesənt] unaufhörlich *44*; **incessantly** [ɪn'sesəntlɪ] unablässig *148*
to incinerate [ɪn'sɪnəreɪt] verbrennen *67*
inconvenient [ˌɪnkən'vi:nɪənt] unbequem *61*
incredibly [ɪn'kredɪblɪ] unglaublich *93*
incurable [ɪn'kjʊərəbl] unheilbar *84*
indecent [ɪn'di:sənt] unanständig, anstößig *119*
indefinite leave [ɪnˌdefɪnət'li:v] Erlaubnis auf eine unbestimmte Zeit *56*
indefinitely [ɪn'defɪnətlɪ] unbestimmt *133*
independent school [ˌɪndɪ'pendənt ˌsku:l] Privatschule *147*
indolence ['ɪndələns] Trägheit *36*
to indulge in s.th. [ɪn'dʌldʒ ɪn ˌsʌmθɪŋ] sich etwas gönnen *45*
ineluctable [ˌɪnɪ'lʌktabl] unvermeidlich *9*
inequitable [ɪ'nekwɪtəbl] ungerecht *29*
inevitable [ɪ'nevɪtəbl] unvermeidlich *137*
influence ['ɪnflʊəns] Einfluss *121*
to infringe [ɪn'frɪndʒ] einschränken *118*
infuriating [ɪn'fjʊərɪeɪtɪŋ] zornig machen *130*

ingrained [ɪn'greɪnd] eingefleischt, verwurzelt *113, 137*
inherently [ɪn'herəntlɪ] von Natur aus *77*; immer schon *132*
initially [ɪ'nɪʃəlɪ] zuerst *95*
innumerate [ɪ'nju:mərət] nicht rechnen können *24*
inquiry [ɪn'kwaɪərɪ] Untersuchung *147*
insanity [ɪn'sænətɪ] Wahnsinn *103*
insect repellent ['ɪnsekt‿rɪˌpelənt] insektenabstoßend *21*
insult ['ɪnsʌlt] Beleidigung *32*
integral ['ɪntɪgrəl] wichtig, integral *32*
intention [ɪn'tenʃn] Absicht *61*
interaction [ˌɪntə'ækʃn] Interaktion *113*
interest rate ['ɪntrəstˌreɪt] Zinssatz *141*
interference [ˌɪntə'fɪərəns] Einmischung *120*
interglacial [ˌɪntə'gleɪsɪəl] [ˌɪntə'gleɪʃl] Periode zwischen zwei Eiszeiten *62*
interminably [ɪn'tɜ:mɪnəblɪ] endlos *149*
international sports body [ˌɪntənæʃənl'spɔ:tsˌbɒdɪ] Internationales Sportkommitee *146*
internship ['ɪntɜ:nʃɪp] Praktikum *12*
to intervene [ˌɪntə'vi:n] sich einschalten, einschreiten *14, 121*
interwoven [ˌɪntə'wəʊvn] eng verbunden *126*
intruder [ɪn'tru:də] Eindringling *82*
ion exchange resin [ˌaɪɒnɪks'tʃeɪndʒˌrezɪn] Ionenaustauscherharz *67*
IPCC [ˌaɪpi:si:'si:] Weltklimarat *63*
iron cage [ˌaɪən'keɪdʒ] eiserner Käfig *12*
irrevocably [ˌɪrɪ'vəʊkəblɪ] [ɪ'revəkəblɪ] unwiderruflich *43*
issue ['ɪʃu:] Thema *62*
it would not do to … [ɪtˌwʊdnɒt‿'du:tʊ…] es wäre nicht damit getan zu … *98*

J

jaunt [dʒɔ:nt] Ausflug, Spritztour *94*
Jean Anthelme Brillat-Savarin ['ʒɑ:nɑ:nˌtelm bri:jæsævə'ra:n] *20*
jet propulsion [ˌdʒet‿prə'pʌlʃn] Düsen-, Strahlantrieb *97*
to jibe with ['dʒaɪb wɪð] übereinstimmen mit *39*
to join forces [ˌdʒɔɪn 'fɔ:sɪz] sich zusammenschließen *144*
joint [dʒɔɪnt] gemeinsam *9*
joint venture [ˌdʒɔɪnt'ventʃə] Gemeinschaftsunternehmen *97*
to jut [dʒʌt] plötzlich heben, hervorstrecken *115*

K

to keep in step [ˌki:p ɪn 'step] Schritt halten *114*
Kenye ['kenjeɪ] *110*
key language [ˌki:'læŋgwɪdʒ] Schlüsselsprache *147*
to kick-start ['kɪkstɑ:t] etwas zügig beginnen *94*
kit [kɪt] Ausrüstung *41*
knickers ['nɪkəz] Slip *41*
Kovic ['kəʊvɪk] *115*
Kuapa Kokoo [ˌkwɑ:pæ'kɒkəʊ] *145*

L

lab [læb] Labor *93*
lace lingerie [ˌleɪs 'lɒnʒərɪ] Spitzendessous *41*
lack of consensus [ˌlækəvkən'sensəs] Mangel an Konsens *23*
to lag behind [ˌlæg bɪ'haɪnd] zurückbleiben (in einer Entwicklung) *82*
Lale [lɑ:lə] *58*
large-scale [ˌlɑ:dʒ'skeɪl] ausgedehnt *144*
Las Cruces [ˌlæs'kru:sez] *95*
the latter [ðə'lætə] Letzterer *32*
launch [lɔ:ntʃ] Veröffentlichung *14*; **to launch** [lɔ:ntʃ] starten, beginnen *29, 50*
laureate ['lɔ:rɪət] Preisträger(in) *29*
lavish ['lævɪʃ] großzügig *33*
lax [læks] lose, locker *119*
to lay s.o. off [ˌleɪ ˌsʌmwʌn 'ɒf] jemanden kündigen *141*
league table ['li:gˌteɪbl] Tabelle *71*
to leak [li:k] durchsickern *105*
to leap [li:p] springen *39*
learned ['lɜ:nɪd] akademisch, wissenschaftlich *82*
to leave a mark on s.th. [ˌli:v ə 'mɑ:k ɒn ˌsʌmθɪŋ] etwas beeinflussen *16*
Lefever [lə'feɪ:və] *43*
legal barrier [ˌli:gl'bærɪə] gesetzmäßiges Hindernis *56*
Legion ['li:dʒən] Organisation amerikanischer Veteranen *115*
Leicester ['lestə] *54*
let alone [ˌletə'ləʊn] ganz zu schweigen von *148*
Liam Byrne [ˌli:əm 'bɜ:n] *56*
liberalisation [ˌlɪbərəlaɪ'zeɪʃn] Freigabe *145*
library ['laɪbrərɪ] Bibliothek *151*
life span ['laɪfspæn] Lebensdauer *78*
life-sustaining ['laɪfsəˌsteɪnɪŋ] ermöglicht das menschliche Überleben *105*
likelihood ['laɪklɪhʊd] Wahrscheinlichkeit *51*
liquefied ['lɪkwɪfaɪd] verflüssigt *71*
lite [laɪt] kalorienarm *47*
Little Miss Naughty [ˌlɪtlˌmɪs'nɔ:tɪ] unanständig *41*
lobbying group ['lɒbɪɪŋˌgru:p] Lobbyisten *71*
to lose out on s.th. [ˌlu:z'aʊt ɒn ˌsʌmθɪŋ] ins Hintertreffen geraten *26*
low-cal [ˌləʊ'kæl] kalorienarm *47*
lunar ['lu:nə] Mond- *93*; **lunar surface** [ˌlu:nə'sɜ:fɪs] Mondoberfläche *101*
to lurch [lɜ:tʃ] rucken, taumeln, schlingern *50, 97*
Luton ['lu:tən] *54*

M

m [em] ['mɪljən] Million *50*
mainstream ['meɪnstri:m] konventionell *29*
to maintain [meɪn'teɪn] bewahren *146*; **maintenance** ['meɪntənəns] Instandhaltung *73*
to make for ['meɪk fɔ:] zu Stande bringen *127*
manufacturing [ˌmænjə'fæktʃərɪŋ] Produktion *142*
to map [mæp] vermessen, kartieren *97*
marginalised ['mɑ:dʒɪnəlaɪzd] an den Rand gedrängt *14*; verdrängt *144*
Marine [mə'ri:n] Mitglied einer bestimmten Abteilung der US-Marine *115*
to mask [mɑ:sk] verstecken, verbergen *24, 52*
massive ['mæsɪv] riesig *120*
maturity [mə'tjʊərətɪ] Reife *14*

Me están volviendo loca [mee'stan bol̩bjendo'loka] Sie machen mich verrückt *52*
to measure one's steps [ˌmeʒə wʌnz‿'steps] gemessenen Schritte gehen *115*
meddling [medlɪŋ] sich einmischend *137*
mediaeval numismatic [ˌmedɪ'i:vl ˌnju:mɪz'mætɪk] Sachverständige(r) für mittelalterliche Münzen *148*
median ['mi:dɪən] Mittelwert *12, 49*
Mediterranean [ˌmedɪtər'eɪnɪən] südländisch *57*
Memorial Day [mə'mɔ:rɪəlˌdeɪ] U.S. Feiertag zu Ehren der im Krieg Gefallenen *114*
mental disorder [ˌmentldɪ'sɔ:də] geistige Störungen *14*
mercury ['mɜ:kjərɪ] Quecksilber *66*
message ['mesɪdʒ] Botschaft *113*
Metamora ['metəmɔ:rə] *117*
methane ['mi:θeɪn] Methan *62*
metric ['metrɪk] Maßsystem *36*
micron ['maɪkrɒn] Mikrometer; ein tausendstel Millimeter *97*
mid-latitudes [ˌmɪd'latɪtju:dz] mittlere Breitengrade *63*
migrant ['maɪgrənt] Migrant(in) *50*
Mikes [maɪks] *148*
minute [maɪ'nju:t] winzig *9*
Minutemen ['mɪnɪtmen] auf Abruf bereitstehende freiwillige Helfer *50*
moan [məʊn] Stöhnen *130*
model ['mɒdl] vorbildlich, ideal *120*
Mojave [məʊ'hɑ:vɪ] *95*
to monitor ['mɒnɪtə] beobachten, überprüfen, überwachen *58, 97, 144*
moral decline [ˌmɒrəldɪ'klaɪn] moralischer Verfall *9*
moral fiber [ˌmɒrəl'faɪbə] Charakterstärke *69*
mortgage ['mɔ:gɪdʒ] Hypothek *94*
motor neurone disease [ˌməʊtə'njʊərəʊndɪˌzi:s] eine Nervenkrankheit *91*
much vaunted [ˌmʌtʃ'vɔ:ntɪd] viel gelobt *135*
much-frowned-upon [ˌmʌtʃ'fraʊndəˌpɒn] verpönt *130*
multilateral [ˌmʌltɪ'lætərəl] multilateral, mehrere Staaten betreffend *135*
murky ['mɜ:kɪ] undurchsichtig *21*

N

nagging ['nægɪŋ] nörgelnd *73*
narrow ['nærəʊ] engstirnig *110*
navel-gazing ['neɪvlˌgeɪzɪŋ] Nabelschau *126*
neglected [nɪ'glektɪd] vernachlässigt *14*
negotiation [nɪˌgəʊʃɪ'eɪʃn] Verhandlung *120*;
negotiator [nɪˌgəʊʃɪ'eɪtə] Verhandlungsführer(in) *32*
nevertheless [ˌnevəðə'les] nichtsdestoweniger, nichtsdestotrotz *71, 107*
Newham ['nju:əm] *54*
nippy ['nɪpɪ] eisig *98*
nitrogen oxide [ˌnaɪtrədʒən'ɒksaɪd] Stickstoffoxid *71*
nitrous oxide [ˌnaɪtrəs'ɒksaɪd] Lachgas, Distickstoffmonoxyd *62*
Nizhne-Novgorod [ˌnɪʒnɪ'nɒvgərɒt] *149*
Nobel laureate [nəʊˌbel‿'lɔ:rɪət] Nobelpreisgewinner(in) *105*
NORAD ['nɔ:ræd] *102*
nostalgia [nɒs'tældʒə] Sehnsucht *137*; Heimweh *149*
nosey/nosy ['nəʊzɪ] neugierig *130*
notion ['nəʊʃn] Idee *121*
to nurture s.th. ['nɜ:tʃə ˌsʌmθɪŋ] etwas fördern *136*

O

obituary [əʊ'bɪtʃʊərɪ] Nachruf *68*
oblivious [ə'blɪvɪəs] die Situation vergessend *130*
obsessively [əb'sesɪvlɪ] zwanghaft *43*
to obtain [əb'teɪn] erhalten *97*
to occupy ['ɒkjʊpaɪ] (Zeit) in Anspruch nehmen *36*
offended [ə'fendɪd] beleidigt *131*
official [ə'fɪʃl] Beamte(r) *151*
on an annual basis [ɒnənˌænjʊəl'beɪsɪs] jährlich *151*
on the polysyllabic lines [ɒn ðə ˌpɒlɪsɪ'læbɪk ˌlaɪnz] Taktik der Mehrsilbigkeit *149*
orgy ['ɔ:dʒɪ] Orgie *44*
origin ['ɒrɪdʒɪn] Abstammung *57*
ostrich ['ɒstrɪtʃ] Strauß; Person, die den Kopf in den Sand steckt *130*
outsourcing ['aʊtsɔ:sɪŋ] Tätigkeiten durch eine Fremdfirma ausführen lassen *142*
overall [ˌəʊvər'ɔ:l] gesamt *142*
to overextend [ˌəʊvərɪk'stend] sich übernehmen *122*
to overhear [ˌəuvə'hɪə] zufällig mitbekommen *102*
overt [əʊ'vɜ:t] offen, unverhohlen *56*
overwhelmingly [ˌəʊvə'welmɪŋglɪ] überwiegend *126*

P

padded bra [ˌpædɪd‿'brɑ:] gepolsterter BH *41*
palpable ['pælpəbl] spürbar *44*
paneled ['pænəld] getäfelt *52*
partially ['pɑ:ʃəlɪ] teilweise *27*
partition [pɑ:'tɪʃn] Aufteilung *132*
pastry ['peɪstrɪ] süßes Teilchen *47*
patio ['pætɪəʊ] Terrasse *44*
pavement ['peɪvmənt] Gehsteig *13*
to pay homage [ˌpeɪ 'hɒmɪdʒ] huldigen *113*
to pay up front [ˌpeɪ‿ʌp'frʌnt] im Voraus bezahlen *95*
to peak [pi:k] einen Höchststand erreichen *95*
pecking order ['pekɪŋˌɔ:də] Hackordnung *147*
pension ['penʃn] Rente *13*
to perceive [pə'si:v] wahrnehmen *32*
perennial hand-wringing [pəˌrenɪəl 'hændˌrɪŋɪŋ] ständiges Klagen *9*
to permit [pə'mɪt] erlauben *14*
persecuted ['pɜ:sɪkju:tɪd] verfolgt werden *57*
to persist [pə'sɪst] andauern, sich halten *23*
pester ['pestə] Quengelei *41*
pesticide ['pestɪsaɪd] Pestizid *21*
to pick a pet [ˌpɪk ə 'pet] einen neuen Liebling auswählen *98*
pickle ['pɪkl] saure Gurke *13*
Picoult [pɪ'kəʊ] *86*
to pigeonhole ['pɪdʒənhəʊl] in eine Schublade stecken *23*
pimiento [pɪ'mjentəʊ] rote Paprika *47*
to place oneself at the sharp end of s.th. [ˌpleɪs wʌnˌself ət‿ðə ˌʃɑ:p'endəv ˌsʌmθɪŋ] sich ins Zentrum des Geschehens rücken *50*
platform ['plætfɔ:m] Podium, Bühne *115*
to plead [pli:d] (dringend) bitten, appellieren *50*
to plod along [ˌplɒd ə'lɒŋ] mühsam vorwärts schreiten, entlangdümpeln *105*

ploy [plɔɪ] List, Dreh 51
to plummet ['plʌmɪt] sinken 24
to point to evidence [ˌpɔɪnt‿tʊ‿ 'evɪdəns] auf Fakten aufmerksam machen 9
a pointed look [ə ˌpɔɪntɪd'lʊk] kritischer Blick 130
pole [pəʊl] Pfosten, Pfahl 50; **pole-dancing** ['pəʊlˌdɑːnsɪŋ] um eine Stange tanzend 41
poll [pəʊl] Meinungsumfrage 93
polyunsaturated [ˌpɒlɪʌn'sætʃəreɪtɪd] mehrfach ungesättigt 47
to pootle off [ˌpuːtl'ɒf] wegfahren 73
poppycock ['pɒpɪkɒk] Quatsch 60
poppyseeds ['pɒpɪsiːdz] Mohn 47
portacath ['pɔːtəkæθ] tragbarer Katheter 87
to pose [pəʊz] darstellen 66
preceding [priː'siːdɪŋ] vorangehend 119
precious ['preʃəs] kostbar 21
predictable [prɪ'dɪktəbl] vorhersehbar 66; **prediction** [prɪ'dɪkʃn] Vorhersage 91
pregnancy ['pregnənsɪ] Schwangerschaft 9
pre-industrial [ˌpriːɪn'dʌstrɪəl] vorindustriell 63
premise ['premɪs] Idee 113
preposterously [prɪ'pɒstərəslɪ] unsinnig 47
preserve [prɪ'zɜːv] Vorrecht 16
pressing ['presɪŋ] dringlich 93
to pressurise ['preʃəraɪz] drängen 41
prestigious [pres'tɪdʒəs] wichtig 91
prevalence ['prevələns] Vorkommen 17
private investigator [ˌpraɪvətɪn'vestɪgeɪtə] Privatdetektiv(in) 51
proceedings [prə'siːdɪŋz] Vorgehensweise 32
to proclaim [prə'kleɪm] erklären 59
profligate ['prɒflɪgət] verschwenderisch 43
profound [prə'faʊnd] tiefgründig 93; wirkungsvoll 141
progression [prə'greʃn] Fortschritt 82
to prohibit [prə'hɪbɪt] verbieten 84
to promote [prə'məʊt] werben 58; fördern, unterstützen 127
promyelocytic leukemia [prəˌmaɪələˌsɪtɪkljuː'kiːmɪə] Promyelozytenleukämie 87
property ['prɒpətɪ] Eigenschaft 81
to prosper ['prɒspə] gedeihen 24; **prosperous** ['prɒspərəs] wohlhabend, florierend 54
psyche ['saɪkiː] Seele 137
to pull s.th. ['pʊl ˌsʌmθɪŋ] etwas zurückziehen 39
purchase ['pɜːtʃəs] Kauf 145
pursuit [pə'sjuːt] [pə'suːt] Verfolgung, Streben nach 97
to put s.th. in a nutshell ['pʊt ˌsʌmθɪŋ ɪnə'nʌtʃel] etwas kurz und bündig sagen 121
to putt [pʌt] (Golf) einlochen 101

Q

quantum entanglement [ˌkwɒntəmɪn'tæŋglmənt] Quantenverschränkung 81
to quash [kwɒʃ] halten 51
quest [kwest] Bestreben 95
queue [kjuː] Warteschlange 56
to quit [kwɪt] aufgeben 99

R

radiation [ˌreɪdɪ'eɪʃn] Strahlung 91
railings ['reɪlɪŋz] Geländer 13
Rainie ['reɪniː] 36
to raise its stock [ˌreɪz ɪts‿'stɒk] den Wert steigern 135
random encounter [ˌrændəmɪn'kaʊntə] unerwartete Begegnung 54
ratio ['reɪʃɪəʊ] Verhältnis 21
to reach the bottom of the barrel [ˌriːtʃ ðəˌbɒtəməvðə'bærəl] unpassend sein 44
Reading ['redɪŋ] 54
real estate ['riːlɪˌsteɪt] Immobilien 21
realm [relm] Reich 124
reams of print [ˌriːmzəv'prɪnt] ganze Bände 130
to reap the fruit of s.th. [ˌriːp ðə 'fruːt‿əv ˌsʌmθɪŋ] die Früchte von etwas ernten 12
to rear [rɪə] großziehen 9
reassuringly [ˌriːə'ʃʊərɪŋlɪ] beruhigend 43
receipt [rɪ'siːt] Kassenzettel 131
recession [rɪ'seʃn] Rezession 151
recipe ['resɪpɪ] Rezept 127
to reciprocate [rɪ'sɪprəkeɪt] erwidern 33
to reckon ['rekən] vermuten 27, 81
to recruit [rɪ'kruːt] rekrutieren, anstellen 57
to refer s.th. [rɪ'fɜː ˌsʌmθɪŋ] etwas weiterleiten 39
to reflect s.th. [rɪ'flekt ˌsʌmθɪŋ] darstellen 20
to refrain from [rɪ'freɪn frəm] Abstand nehmen von 126
refuge ['refjuːdʒ] Zuflucht 21
to regulate a language [ˌregjəleɪt ə 'læŋgwɪdʒ] Sprachregeln einführen 146
to rehome [ˌriː'həʊm] einen neuen Besitzer finden 44
reincarnation [ˌriːɪnkɑː'neɪʃn] Wiedergeburt 85
to reinforce [ˌriːɪn'fɔːs] verstärken, betonen 127
relapse [rɪ'læps] ['riːlæps] Rückfall 87
release [rɪ'liːs] Erleichterung 44
relentless [rɪ'lentləs] unerbittlich 20
reliability [rɪˌlaɪə'bɪlətɪ] Zuverlässigkeit 81; **reliance** [rɪ'laɪəns] Verlass 26
religious affiliation [rɪˌlɪdʒəsəˌfɪlɪ'eɪʃn] Glaubenszugehörigkeit 132
reluctance [rɪ'lʌktəns] Abneigung, Widerwillen 122
to remain [rɪ'meɪn] bleiben 56; **remains** [rɪ'meɪnz] Überreste 101
reminiscent [ˌremɪ'nɪsənt] erinnernd 126
remote [rɪ'məʊt] entlegen 51; **remote working** [rɪˌməʊt'wɜːkɪŋ] Telearbeit 27
to remove [rɪ'muːv] entfernen 39
renewable [rɪ'njuːəbl] erneuerbar 70; **renewed** [rɪ'njuːd] erneut, wiederholt 122
renowned [rɪ'naʊnd] angesehen, berühmt 95
repercussion [ˌriːpə'kʌʃn] eine negative Auswirkung 122
reprocessing [ˌriː'prəʊsesɪŋ] Wiederaufbereitung 66
resentment [rɪ'zentmənt] Groll, Vorbehalte 56
resident ['rezɪdənt] wohnhaft, ansässig 53
resource [rɪ'zɔːs] (finanzielle) Mittel 56
respite ['respɪt] ['respaɪt] Ruhepause 132
to respond [rɪ'spɒnd] reagieren 145
to retain [rɪ'teɪn] behalten 56
retiree [rɪˌtaɪə'riː] Rentner(in) 51; **retirement** [rɪ'taɪəmənt] Ruhestand 26

to retreat [rɪ'tri:t] sich zurückziehen *62*
to reveal [rɪ'vi:l] bekannt geben *147*
revolutions per minute [revəˌlu:ʃnz pə'mɪnɪt] Umdrehungen pro Minute *75*
reward [rɪ'wɔ:d] Belohnung *29*
rigid ['rɪdʒɪd] streng *67*
to rile [raɪl] ärgern, reizen *98*
riot [raɪət] Aufruhr *151*
rogue [rəʊg] ungewöhnlich laut *130*
root [ru:t] Wurzel *113*
to rotate [rəʊ'teɪt] rotieren *151*
rotten ['rɒtn] verzogen *68*
row [raʊ] Auseinandersetzung *9*
rumbling ['rʌmblɪŋ] Grollen *61*
to run headlong [ˌrʌn 'hedlɒŋ] sich unbeschwert ins Erwachsenwerden stürzen *87*
to run in the family [ˌrʌn ɪn ðə 'fæməlɪ] in der Familie liegen *9*
to run interference [ˌrʌn ˌɪntə'fɪərəns] von etwas ablenken *103*

S

S.E.T.I. Institute ['seti:‿ˌɪnstɪtju:t] *101*
sacrifice ['sækrɪfaɪs] Opfer *115*
safety precaution ['seɪftɪprɪˌkɔ:ʃn] Sicherheitsvorkehrung *93*
sample ['sɑ:mpl] Kostprobe *13*
SAT [ˌeseɪ'ti:] Qualifizierungstests für die Zulassung zum Studium *87*
saviour ['seɪvjə] Rettung *144*
to savor ['seɪvə] genießen *12*
scale [skeɪl] Umfang *142*
to scan [skæn] absuchen *101*
scarce [skeəs] knapp *56, 63*
scope [skəʊp] Ausmass, Umfang *142*
score [skɔ:] Anzahl *54*
scourge of s.th. ['skɜ:dʒ əv ˌsʌmθɪŋ] Plage, Geißel *135*
to scout [skaʊt] erkunden, auskundschaften *51*
scratch [skrætʃ] Kratzer *67*
scrubland ['skrʌblænd] Buschland *63*
to seal [si:l] verschließen *67*; **to seal off** [si:l 'ɒf] absperren, abriegeln *119*
to sear [sɪə] versengen, verbrennen *105*
to seek, sought, sought [si:k, sɔ:t, sɔ:t] versuchen *29*; suchen *57*
self-esteem [ˌselfɪ'sti:m] Selbstwertgefühl *43*
sell-out ['selaʊt] Verräter(in) *111*
sensitive ['sensɪtɪv] heikel *59*
sequential [sɪ'kwenʃl] regelmäßig, fortlaufend *101*; **sequentially** [sɪ'kwenʃəlɪ] nacheinander *33*
to set in train [ˌset ɪn 'treɪn] in Gang setzen *59*
to set s.o. back [ˌset sʌmwʌn 'bæk] jemanden kosten *73*
to set s.th. apart [set ˌsʌmθɪŋ‿ə'pɑ:t] etwas absetzen *58*
to set the Cassandras wailing [ˌset‿ðə kə'sændrəz ˌweɪlɪŋ] Cassandrarufe verursachen *9*
settlement ['setlmənt] Übereinkunft, Regelung *121*
Seunghui [ˌsʌŋ'hi:] *119*
severely [sə'vɪəlɪ] außerordentlich *113*
shade grown [ˌʃeɪd'grəʊn] im Schatten angebaut *144*
to shake up [ʃeɪk 'ʌp] etwas ändern *61*
to shame s.o. ['ʃeɪm ˌsʌmwʌn] jemanden beschämen *51*
Shami Chakrabarti [ˌʃɑ:mɪ ˌtʃækrə'bɑ:tɪ] *127*
share price ['ʃeəˌpraɪs] Wert *135*
sheik [ʃeɪk] [ʃi:k] [ʃek] Scheich *68*
shielded ['ʃi:ldɪd] abgeschirmt *66*
shift [ʃɪft] Veränderung *12, 97*; **to shift** [ʃɪft] sich verlagern *63*
shortcoming ['ʃɔ:tˌkʌmɪŋ] Mangel, Fehler *77*
shovel ['ʃʌvl] Schaufel *69*
to shrug s.th. off [ˌʃrʌg ˌsʌmθɪŋ 'ɒf] etwas als unwichtig abtun *117*
to sift through [ˌsɪft‿'θru:] sichten, durchgehen *101*
significant [sɪg'nɪfɪkənt] wichtig, bezeichnend *36*
sincerity [sɪn'serətɪ] Aufrichtigkeit *32*
single ['sɪŋgl] (einzelnes) Lied *44*
to sink [sɪŋk] ignorieren *59*
skilled [skɪld] qualifiziert *141*
skin graft ['skɪnˌgrɑ:ft] Hauttransplantation *117*
skin-care ['skɪnˌkeə] Hautpflege *94*
to skip s.th. ['skɪp ˌsʌmθɪŋ] etwas auslassen *27*
to skyrocket ['skaɪˌrɒkɪt] in die Höhe schießen *122*
slacker ['slækə] Person, die ziellos herumdriftet *12*
Slade [sleɪd] britische Band aus den 1970ern *44*
slight [slaɪt] leicht *149*
to sling, slung, slung [slɪŋ, slʌŋ, slʌŋ] umhängen *50*
slope [sləʊp] Hang *68*
Slough [slaʊ] *54*
sludge [slʌdʒ] Schlamm *67*
to slump [slʌmp] sich fallen lassen (z.B. auf einen Stuhl) *102*
smooth [smu:ð] flüssig *52*
to snap to attention [ˌsnæptʊə'tenʃn] zackig Haltung annehmen *102*
to soar [sɔ:] hochschnellen *79*
sobriety [səʊ'braɪətɪ] Nüchternheit, Ernst *13*
social cohesion [ˌsəʊʃlkəʊ'hi:ʒn] Zusammenhalt *23*
sociopath ['səʊsɪəʊpæθ] Soziopath *9*
solar array [ˌsəʊlər‿ə'reɪ] Solarmodul *92*
solicitor [sə'lɪsɪtə] Anwalt/Anwältin *27*
to somersault ['sʌməsɔ:lt] ['sʌməsɒlt] einen Salto/Purzelbaum machen *95*
sophistication [səˌfɪstɪ'keɪʃn] hoher Entwicklungsstand, Komplexität *93*
sourdough ['saʊədəʊ] Sauerteig *47*
space [speɪs] Zeitraum *43*
spectre ['spektə] Gespenst *9*
to speed up [spi:d 'ʌp] beschleunigen *20*
spent [spent] verbraucht *67*
spin [spɪn] Spin *81*
to spiral out of control [ˌspaɪərəl ˌaʊtəvkən'trəʊl] völlig außer Kontrolle geraten *43*
to spit [spɪt] spucken *13*
to split [splɪt] (auf)spalten *113*
to sport [spɔ:t] zur Schau stellen *16*
spouse [spaʊs] Ehemann oder Ehefrau *130*
sprawl [sprɔ:l] Ausbreitung *132*
spree [spri:] große Einkaufstour *43*
squash [skwɒʃ] Squash, Butternutkürbis *21*
Squyres [skwaɪəz] *93*
stab [stæb] Stich *43*
stag night ['stægˌnaɪt] Junggesellenabend *16*
to stagger ['stægə] schwanken, wanken *115*
to stall [stɔ:l] stecken bleiben *12*

stanchion ['stænʃn] Stütze *50*
stand-off ['stændɒf] Patt(situation) *121*
state of affairs [ˌsteɪtəvə'feəz] Situation *29*
statutory paternity leave [ˌstætjətrɪ pə'tɜ:nətɪˌli:v] gesetzlicher Vaterschaftsurlaub *26*
steamer ['sti:mə] Dampfer *113*
to stem [stem] aufhalten *122*
stem cell ['stemˌsel] Stammzelle *84*
stern [stɜ:n] ernst *103*
Stetson ['stetsən] Cowboyhut *51*
to sting s.o. ['stɪŋ ˌsʌmwʌn] jemanden treffen, schmerzen *103*
to stock [stɒk] auf Lager haben *145*
stoically ['stəʊɪkəlɪ] stoisch *117*
story line ['stɔ:rɪlaɪn] Handlung *113*
strain [streɪn] Belastung, Anstrengung *23, 148*
strains [streɪnz] Melodie *44*
a strand of racism [ə ˌstrændəv'reɪsɪzm] Rassismusanteil *126*
to stride [straɪd] schreiten *82*
strife [straɪf] Konflikt *113*
to strive, strove, striven [straɪv, strəʊv, strɪvn] streben nach *126*
stubborn ['stʌbən] hartnäckig *26*
submerged [səb'mɜ:dʒd] überschwemmt *60*
suborbital [ˌsʌb'ɔ:bɪtl] unterhalb der Umlaufbahn *95*
substantial [səb'stænʃl] beträchtlich, umfangreich *53, 71*
to substitute ['sʌbstɪtju:t] ersetzen *43*; **substitution** [ˌsʌbstɪ'tju:ʃn] Ersatz *71*
successor [sək'sesə] Nachfolger(in) *120*
Suez debacle ['su:ɪzdeɪˌbɑ:kl] Krise um den Suezkanal *137*
sufficient [sə'fɪʃənt] ausreichend *23*; **sufficiently** [sə'fɪʃəntlɪ] ausreichend *39*
to not suit s.o. [nɒt 'su:t ˌsʌmwʌn] jemandem nicht stehen *13*
sullenly ['sʌlənlɪ] mürrisch, missmutig *102*
summit ['sʌmɪt] Gipfeltreffen *151*
supervision [ˌsu:pə'vɪʒn] Aufsicht *27*
supplemental [ˌsʌplɪ'mentl] zusätzlich *36*
to supply [sə'plaɪ] liefern *145*
to support [sə'pɔ:t] unterstützen *115*
surgeon ['sɜ:dʒən] Chirurg(in) *16*
suspicion [sə'spɪʃn] Argwohn *59*
to sustain [sə'steɪn] erleiden *67, 102*; unterstützen *132*; **sustainable** [sə'steɪnəbl] nachhaltig *26, 70, 71*
to sway [sweɪ] schwanken *50*
to swear [sweə] fluchen *13*
sweep [swi:p] Bewegung *79*
swift [swɪft] schnell *20*
to swipe a card [ˌswaɪp ə 'kɑ:d] ein Karte lesen lassen *73*

T

tactile ['tæktaɪl] taktil *32*
to tailor ['teɪlə] anpassen *32*
to take off [teɪk 'ɒf] sich weit verbreiten *79*
take-up ['teɪkʌp] Akzeptanz *147*
talk radio ['tɔ:kˌreɪdɪəʊ] Radiosender mit Talkshows und Zuhörerbeteiligung *119*
to tap [tæp] durchdringen *16*; nutzen *23*; anzapfen *81*; **to tap into s.th.** [ˌtæp'ɪntʊ ˌsʌmθɪŋ] mit etwas vertraut sein *36*
to target s.th. ['tɑ:gɪt ˌsʌmθɪŋ] sich auf etwas konzentrieren *142*
tariff barrier ['tærɪfˌbærɪə] Zollschranke *142*
to tax away [ˌtæks ə'weɪ] (über Gebühr) besteuern *99*
the bottom line is ... [ðəˌbɒtem'laɪn ɪz...] Tatsache ist.../alles in allem *108*
"The Sky Is Falling" [ðə'skaɪ‿ɪz ˌfɔ:lɪŋ] übertriebene Katastrophenmeldung *60*
theatre ['θɪətə] Kriegsschauplatz *121*
think tank ['θɪŋkˌtæŋk] Expertenkommission *26, 51*
this remains to be seen [ðɪsrɪˌmeɪnztəbɪ'si:n] man wird sehen/wir werden sehen *79*
thorough ['θʌrə] gründlich *119*
thronged [θrɒŋd] voll (mit Menschen) *45*
thus [ðʌs] so, somit *142*
to tie for second place [ˌtaɪ fə ˌsekənd‿'pleɪs] zusammen auf Platz zwei folgen *62*
tied to s.th. ['taɪd‿tʊ ˌsʌmθɪŋ] mit etwas verbunden *137*
tightrope ['taɪtrəʊp] Hochseil *26*
time-consuming ['taɪmkənˌsju:mɪŋ] zeitaufwändig *47*
to tinker with ['tɪŋkə wɪð] herumpfuschen an *98*
tiny ['taɪnɪ] klein, winzig *97*
to s.o.'s cost [tʊ ˌsʌmwʌnz 'kɒst] auf jemands Kosten *59*
to toil [tɔɪl] sich abmühen, plagen *50*
token ['təʊkən] Merkmal *52*
tool belt ['tu:lˌbelt] Werkzeuggürtel *50*
tour guide ['tʊəˌgaɪd] Reiseführer(in) *141*
toxic ['tɒksɪk] giftig *66*
to track [træk] aufspüren, verfolgen *142*
trade [treɪd] Berufszweig *16*; **trade off** ['treɪdɒf] Kompromiss *71*
trade regime ['treɪdreɪˌʒi:m] Handelsmacht *135*
trait [treɪt] Charakterzug *43*
to transcend [træn'send] übersteigen *126*
a transitional never-neverland [ə trænˌzɪʃənl ˌneve'nevəˌlænd] Durchgangsstadium *12*
transmission [trænz'mɪʃn] Übertragung *17*
transmitted [trænz'mɪtɪd] übertragen *14*
transparency [træn'spærənsɪ] Folie *102*
to trap [træp] etwas am Entweichen hindern *62*; **trapped** [træpt] gefangen *61*
to treasure ['treʒə] schätzen, wertschätzen *107*
treat [tri:t] Vergnügen, Freude *41*; **to treat oneself** ['tri:t wʌnˌself] sich etwas Gutes tun *43*
tremendously [trə'mendəslɪ] äußerst, ausgesprochen *130*
trunk [trʌŋk] Kofferraum *115*
Tseng Tan-Kiang [ˌtseŋˌtænkɪ'æŋ] *111*
Tucson ['tu:sɒn] *50*
turbot ['tɜ:bət] Steinbutt *20*
turd [tɜ:d] Scheißhaufen *102*
to turn a profit [ˌtɜ:n ə 'prɒfɪt] Gewinn erzielen *95*
to tut [tʌt] Mißmut ausdrücken *130*

U

ultimate ['ʌltɪmət] größtmöglich *93*
umbrella body [ʌm'breləˌbɒdɪ] Dachorganisation *59*
to undermine s.th. [ˌʌndə'maɪn ˌsʌmθɪŋ] etwas untergraben *137*
unheralded [ʌn'herəldɪd] nicht angekündigt, unerwartet *82*

unprecedented [ʌn'presɪdəntɪd] nie dagewesen *63, 79, 141*
unregulated [ʌn'regjəleɪtɪd] nicht (gesetzlich) geregelt *16*
unresolved [ˌʌnrɪ'zɒlvd] nicht endgültig festgelegt *132*
unseemly [ʌn'si:mlɪ] unpassend *130*
to uphold s.th. [ʌp'həʊld ˌsʌmθɪŋ] etwas aufrechterhalten *135*
to urge [3:dʒ] drängen *44*; **urgency** ['3:dʒənsɪ] Dringlichkeit *32*
to usher in [ˌʌʃər‿'ɪn] (ein neues Zeitalter) einleiten *120*
utter pointlessness [ˌʌtə 'pɔɪntləsnəs] absolute Sinnlosigkeit *130*; **utterly** ['ʌtəlɪ] vollständig *73*

V

vacant ['veɪkənt] frei *99*
to vacation [və'keɪʃn] Urlaub machen *86*
to value ['vælju:] (wert)schätzen *36*; **value** ['vælju:] Wert *58*; **valued** ['vælju:d] geschätzt *27*
vapour ['veɪpə] Dampf *62*
vault [vɔ:lt] [vɒlt] (Keller)gewölbe *67*
velocity [vɪ'lɒsətɪ] Geschwindigkeit *36*
to vent [vent] deutliche Kritik üben *39*
venture ['ventʃə] Unternehmen *91*; **to venture out** [ˌventʃər‿'aʊt] sich hinaus wagen *56*
vet [vet] Veteran *114*
vibe [vaɪb] Stimmung *43*
vicious circle [ˌvɪʃəs‿'s3:kl] Teufelskreis *43*
to vindicate ['vɪndɪkeɪt] rechtfertigen, bestätigen *119*
to violate ['vaɪəleɪt] verletzen *130*
vital ['vaɪtl] unerlässlich, lebensnotwendig *91*
vocational [vəʊ'keɪʃənl] Berufs- *23*
to voice [vɔɪs] äußern, zum Ausdruck bringen *56*
void [vɔɪd] Leere *43*
voucher scheme ['vaʊtʃəˌski:m] Rabattcouponaktion *41*

W

to wage [weɪdʒ] führen *121*
waist [weɪst] Taille *115*
warp drive ['wɔ:pˌdraɪv] Warpantrieb *91*
watershed ['wɔ:təʃed] Zeitpunkt, vor dem Fernsehsendungen, die für Kinder ungeeignet sind, nicht gezeigt werden dürfen *41*
waxy ['wæksɪ] glänzend *21*
wear and tear [ˌweərən'teə] Verschleiss *73*
to wear off [weər‿'ɒf] nachlassen *43*
wearily ['wɪərəlɪ] abgespannt, erschöpft *99*
well-off [ˌwel'ɒf] gut dran *111*
well-to-wheel [ˌweltə'wi:l] bezüglich der Brennstoffproduktion von der Quelle bis zur Verwendung im Fahrzeug *71*
Westminster model [west'mɪnstəˌmɒdl] Parlamentssystem, benannt nach dem britischen Parlament
wetland drainage [ˌwetlænd‿'dreɪnɪdʒ] Trockenlegung von Feuchtgebieten *97*
what possesses anyone to do s.th. [ˌwɒt‿pəˌzesɪz 'enɪwʌn tʊ 'du: ˌsʌmθɪŋ] was treibt jemanden dazu etwas zu machen *44*
whipped cream [ˌwɪpt'kri:m] Schlagsahne *47*
white goods ['waɪt‿ˌgʊdz] weiße Ware *79*
win-win situation [ˌwɪn'wɪnsɪtjʊˌeɪʃn] ein Gewinn für beide Seiten *145*
withdrawal [wɪð'drɔ:əl] Rückzug, Abzug *122*
witty ['wɪtɪ] geistreich *130*
work placement ['w3:kˌpleɪsmənt] Praktikum *23*
World's Series [ˌw3:ldz‿'sɪəri:z] Endspiel im Baseball *98*
wrinkled ['rɪŋkld] faltig, runzelig *98*

Y

Yankee Doodle [ˌjæŋkɪ'du:dl] patriotisch *114*
Yasmin Alibhai-Brown [ˌjæzmɪn ˌælɪbaɪ'braʊn] *126*
yearning ['j3:nɪŋ] Verlangen *113*
You can't take it with you. [jʊˌkɑ:nt‿teɪkɪt'wɪðju:] Du kannst es nicht mit ins Grab nehmen. *69*
You're more likely to... [jɔ:ˌmɔ:'laɪklɪ tʊ...] Die Wahrscheinlichkeit ist größer, dass Sie... *27*

Glossary

The glossary explains literary terms and terms which you need to understand when working with texts and completing tasks in English. The words in **blue print** are explained in their own glossary entry.

abbreviation short form of a word or phrase made by leaving out some of the letters or only using the first few letters of a word. Example: 'Rd' is the abbreviation for 'Road'.

acronym short form of a phrase in which a new 'word' is made by using the first letters of the words in the phrase. Example: AIDS is an acronym for Acquired Immune Deficiency Syndrome.

alliteration repetition of sounds, especially consonants, either at the beginning of each word in a group or on certain syllables within each of the words. Example: 'seven singing sisters'.

allusion reference to a well-known person or event. These persons or events may come from a historical, religious or literary context.

antagonist the character who is opposed to, or is in conflict with, the main character or **protagonist** in a **novel**, **play** or **short story**.

antonym see **opposite**.

assonance repetition of the same or similar vowel sounds within stressed syllables of neighbouring words. Example: "on the dole with nowhere to go".

atmosphere the dominant feeling or mood in a text often created by the writer's use of **setting** and description.

character person in a piece of fiction whose personality develops through action, description, language and way of speaking.
- Flat characters lack depth and represent constant, non-changing types rather than full personalities.
- Round characters are like real people who can change and develop.

characterization how a character is presented. When a character is presented directly, the **narrator** or another figure tells the reader what the character is like. When a character is presented indirectly, the reader has to find out what the character is like by analysing his or her actions, thoughts, words, etc.

cliché description of a group of things or people in a way that has been done so often before that it is no longer interesting. See **stereotype**.

climax the most intense point in a novel, short story or drama. This point in the plot often coincides with the crisis or turning point, when the protagonist experiences a dramatic change that will better or worsen his situation

collocation words which often appear combined as a unit. Example: to take a photo, a good laugh.

colloquial language **synonym** for **informal language**. A 'colloquialism' is a colloquial word or phrase.

comment short **essay** giving your opinion on a topic (usually about 200 words). See *skills file* on page 157.

connotation additional meaning of a word beyond its dictionary definition(s).

curriculum vitae (CV) short formal written account of personal details, education, work experience, etc. usually sent with a letter when applying for a job. (See *skills file* on p. 174.)

denotation actual meaning of a word as defined in a dictionary.

drama piece of fiction, also known as a **play**, usually written for performance on stage, in films or on TV. It is characterized by dialogue and **stage directions**. It may be written as a **poem** or **prose**.

essay piece of writing usually between 300–600 words. See *skills file* on p. 157.

euphemism device used to make something unpleasant sound nicer by expressing it in a more pleasant, less direct way. Example: 'to pass away' is a euphemism of 'to die'.

exposition structural element at the beginning of a longer text, in which the main **characters** are introduced, the **setting** is described, and first indications of the **atmosphere** and **tone** are made.

falling action the part of a **fictional** text which occurs after the crisis has been reached, when the conflict is resolved and there is a clear reduction of suspense.

fictional not real, invented by a writer.

figurative language words (figures of speech) used in an imaginative, abstract context rather than with their literal definitions. Metaphors, similes, and personification are examples of figurative language. Example: "Girls are like cats". The term imagery is a synonym for figurative language.

flashback interruption of the chronological order of a text in order to go back in time and show what happened earlier.

foreshadowing anticipating events that will occur later in the story.

formal language used to address people you don't know well. A formal style shows detachment and respect. It typically uses precise and often difficult vocabulary, full forms and frequently long, complex sentences.

genre type of text such as poetry, drama, fiction and non-fiction.

hyperbole statement which is exaggerated for effect. Example: "The way he put his car keys on the desk indicated that he had a fleet of Cadillacs parked outside".

imagery see figurative language.

informal language relaxed, personal and subjective communication. It typically involves the use of quite simple language, short forms, uncomplicated sentence patterns and fillers.

irony a statement expressing the opposite of what is really meant. The reader is expected to realize the true meaning. Example: You say, "What a lovely day!" when the weather is terrible.

literal meaning of a word as defined in a dictionary.

literary devices synonym for rhetorical devices (see also *skills file* on p. 164).

metaphor way of describing something by saying it is something else. Example: Journalists are vultures.

narrator the narrator is the person who tells a story in a novel or short story. The narrator is not identical with the writer. If the story is written as if someone was telling it themselves, using the 'I' form, the narrator is a first-person narrator. The first-person narrator can only tell you what he/she does, thinks, and feels, so he/she always has a limited point of view. A third-person narrator is not a character in the story, but stands outside it. The story is told in the third person (he/she/they). The point of view of a third-person narrator can be limited or omniscient (unlimited).

non-fictional true to life; the writer refers only to real people and places and to events that do or did take place.

note making writing down, in short form, information you are given from a written source.

note taking writing down, in short form, information you are given from a spoken source.

novel long and complex fictional story, written in prose, which typically includes characters, setting(s) and a plot.

opposite (also known as **antonym**) word or term which has roughly the opposite meaning of another word. Example: soft ≠ hard.

parody fictional text which imitates the form or language of a well-known piece of writing.

personification technique of presenting animals, plants, objects, the forces of nature or abstract ideas as if they were human beings and had human qualities. Example: "Atlanta was young for her years."

plot the writer's careful selection and arrangement of related events. A plot, found in most novels, short stories or dramas, typically consists of a conflict, which develops during the rising action and reaches a climax, which is then followed by falling action and finally a resolution of the conflict.

poem writing divided into single lines that express ideas, experiences and feelings through the use of descriptive and figurative language. Traditional poetry uses four poetic devices:

- metre = the regular pattern of stressed and unstressed syllables;
- stanza = the usually regular number of lines which form a unit;
- rhythm = the sound pattern which is created primarily by the metre;
- rhyme = the repetition of the same or similar sounds, often found at the ends of words.

Modern poetry often does not have a regular rhythm or rhyme scheme (the pattern created by rhymed words).

point of view perspective or position from which the narrator presents the story to the reader.

project a major assignment which usually involves some kind of research.

prose writing which is used for articles, essays,

novels, short stories and most dramas. This type of 'everyday language' is composed of lines of various lengths which flow together and are divided into paragraphs.

protagonist the main character in a novel, play or short story.

pun play on words. Example: "The sole has no feet and therefore no soul, poor soul."

quotation a sentence or phrase taken word for word from another source. If you quote someone, or quote from a text, you use the exact words spoken or written, usually to support an argument.

report factual text written objectively describing a particular event or point.

rhetorical devices synonym for literary devices (see *skills file* on p. 164).

rhetorical question question to which an answer is not expected; it is used for emphasis or organizational purposes.

rising action structural element of a fictional text, marked by an increase in suspense and an intensifying of the conflict.

sarcasm bitter or aggressive remark used to express disapproval or mockery.

satire a humorous, fictional text that criticizes certain conditions, events or people by making them appear ridiculous. It differs from comedy in that it tries to correct and improve rather than to be only funny.

science fiction literary genre in which fantastic adventures take place on Earth, on other planets or in other worlds, mostly in the future. Fictional technological developments and inventions play a major part in this genre.

setting the place and time in which the action in a piece of writing occurs.

short story short, fictional narrative which typically has a tight plot, and is limited in theme, setting, number of events and characters.

simile a simile describes someone or something as being like something else. Example: She runs like a hare.

speaker the voice speaking in a poem, which is not necessarily identical to the voice of the writer.

stage direction writer's notes in a drama on how it is to be performed.

stanza group of lines in a poem.

stereotype a fixed set of general characteristics that people believe are typical of a particular group of people or things (see also cliché).

suspense feeling of tension and expectation about what is about to happen in a book, play or film.

symbol an object which stands not only for itself but for some abstract idea as well. Example: The 'dove' is often used as a symbol of peace.

synonym a word or term that means the same or nearly the same as another, Example: 'clever' and 'intelligent'.

technical term word or phrase used in a special area. Example: memory stick, blu-ray disc.

text form a kind of text such as a comment, a novel, a report, a manual (see *skills file* on p. 162).

text type classification of texts based on the writer's intentions (see also *skills file* on p. 163). Example:
- An argumentative or persuasive text tries to convince the reader of a certain point of view;
- An instructive text is neutral and tells the reader what to do or how to do something,
- A narrative text tells the story of a fictional or non-fictional event in chronological order.
- A descriptive text describes people, places, objects.
- An expository text explains and analyses complex topics or issues.

theme the central idea or 'message' in a text. A theme is an abstract idea that is not usually stated directly but may be demonstrated through the use of symbols or recurring events and/or images.

tone the writer's attitude towards the subject, character(s) and especially towards the reader, as reflected in the text. Example: The tone can be serious or playful, humorous or solemn, arrogant or modest.

turning point structural element of a fictional text that marks a change in the conflict or suspense.

understatement statement that is deliberately weak. It puts less emphasis on something than it deserves and it is often used in the form of irony.

utopia fictional text dealing with an ideal society, place or world.

word family a base word plus the other words which can be formed from it. Example: the noun, verb, adjective, or adverb forms; combinations with prefixes and suffixes, etc.

word field a group of words relating to the same topic or category. A word field can include nouns, adjectives, verbs, phrases, etc.

Acknowledgements

The editors wish to thank all authors, publishers and literary agencies who have given permission to use copyright material. Sources are given next to the texts.
Every effort has been made to locate owners of copyright material, but in a few cases this has not proved possible and repeated inquiries have remained unanswered. The publishers would be glad to hear from any further copyright owners of material reproduced in this book.

Picture credits

COV: Corbis (Duomo / Sallaz), Düsseldorf • COV: Corbis (Micro Discovery), Düsseldorf • COV: Fotosearch RF (PhotoDisc), Waukesha, WI • COV: JupiterImages (photos.com), Tucson, AZ • S.3: Dreamstime (Ruta Saulyte-laurin), Brentwood, TN • S.3: MEV, Augsburg • S.4: Getty Images (Alexander Hassenstein), München • S.4: iStockphoto (Ian Schlueter), Calgary, Alberta • S.5: picturemaxx AG (defd movies), München • S.5: AP (GEORGE NIKITIN), Frankfurt • S.5: Honda Motor Europe, Offenbach am Main • S.6: Picture-Alliance (epa / Kirsty Wigglesw), Frankfurt • S.6: JupiterImages (RF / photos.com), Tucson, AZ • S.6: Commonwealth Secretariat (Games), London • S.19: Klett-Archiv (A. Raftaki), Stuttgart • S.8: iStockphoto (Sean Locke), Calgary, Alberta • S.8: Avenue Images GmbH (Corbis RF / Hill Street Studios), Hamburg • S.8: JupiterImages (photos.com), Tucson, AZ • S.8: Dreamstime (Ruta Saulyte-laurinaviciene), Brentwood, TN • S.10: www.cartoonstock.com (Wilbur-Dawbarn-), Lansdown Mews, Bath, Avon • S.12: iStockphoto (mihaicalin), Calgary, Alberta • S.13: MEV, Augsburg • S.13: MEV, Augsburg • S.13: iStockphoto (iofoto), Calgary, Alberta • S.14: shutterstock (Marcin Balcerzak), New York, NY • S.15: shutterstock (Khafizov Ivan Harisovich), New York, NY • S.15: JupiterImages (photos.com), Tucson, AZ • S.15: shutterstock (malle), New York, NY • S.15: iStockphoto (ronen), Calgary, Alberta • S.15: shutterstock (Nataliya Peregudova), New York, NY • S.17: shutterstock (iofoto), New York, NY • S.18: The Spectator Limited, London • S.18: The Spectator Limited, London • S.18: The Spectator Limited, London • S.18: The Spectator Limited, London • S.19: iStockphoto (Quavondo Nguyen), Calgary, Alberta • S.19: Klett-Archiv (A. Raftaki), Stuttgart • S.19: shutterstock (Artix Studio), New York, NY • S.20: Corbis (Caste / Photo-Cuisine), Düsseldorf • S.22: www.cartoonstock.com (Piero Tonin), Lansdown Mews, Bath, Avon • S.22: www.cartoonstock.com (McLachlan, Ed), Lansdown Mews, Bath, Avon • S.22: www.cartoonstock.com (Tonin, Piero), Lansdown Mews, Bath, Avon • S.22: www.cartoonstock.com (Bacall, Aaron), Lansdown Mews, Bath, Avon • S.22: www.cartoonstock.com (Martin Guh), Lansdown Mews, Bath, Avon • S.23: Wolfram Büchel, Remshalden • S.26: MEV, Augsburg • S.27: shutterstock (mihaicalin), New York, NY • S.28: www.cartoonstock.com (Shapiro, Mike), Lansdown Mews, Bath, Avon • S.29: laif (Hahn), Köln • S.31: iStockphoto (Justin Horrocks), Calgary, Alberta • S.32: Fotosearch RF (PhotoDisc), Waukesha, WI • S.33: Getty Images (PhotoDisc), München • S.34: Das Fotoarchiv (Xinhua), Essen • S.34: Corel Corporation, Unterschleissheim • S.34: Picture-Alliance (dpa / ATP Arthur Thill), Frankfurt • S.35: The Library of Congress, Washington, D.C. • S.36: iStockphoto (RF / Ronen), Calgary, Alberta • S.37: CartoonStock (Thompson, Robert), Bath • S.39: Volkswagen AG (Hartmann), Wolfsburg • S.41: shutterstock (RF / Losevsky Pavel), New York, NY • S.42: CartoonStock (Baldwin, Mike), Bath • S.42: CartoonStock (Therien, Ron), Bath • S.43: shutterstock (RF / Nikolay Okhitin), New York, NY • S.45: iStockphoto (RF / photos.com), Calgary, Alberta • S.46: Picture-Alliance (photoshot), Frankfurt • S.48: Keystone (Ariel Ramerez), Hamburg • S.48: Getty Images (Alexander Hassenstein / Bongarts), München • S.48: laif (Gerster), Köln • S.48: Action Press (SPLASH), Hamburg • S.48: laif (Gluecklich), Köln • S.49: Avenue Images GmbH (Digital Vision, RF), Hamburg • S.50: shutterstock (Jim Parkin), New York, NY • S.51: Andy Singer, St. Paul, MN • S.52: We Love Children's Books, Ridley Park, PA 19078 • S.53: Corbis (Gideon Mendel), Düsseldorf • S.54: Picture-Alliance (FT Eggitt), Frankfurt • S.55: www.cartoonstock.com (Goddard, Clive), Lansdown Mews, Bath, Avon • S.56: iStockphoto (Chris Schmidt), Calgary, Alberta • S.57: shutterstock (salamanderman), New York, NY • S.58: iStockphoto (Chris Schmidt), Calgary, Alberta • S.60: Steve Greenberg, Camarillo • S.61: picturemaxx AG (defd movies), München • S.62: iStockphoto (Wendy Zilver), Calgary, Alberta • S.63: iStockphoto (Andy Green), Calgary, Alberta • S.65: iStockphoto (Ian Schlueter), Calgary, Alberta • S.66: MEV, Augsburg • S.66: Sellafield Site, Cheshire • S.66: Sellafield Site, Cheshire • S.67: Sellafield Site, Cheshire • S.67: Sellafield Site, Cheshire • S.70: Corbis (Tim Rue), Düsseldorf • S.70: Picture-Alliance (epa efe Moreira), Frankfurt • S.73: Mauritius (Photononstop), Mittenwald • S.74: Cagle Cartoons (Andy Singer), Santa Barbara, CA • S.76: Historisch-Techn. Informationszentrum, Peenemünde •

S. 76: Historisch-Techn. Informationszentrum, Peenemünde • S. 76: Historisch-Techn. Informationszentrum, Peenemünde • S. 77: iStockphoto (clu), Calgary, Alberta • S. 77: Intel, Feldkirchen • S. 77: JupiterImages (photos.com), Tucson, AZ • S. 77: JupiterImages (photos.com), Tucson, AZ • S. 78: iStockphoto (Sharon Dominick), Calgary, Alberta • S. 79: iRobot Corporation, Burlington, MA 01803 • S. 81: Cinetext, Frankfurt • S. 82: Honda Motor Europe, Offenbach am Main • S. 82: The Department of Defense, Washington, DC 20310-1400 • S. 82: The Department of Defense, Washington, DC • S. 83: www.cartoonstock.com (Thomas Bros.), Lansdown Mews, Bath, Avon • S. 83: www.cartoonstock.com (Fischer, Ed), Lansdown Mews, Bath, Avon • S. 85: iStockphoto (Andrei Tchernov), Calgary, Alberta • S. 85: iStockphoto (Elena Korenbaum), Calgary, Alberta • S. 86: Atria Books and Pocket Books, New York • S. 88: iStockphoto (Eliza Snow), Calgary, Alberta • S. 88: Getty Images, München • S. 88: Astrofoto, Sörth • S. 88: NASA, Washington, D.C. • S. 88: shutterstock (Iva Villi), New York, NY • S. 88: JupiterImages (photos.com), Tucson, AZ • S. 88: picturemaxx AG (defd movies), München • S. 91: Corbis (Reuters), Düsseldorf • S. 92: NASA, Washington, D.C. • S. 94: Corbis (Ben Chrisman / Reuters), Düsseldorf • S. 96: The Tech Museum of Innovation, San Jose, CA • S. 96: Greenpeace, Hamburg • S. 97: NASA Goddard Space Flight Center, Greenbelt, Maryland • S. 98: Corbis (Zack Seckler), Düsseldorf • S. 100: picturemaxx AG (KPA), München • S. 104: www.cartoonstock.com, Lansdown Mews, Bath, Avon • S. 105: NASA Goddard Space Flight Center (esa), Greenbelt, Maryland • S. 106: shutterstock (Richard Sargeant), New York, NY • S. 106: Corbis (Wally McNamee), Düsseldorf • S. 106: Corbis (Kim Kulish), Düsseldorf • S. 106: AP (GEORGE NIKITIN), Frankfurt • S. 107: shutterstock (Alan C. Heison), New York, NY • S. 107: iStockphoto (Björn Kindler), Calgary, Alberta • S. 110: iStockphoto (Luis Sierra), Calgary, Alberta • S. 110: iStockphoto (Sandra O'Claire), Calgary, Alberta • S. 110: iStockphoto (Dan Brandenburg), Calgary, Alberta • S. 111: iStockphoto (Jose Gil), Calgary, Alberta • S. 111: iStockphoto (Jason van der Valk), Calgary, Alberta • S. 111: iStockphoto (Cliff Parnell), Calgary, Alberta • S. 111: shutterstock (Tan Kian Khoon), New York, NY • S. 112: shutterstock (RF / pmphoto), New York, NY • S. 112: Corbis (Bettmann), Düsseldorf • S. 115: Getty Images (EVA-LOTTA JANSSON / AFP), München • S. 116: PWE-Verlag Gesellschaft für Medien, Hamburg • S. 117: iStockphoto (Craig DeBourbon), Calgary, Alberta • S. 120: Corbis (Burstein Collection), Düsseldorf • S. 121: Wikimedia Foundation Inc. (PD), St. Petersburg FL • S. 123: laif (Heiko Specht), Köln • S. 124: Picture-Alliance (epa / Kirsty Wigglesworth), Frankfurt • S. 126: shutterstock (Mark William Richardson), New York, NY • S. 127: iStockphoto (Marcel Pelletier), Calgary, Alberta • S. 127: shutterstock (MAT), New York, NY • S. 127: iStockphoto (Wing Tang), Calgary, Alberta • S. 129: Privacy Victoria (Scott Bartlett), Melbourne Victoria 3000 • S. 131: Fotosearch RF (Imagesource), Waukesha, WI • S. 133: Commonwealth Secretariat (Games), London • S. 134: Picture-Alliance (PA Tim Ockenden), Frankfurt • S. 135: Commonwealth Secretariat, London • S. 137: iStockphoto (De Meyer), Calgary, Alberta • S. 139: www.cartoonstock.com (Goddard, Clive), Lansdown Mews, Bath, Avon • S. 140: gepa, Wuppertal • S. 140: iStockphoto (Rebecca Ellis), Calgary, Alberta • S. 140: shutterstock (Dragan Trifunovic), New York, NY • S. 140: shutterstock (Khafizov Ivan Harisovich), New York, NY • S. 140: Action Press (PKP x), Hamburg • S. 140: JupiterImages (RF / photos.com), Tucson, AZ • S. 141: Dreamstime (Christian Bernfeld), Brentwood, TN • S. 143: shutterstock (Chee Choon Fat), New York, NY • S. 143: iStockphoto (art-4-art), Calgary, Alberta • S. 143: www.cartoonstock.com (Whyman, Gerard), Lansdown Mews, Bath, Avon • S. 146: www.cartoonstock.com (Fran), Lansdown Mews, Bath, Avon • S. 147: shutterstock (PhotoCreate), New York, NY • S. 151: Picture-Alliance (Peter Kneffel), Frankfurt

Abbreviations and symbols

AE	American English
BE	British English
b.	born
cf.	compare, see
e.g.	for example
esp.	especially
etc.	et cetera, and so on
GB	refers to a British phenomenon
i.e.	that is
L	line/lines
p./pp.	page/pages
s.o.	someone
s.th.	something
US	refers to an American phenomenon

2|5

Text on CD; the first number refers to the number of the CD in the *Teacher's Resource Book* (CD1 or CD2); the second number refers to the track number on the CD.

801005-0002

Go to www.klett.de and type in the online link to download vocabulary (mp3 files), and to check grammar points.

Irregular Verbs

be, was/were, been	sein	**leave, left, left**	(ver)lassen
beat, beat, beaten	schlagen	**lend, lent, lent**	(ver)leihen
become, became, become	werden	**let, let, let**	lassen
begin, began, begun	anfangen	**lie, lay, lain**	liegen
bite, bit, bitten	beißen	**lose, lost, lost**	verlieren
break, broke, broken	(zer)brechen	**make, made, made**	machen
bring, brought, brought	(mit)bringen	**mean, meant, meant**	meinen, bedeuten
build, built, built	bauen	**meet, met, met**	treffen
buy, bought, bought	kaufen	**pay, paid, paid**	bezahlen
can, could, —	können	**put, put, put**	legen, stellen, setzen
catch, caught, caught	fangen	**read, read, read**	lesen
choose, chose, chosen	wählen	**ride, rode, ridden**	reiten, fahren
come, came, come	kommen	**ring, rang, rung**	klingeln
cost, cost, cost	kosten	**rise, rose, risen**	steigen
cut, cut, cut	schneiden	**run, ran, run**	laufen
do, did, done	tun, machen	**say, said, said**	sagen
draw, drew, drawn	zeichnen	**see, saw, seen**	sehen
drink, drank, drunk	trinken	**sell, sold, sold**	verkaufen
drive, drove, driven	fahren	**send, sent, sent**	senden
eat, ate, eaten	essen	**shoot, shot, shot**	(er)schießen
fall, fell, fallen	fallen	**show, showed, shown**	zeigen
feel, felt, felt	(sich) fühlen	**shut, shut, shut**	schließen
fight, fought, fought	(be)kämpfen	**sing, sang, sung**	singen
find, found, found	finden	**sink, sank, sunk**	sinken
fly, flew, flown	fliegen	**sit, sat, sat**	sitzen
forbid, forbade, forbidden	verbieten	**sleep, slept, slept**	schlafen
forget, forgot, forgotten	vergessen	**speak, spoke, spoken**	sprechen
freeze, froze, frozen	frieren	**spend, spent, spent**	ausgeben; verbringen
get, got, got	bekommen	**stand, stood, stood**	stehen
give, gave, given	geben	**steal, stole, stolen**	stehlen
go, went, gone	gehen, fahren	**swim, swam, swum**	schwimmen
grow, grew, grown	wachsen	**take, took, taken**	nehmen
hang, hung, hung	hängen	**teach, taught, taught**	unterrichten
have, had, had	haben	**tear, tore, torn**	zerreißen
hear, heard, heard	hören	**tell, told, told**	sagen; erzählen
hide, hid, hidden	(sich) verstecken	**think, thought, thought**	denken
hit, hit, hit	schlagen	**throw, threw, thrown**	werfen
hold, held, held	(fest)halten	**understand, understood, understood**	verstehen
hurt, hurt, hurt	(sich) wehtun	**wake, woke, woken**	aufwachen
keep, kept, kept	aufbewahren	**wear, wore, worn**	tragen
know, knew, known	wissen; kennen	**win, won, won**	gewinnen
lead, led, led	führen	**write, wrote, written**	schreiben

Shetland Islands
United Kingdom
Yell
Unst
450
Fetlar
Foula
Lerwick
Mainland
Fair Isle
ATLANTIC
OCEAN
Orkney Islands
United Kingdom
Kirkwall
Lewis
Wick
St Kilda
United Kingdom
Stornoway
Outer Hebrides
The Minch
Skye
Inverness
Elgin
Loch
Ness
NORTH
SEA
Rhum
Aberdeen
1343
Ben Nevis
Grampians Mts
Mull
Oban
SCOTLAND
Arbroath
Perth
Dundee
Jura
Lochgilphead
Stirling
Dunfermline
Kirkcaldy
Greenock
Edinburgh
Paisley
Islay
Glasgow
Motherwell
Kilmarnock
North Channel
Arran
Ayr
Berwick-upon-Tweed
Londonderry
Coleraine
NORTHERN
IRELAND
Lifford
Ballymena
Hawick
Great
Donegal Bay
Omagh
Larne
Dumfries
Lough Neagh
Newcastle upon Tyne
Sligo
Ireland
Belfast
UNITED KINGDOM
South Shields
Sunderland
Workington
978
Scafell Pikes
Monaghan
Stockton-on-Tees
Hartlepool
Castlebar
Carrick-on-Shannon
Cavan
Newry
ISLE OF MAN
Darlington
Middlesbrough
Dundalk
Douglas
Roscommon
Longford
Isle of Man
Barrow-in-Furness
Britain
Drogheda
Lancaster
Galway
Galway
Bay
Mullingar
Trim
IRISH SEA
Blackpool
Bradford
York
Preston
Leeds
DUBLIN
Blackburn
Kingston upon Hull
Tullamore
Shannon
Dún Laoghaire
Bolton
Manchester
Nass
Scunthorpe
Ennis
Portlaoise
Bray
Holyhead
Liverpool
Great Grimsby
Anglesey
Birkenhead
Warrington
Sheffield
Limerick
IRELAND
Wicklow
Caernarfon
Carlow
Chester
Lincoln
1085
Snowdon
Trent
ENGLAND
Tralee
Cashel
Kilkenny
Stoke-on-Trent
Derby
Nottingham
Clonmel
Boston
Cardigan
Bay
WALES
Shrewsbury
1038
Carrantuohill
Killarney
Wexford
St Georges Channel
Waterford
Aberystwyth
Dudley
Walsall
Leicester
King's Lynn
Cork
Norwich
Birmingham
Peterborough
Coventry
Great Yarmouth
Severn
Worcester
Lowestoft
Cambridge
Hereford
Northampton
Carmarthen
Bury St Edmunds
Bedford
Merthyr Tydfil
Gloucester
Cheltenham
Ipswich
Luton
Swansea
Oxford
Harlow
Colchester
Bristol Channel
Newport
Chelmsford
Cardiff
Bristol
Swindon
Watford
Thames
Basildon
CELTIC SEA
Weston-Super-Mare
Bath
Reading
Southend-on-Sea
Barnstaple
LONDON
Margate
Taunton
Guildford
Maidstone
Crawley
Dover
Exeter
Southampton
Folkestone
Strait of Dover
Oostende
Bournemouth
Brighton
Dunkerque
621
High Willhays
Channel Tunnel
Calais
Weymouth
Poole
Portsmouth
Hastings
BELGI
Plymouth
Torquay
Eastbourne
Boulogne-sur-Mer
Tourcoing
Roubaix
Isle of Wight
Penzance
Falmouth
Béthune
Lille
Isles of Scilly
Lens
ENGLISH CHANNEL
Arras
Abbeville
Dieppe
Guernsey
Amiens
St-Quen
St Peter Port
Cherbourg
Fécamp

World Time Zones
Date Line
Deviation in hours
-12 -11 -10 -9 -8 -7 -6 -5 -4 -3 -2 -1 0 +1 +2 +3 +4 +5 +6 +7 +8 +9 +10 +11 +12
World languages
English
Spanish
Portuguese
French
Arabic
Chinese
Countries with economic agreements:
NAFTA
G8
EU
Borders of the economic areas
ARCTIC OCEAN
GREENLAND
(Kalaallit Nunaat)
DENMARK
GREENLAND SEA
NORWEGIAN SEA
BARENTS SEA
BEAUFORT SEA
Baffin Bay
Hudson Bay
LABRADOR SEA
Gulf of Alaska
BERING SEA
ALASKA
UNITED STATES OF AMERICA
CANADA
UNITED STATES OF AMERICA
MEXICO
Gulf of Mexico
NORTH PACIFIC OCEAN
NORTH ATLANTIC OCEAN
SOUTH ATLANTIC OCEAN
SOUTH PACIFIC OCEAN
INDIAN OCEAN
RUSSIAN FEDERATION
KAZAKHSTAN
MONGOLIA
CHINA
JAPAN
INDIA
IRAN
SAUDI ARABIA
EGYPT
LIBYA
ALGERIA
SUDAN
BRAZIL
ARGENTINA
CHILE
AUSTRALIA
SOUTH AFRICA
INDONESIA
ICELAND
TASMAN SEA